The Socratic Classroom

☎ 01603 773114
email: tis@ccn.ac.uk

21 DAY LOAN ITEM

2 1 OCT 2022

Please return <u>on or before</u> the last date stamped above

A fine will be charged for overdue items

CITY
COLLEGE
NORWICH

The Socratic Classroom

Reflective Thinking Through Collaborative Inquiry

Sarah Davey Chesters
Queensland University of Technology, Brisbane, Australia

SENSE PUBLISHERS
ROTTERDAM/BOSTON/TAIPEI

A C.I.P. record for this book is available from the Library of Congress.

ISBN: 978-94-6091-853-7 (paperback)
ISBN: 978-94-6091-854-4 (hardback)
ISBN: 978-94-6091-855-1 (e-book)

Published by: Sense Publishers,
P.O. Box 21858,
3001 AW Rotterdam,
The Netherlands
https://www.sensepublishers.com/

Printed on acid-free paper

TABLE OF CONTENTS

PREFACE

This book was written to serve two functions. First it is an exploration of what I have called Socratic pedagogy, a collaborative inquiry-based approach to teaching and learning suitable not only to formal educational settings such as the school classroom but to all educational settings. The term is intended to capture a variety of philosophical approaches to classroom practice that could broadly be described Socratic in form. The term 'philosophy in schools' is ambiguous and could refer to teaching university style philosophy to high school students or to the teaching of philosophy and logic or critical reasoning in senior years of high school. It is also used to describe the teaching of philosophy in schools generally. In the early and middle phases of schooling the term philosophy for children is often used. But this too is ambiguous as the name was adopted from Matthew Lipman's Philosophy for Children curriculum that he and his colleagues at the Institute for the Advancement of Philosophy for Children developed. In Britain the term 'philosophy with children' is sometimes employed to mark two methods of teaching that have Socratic roots but have distinct differences, namely Philosophy for Children and Socratic Dialogue developed by Leonard Nelson. The use of the term Socratic pedagogy and its companion term Socratic classroom (to refer to the kind of classroom that employs Socratic teaching) avoids the problem of distinguishing between various approaches to philosophical inquiry in the Socratic tradition but also separates it from the 'study of philosophy', such as university style philosophy or other approaches which place little or no emphasis on collaborative inquiry-based teaching and learning.

The second function builds from the first. It is to develop an effective framework for understanding the relationship between what I call the generative, evaluative and connective aspects of communal dialogue, which I think are necessary to the Socratic notion of inquiry. In doing so it is hoped that this book offers some way to show how philosophy as inquiry can contribute to educational theory and practice, while also demonstrating how it can be an effective way to approach teaching and learning. This has meant striking a balance between speaking to philosophers and to teachers and educators together, with the view that both see the virtues of such a project.

In the strictest sense this book is not philosophy *of* education, insofar as its chief focus is not on the analysis of concepts or formulation of definitions specific to education with the aim of formulating directives that guide educational practice. It relinquishes the role of philosopher as 'spectator', to one of philosopher 'immersed in matter' – in this case philosophical issues in education, specifically those related to philosophical inquiry, pedagogy and classroom practice. Put another way, it is a book about philosophical education.

ACKNOWLEDGEMENT

I must firstly acknowledge Dr Gilbert Burgh, without whom this book would not have evolved. The ideas developed herein are a result of years of dialogue that reflect a true process of inquiry. My experience of a philosophical approach to teaching and learning as a student provided the impetus for my further inquiry into education as a discipline and philosophy's possible contribution. This book, which is an attempt to capture the pedagogical process introduced to me by Dr Burgh is attributed to him.

I would like to formally acknowledge the support given to me both financially and academically from the University of Queensland, University of Southern Queensland and Queensland University of Technology with whom I was affiliated during the writing of this book. Particular thanks must go to Alan Rix, Fred D'Agostino, Nita Temmerman, Lindsay Parry, Wendy Patton and Annette Patterson.

Thanks must also go to Megan Laverty, Philip Cam, Trevor Curnow, and Mia O'Brien whose feedback helped to shape this manuscript and to Clare O'Farrell who encouraged me to see value in my writing.

To the practitioners of philosophical inquiry, in particular Lynne Hinton, Liz Fynes-Clinton, and Rosie Scholl, thank you for continually opening my eyes and demonstrating new ways of seeing philosophy in the classroom.

Thank you to the teachers and students I have had the privilege of working with, past and present who have embraced philosophy in their own classrooms, whose continued enthusiasm and commitment means that philosophy will have a place in education in the future.

Lastly, to my family and friends who have supported me throughout this process - thank you to my parents and my husband who have always, and continue to encourage, my sense of wonder and who teach me so much about life.

Some ideas in this book can be found in condensed form in the following publications and conference proceedings: Davey Chesters, S. (2010). Engagement through dialogue : an exploration of collaborative inquiry and dimensions of thinking. In Brune, Jens Peter, Gronke, Horst, & Krohn, Dieter (Eds.) *The Challenge of Dialogue : Socratic Dialogue and Other Forms of Dialogue in Different Political Systems and Cultures* (pp. 73–96). LIT-Verlag, Munster; Davey Chesters (2009, 3–6 December) *Technologies of Silence*. Paper presented at the Dialogue and Difference Conference, Philosophy of Education Society of Australasia, Hawaii; Davey, S. (2004). Consensus, Caring and Community: An Inquiry into Dialogue. *Analytic Teaching, 25*(1), 18–51; Davey, S. (2005, 14–16 July). *Creative, Critical and Caring Engagements: Philosophy through Inquiry.* Paper presented at the Creative Engagements Conference; Thinking with Children Conference, Oxford University. Thank you to the editors for their permission to include this work.

SOCRATIC EDUCATION: A SCHOOL OF FREEDOM

This book, simply put, explores the potential of Socratic pedagogy as an effective educational strategy that develops the social and intellectual capacities for active citizenship in a democratic society. The assumption that underpins this claim is that certain kinds of educational arrangement lend more support to democracy than others (Lipman, 2003; Cam, 2006; Burgh, 2003). I am mindful that such a claim is contestable, so let me begin by situating this book in the wider context of philosophy in education. This book began as an exploration of various philosophical approaches to classroom practice that could be described as typically Socratic in form, as well as an attempt to open up discussion about what these approaches have in common—thinking through dialogue. It became apparent that there are also distinct differences between them, and that these differences have important practical implications, to which the pages of this book also attest. These differences notwithstanding, all teaching methods inspired by Socrates have in common questioning and inquiry, in which all answers are subject to further questioning. There is a proliferation of literature on the virtues of philosophical inquiry as a classroom strategy, either as an exemplar of democratic practice or as having the capacity to cultivate democratic dispositions and skills necessary for active citizenship. This has been affirmed in the 2008 UNESCO report, *Philosophy: A School of Freedom.*

This report, based on the results of a worldwide study on the teaching of philosophy, not only made clearer the purpose of the book, but also offered practical grounds for the arguments presented within. The overwhelming need for pedagogy that promotes thinking resonates from the study. It is the ability to think about problems and issues of all kinds that sows the seeds for liberating the powers of the individual and developing the social and intellectual capacities and dispositions needed for active citizenship. While education theorists aim to cultivate thinking for freedom, thinking for harmony or thinking for societal change, what lies at the heart of these aspirations is really about enhancing, quite simply, 'good thinking'. This book, in retrospect, is a response to this study; it makes suggestions for how we might go about cultivating thinking well (that is the key to leading the 'good life') through the development of Socratic classrooms.

My chief concern is to look at philosophy in the tradition of reflective education, of which Socrates was a forerunner; that is, the tradition of promoting learning to think as a foundation for educational aims and practices. The Socratic Method, a form of philosophical inquiry, or more precisely, a dialectic method of inquiry used by Socrates mainly for the purpose of examining key moral concepts and first illustrated in Plato's early dialogues, is a distinctive pedagogy to encourage people to develop independent thinking by questioning claims about knowledge, to argue about ideas, and to engage in dialogue about important issues of life. While the Socratic Method described in Plato's dialogues would require little scrutiny to come to the conclusion that the practices and views on knowledge purportedly held by Socrates are questionable in terms of their relevance to inquiry about what constitutes a good life, there is much to applaud in relation to the development of higher-order thinking and the acquisition of the knowledge, skills and attitudes considered necessary to function in an increasingly changing and diverse world.[1] It is for this reason that the notion of the Socratic Method as philosophical inquiry and as pedagogy is central to the argument that I present in this book, in particular to teaching students to think well in the context of their lives.

PHILOSOPHY: A SCHOOL OF FREEDOM

The primary purpose of the UNESCO study is to investigate the ways in which philosophy can contribute to teaching and learning. It states:

> If we support the teaching of philosophy to children in principle, we still need to answer a pedagogical question. How? What teaching methods or approaches should be used? How can teachers learn to teach philosophy in a way that children can learn to philosophize? Again there has been much debate over these questions. (p. 9)

It is noteworthy that the UNESCO study claims to not presume any method or philosophical orientation. Yet at the outset of Chapter 1, entitled 'Teaching philosophy and learning to philosophize at pre-school and primary school levels', the reader could be forgiven for thinking that the study points to a particular orientation, namely Philosophy for Children or P4C, which has its roots in the educational theories of John Dewey and has been subsequently developed by Matthew Lipman. It is undeniable, as the report states, that (1) Lipman's groundbreaking work on engaging in the practice of philosophy for children represents a certain change in the objectives of teaching, and (2) that it sparked curiosity and interest in his Philosophy for Children curriculum, particularly the emphasis on narratives for children and the notion of converting classrooms into communities of inquiry. However, the entire chapter makes no mention of other classroom practices and strategies for engaging children in philosophy suitable for pre-school and primary school levels. This is somewhat misleading as there are other methods of teaching philosophy in the Socratic tradition that could be said to have similar objectives to those of Lipman. While Lipman drew on Dewey's modern conception of education, he also found parallels in the more ancient teaching methods of Socrates.

In response, I propose a framework for Socratic pedagogy that uses a multi-dimensional approach to thinking. In this book, we will explore three contemporary approaches to collaborative, inquiry-based teaching and learning through philosophy which could be described as Socratic in form, namely Matthew

Lipman's 'Community of Inquiry', Leonard Nelson's 'Socratic Dialogue', and David Bohm's 'Dialogue'. All three can be successfully used in Socratic pedagogy. The framework that I propose is multi-dimensional; comprised of generative, evaluative and connective thinking. By describing each of the dimensions of multi-dimensional thinking in terms of the function they perform, we are able to escape the confusion created by the vagueness of the terms critical, creative and caring thinking. When we look at creative thinking as generative thinking, critical thinking as evaluative thinking, and caring thinking as connective thinking, we move away from the prejudices and disagreements that surround the previously adopted terms. This allows for a greater understanding of the kind of contribution they make to Socratic pedagogy, which in turn informs classroom practice. It also offers a renewed understanding of Socratic pedagogy and a new starting point for discussion on theory and practice.

It is noteworthy that there has previously been little intellectual exchange between the proponents of the three approaches to dialogue featured in this book, despite there being much written on the benefits of each of them. Notwithstanding the recent publication *The Challenge of Dialogue; Socratic Dialogue and Other Forms of Dialogue in Different Political Systems and Cultures* (Brune et al, 2010), the inclusion of an article by Nelson and another by Bohm, which both appear in *Thinking Children and Education*, a collection of works edited by Lipman (1993), a paper by Trevor Curnow and another by Karen Murris and Joanna Haynes, which appear in a collection of papers on philosophy in practice compiled in *Thinking through Dialogue: Essays on Philosophy and Practice*, edited by Curnow (2001), and less than a handful of articles scattered in various journals, intellectual discussion, particularly any extensive comparative analysis, of these different approaches to thinking through dialogue in education, remains largely underdeveloped.

There are many different directions in which these three approaches to thinking through dialogue have developed. For example, Lou Marinoff's emphasis on Socratic Dialogue within the context of philosophical counselling and practice, the development of philosophy for children in schools internationally as evidenced by changes in terminology in Britain to 'philosophy with children', and in Australia to 'philosophy in schools', or more generally 'philosophical inquiry in the classroom', and the use of Bohmian Dialogue in corporate leadership programs and in prisons across Britain and Europe. While my concern is foremost with philosophical inquiry as an educative practice, by bringing these approaches together in order to examine their commonalities and differences, it is hoped that the result of this examination will contribute to a much needed discussion, not only because each approach has much to offer classroom practice, but also because it would broaden the scope for discussion on thinking through dialogue.

It should be noted that the use of the term 'classroom' as it is used in this book does not strictly apply only to the school classroom, or even to tertiary educational settings, but it also has application generally to settings outside of what traditionally is considered to be an educational setting. For example, the classroom can be the staffroom or the boardroom. This view echoes the view of Socrates, widely considered to be an 'educator', whose purpose was to 'rouse, persuade and rebuke' (Plato in Kolak, 2000). His interlocutors weren't students in a classroom, but Athenian citizens with whom he met by chance, usually in the agora, which was both the market-place and the centre of public life; a place to gather. Education is anywhere that learning can occur, and hence the classroom has many manifestations—it is not simply the right of the child that should be considered but all who come to education at any stage of life. My emphasis on lifelong learning notwithstanding, it is undeniable that the approach to pedagogy that I outline here is directly applicable for school-aged students.

THE FREEDOM INHERENT IN PHILOSOPHY

In a statement by Pierre Sané, Assistant Director-General of Human Sciences (UNESCO), the initiative for the UNESCO study is a response to promoting philosophy and encouraging its teaching as outlined in UNESCO's Intersectoral Strategy on Philosophy, which "is built on three key pillars of action: i) Philosophy facing world problems: dialogue, analysis and questioning of contemporary society; ii) teaching philosophy in the world: fostering critical reflection and independent thinking; and iii) promotion of philosophical thought and research" (p. xi). The notion of 'thinking as freedom', and the corresponding principle that the enhancement of thinking is a basic right of the child,[2] attempt to provide ethical and political justification for the claim that philosophy in education is imperative to the 'three key pillars of action' for promoting philosophy and encouraging its teaching. The report explicitly highlights the need for independent thinking, which is a necessary requirement for freedom of thought. The capacity for freedom of thought is becoming increasingly urgent in a contemporary society that sees students being connected to information via state-of-the art multi-media information and communications technologies. With information becoming more accessible, what is required is the disposition and capacity to think reflectively in order to process the increasing amount of information available.

> All too often individuals, families, organizations, communities and sections of society live with the consequences of poorly thought-out decisions, faulty reasoning, biased judgements, unreasonable conduct, narrow perspectives, unexamined values and unfulfilled lives. If only people were better at asking appropriate questions, articulating problems and issues, imagining life's possibilities, seeing where things lead, evaluating the alternatives open to them, engaging in discussion with one another, and thinking collaboratively, then we would all be so much better off. (Cam, 2006, p.2)

Basically, what Cam is referring to is philosophy as liberty, the freedom to think independently and to think for oneself collaboratively. What is inherent in the freedom of thought is the ability to ask questions about 'what is a good life?' which was the question that underpinned Socrates' motivation for engaging people in dialogue.

PHILOSOPHY'S CONTRIBUTION TO THE THINKING CURRICULUM

As stated earlier, there is mounting pressure on teachers to engage students in higher-order thinking. This means more than paying attention to literacy and numeracy; it requires placing *inquiry* at the heart of education, lest we allow for the continuation of sections of society that are basically 'insocratic'.[3] If we are to promote thinking that is based on inquiry, then we must ourselves engage in inquiry into various models for good practice. What I propose is an approach to *pedagogy* that is Socratic, i.e., an approach to teaching and learning to develop and enhance Socratic classroom strategies and practices. This is not restricted to but may include methodology.

It is a Socratic pedagogy and not just a philosophical pedagogy as it is necessarily dialogical. Philosophy in general may not pertain to inquiry that is dialogical. It is thinking both philosophically *and* dialogically that is important for Socratic pedagogy. So why is it pedagogy and why is pedagogy important rather than just methodology or curriculum? It is pedagogy and not just a methodology or a method because it is an *underpinning* philosophy of teaching and learning. Throughout this book I will be offering a framework for Socratic pedagogy that should be read as a theoretical way of approaching teaching and learning and should not be mistaken as just a methodology. It is important because in theory and in practice we need to teach to take advantage of when situations arise that may allow for dialogue into matters of importance. We need to educate with an openness to inquiry through embracing wonder. Marshall Gregory (2001) gives us a further understanding as to why we need to focus on pedagogy:

> The fundamental reason *why* pedagogy deserves careful thought is that pedagogy is the primary force, the engine, that accomplishes the "leading out" (from Latin *educare*) that lies as the etymological source of *educate* and that also describes education's most basic aim. Since at birth all human skills and forms of development are mere potentialities, it follows that we have to go someplace else in the world from where we are at any given time—we have to be led out, or educated—in order to turn those potentialities into realities. As Bartlett Giamatti (1976: 194) has said, "Teaching is an instinctual art, mindful of potential, craving of realization." The content of any curriculum, whether a single course or a whole program of study, seldom exerts a sufficient pull on a person's imagination to draw him or her out of the inertia of being a standing body and into the activity that takes mind and heart to new places and new levels of development. (p.73)

This passage further explains why philosophy must be adopted as *pedagogy*; as an underpinning for how we teach and not simply a discipline that we teach. It is not a curriculum, but it contributes to curriculum. It is pedagogy because it needs to underpin how and why we teach. We must develop a learning environment that embraces wonder. The development of such learning environments may be formed by the influences of three approaches analysed in this book that provide various approaches to education in the Socratic tradition. However, I stress that this is simply a starting point for an exploration into how to approach thinking through dialogue.

There is a large body of literature devoted to philosophy and education. Historically this has consisted of formulating philosophical foundations that would guide educational practice. While painstaking attention to analysis of concepts, presuppositions, and the grounds of knowledge are necessary for philosophical exploration it is also important to keep in mind that education is also concerned with the analysis and justification of practical questions. On the other hand, to abandon philosophical points entirely would be a gross misunderstanding of the contribution philosophical inquiry can make to educational theory. What education and philosophy have in common is that they are both concerned with human affairs. This book attempts to maintain a balance between the issues of interest to philosophers of education, and to teachers and educators together, in the hope that both will see the virtues of such a project.

Chapter 1 examines the relationship between dialogue and the improvement of thinking. To begin, I compare and contrast dialogue with other forms of communication such as conversation and debate. Next, I examine the relationship between monologue, internal dialogue and engaging in dialogue with others. I also point to the importance of identifying silence in dialogue. I refer to what are termed 'Technologies of Silence' to illustrate the many ways in which people may be silenced. Silence is also a part of dialogue and can be used to replace words, to make a point. Similarly, silence can be a time for critical reflection during dialogue and may not necessarily be an inhibitor to dialogue. The Socratic Method also forms the basis of Chapter 1. There are various interpretations of the Socratic Method as a dialectic method of inquiry, ranging from a form of 'cold calling' in universities to a pedagogical method that underpins collaborative classroom inquiry. I refer to the metaphors used to describe Socrates as a facilitator of dialogue—as gadfly, as midwife and as stinging ray—to convey the different types of thinking that may be promoted by using this method in the classroom.

It is not always easy to imagine what the Socratic Method would look like in a contemporary educational setting. Chapter 2, therefore, explores three models of dialogue that share fundamental characteristics of the Socratic Method: the Community of Inquiry, Socratic Dialogue, and Bohmian Dialogue. Firstly, I introduce the Community of Inquiry, a philosophical pedagogy developed by Matthew Lipman, who in the late 1960s commenced development on a series of curriculum materials for children, consisting of novels and accompanying teachers' manuals, aimed at improving children's thinking skills, which he argued would improve the relationship between deliberative judgments and democratic decision-making. I give an overview of Lipman's views on the importance of learning to think; a central theme in his educational theory and practice. To draw out the ties between Lipman's view on thinking, education, and democracy, I examine the ideas of educationalist and philosopher John Dewey and his predecessor, pragmatist philosopher Charles Peirce, as well as Russian psychologist Lev Vygotsky, all of whom supply a theoretical basis for Lipman's theory and practice. Such an understanding sheds light on Lipman's claim that learning to think together is necessary to develop social and intellectual dispositions and capacities for active citizenship.

Next, I focus on Leonard Nelson, Gustav Heckmann and Jos Kessels, who all contributed to the development of what is known as Socratic Dialogue. Nelson's aim was to educate children to want to seek truth, and to encourage self-esteem. To achieve this, he extended the Socratic Method to large groups. Whereas Nelson gave few guidelines on how to employ the method, his pupil Heckman developed guidelines for how discussion should be conducted. In order to compare Socratic Dialogue with the other two models of philosophical inquiry, I outline the rules for Socratic Dialogue, the role of the facilitator, and the importance of reflecting on experiences common to all participants.

Lastly, I examine a type of dialogue formulated by David Bohm, who emphasised the central place of 'meta-dialogue', but moreover that the actual process of dialogue and thinking is as important, if not more important, than the content. I argue that Bohmian Dialogue can assist in our understanding of the communal dimension of inquiry, and the role of care in the development of genuine engagement through dialogue. In particular, I analyse Bohm's views on listening and social function, especially on listening as key to understanding, and on relationships in the dialogue and the connection between these relationships and thought.

Chapter 3 highlights the metaphors used by proponents of each of the different approaches to dialogue to illustrate their aims and purposes, highlight important distinctions, and to initiate discussion so as to not be uncritical about different ways of understanding dialogue and the way in which dialogue may be implemented in the classroom. I discuss two aspects of the Socratic Method— elenchus, a technique of examination to critically investigate the nature or definition of concepts, and aporia, a state of doubt or perplexity. Next, I examine Lipman's view of the Community of Inquiry as a process of thinking similar to chamber music, whereby each player embellishes on the ideas and notes of others to follow the music where it leads, or in the case of philosophical inquiry, to follow the argument or logic where it leads. I also explain how Nelson compares the process of Socratic Dialogue to that of an hourglass where ideas are narrowed down and then reapplied in a larger context. This metaphor highlights the emphasis on conceptual analysis that characterises Socratic Dialogue. Finally, I turn to Bohm, who uses the metaphor of a dance to illustrate the type of relationship that occurs in his approach to dialogue.

In the next three chapters, I address creative, critical and caring thinking and how each dimension of thinking contributes to inquiry. In Chapter 4, I address creative thinking as a form of divergent thinking. Inherent in divergent thinking is risk. I also make the distinction between creative thinking and creativity. Creative thinking, according to Lipman, is concerned with thinking for oneself. He argues that developing, exploring and extending ideas is at the very heart of creative thinking. Because dialogue is based on the ideas of the participants and following the argument where it leads, generating ideas requires inventiveness. Engagement of a creative kind occurs when we let the argument lead because the ideas must be developed by the participants themselves and cannot be predetermined. I look at Lipman's metaphor of chamber music and the idea that this kind of thinking is concerned with building on ideas. I then draw on the characteristics of creative thinking that are integral to the development of Socratic pedagogy. This is generative thinking. I assert here that the Community of Inquiry has much to contribute to a model of generative thinking in classroom collaborative inquiry.

In Chapter 5, I explore critical thinking as conceptual exploration, reasoning and logic. The main concern of this chapter is with the application of critical thinking to philosophical inquiry in the classroom and what I think is central to Socratic pedagogy, that is, evaluative thinking. Socratic Dialogue places a great emphasis on conceptual analysis and the use of consensus. Nelson's metaphor of the hourglass describes the process of evaluative thinking, and clearly illustrates the kind of thinking intended through Socratic Dialogue. Participants move from a general definition of a concept to a narrow definition agreed upon by the group through reaching consensus.

Chapter 6 examines care as the other dimension of multidimensional thinking. While there are different ways of understanding care, my concern is with the conception of care first described by Carol Gilligan in her studies on moral development and reasoning. Her work has since gained wide attention, in particular from Nel Noddings, whose work has become a major reference point for an analysis of caring and its place in ethics and education. This chapter aims to initiate discussion on the place of care in communal dialogue. I examine three aspects of care in collaborative classroom inquiry: (1) care for the inquiry, (2) care with others, and (3) care for problems deemed worthy. I also redefine caring thinking as connective thinking which is central to Socratic pedagogy. I argue that connective thinking is necessary to the achievement of collaborative, inquiry-based teaching and learning, and that it works in concert with the generative and evaluative dimensions of thinking.

In the concluding chapter, I propose a framework for Socratic pedagogy and examine the contributions of the three models of dialogue to this framework. The Community of Inquiry has much to offer approaches to generative thinking, whereas Socratic Dialogue can inform evaluative thinking. Bohmian Dialogue highlights what is central to connective thinking. Bohm's exploration of the connections between thinking and dialogue has much to contribute to Socratic pedagogy. I do not attempt to recommend one model of dialogue over another but show how their emphasis on generative, evaluative and connective thinking may contribute to the development of Socratic pedagogy.

By beginning a dialogue between proponents of philosophy, educators and philosophers can continue to think innovatively, reflectively and, most importantly, collaboratively about philosophy as pedagogy and to continue to reconstruct the Socratic classroom. What is consistent, however, is the overarching need for Socratic pedagogy in order to create thoughtful, reflective citizens in any educational context. With this in mind, let us begin the exploration.

NOTES

[1] The character of Socrates is a reconstruction from the evidence of others, mainly from Plato's dialogues written after Socrates' death and to some extent the writing of Xenophon. He also appears

as a caricature in Aristophanes' *Clouds*. My concern is not with Socrates, actual or reconstruction, but with what has been described as the Socratic Method—the dialectic processes of seeking truth.

[2] See the Convention of the Rights of the Child (1989) that stipulates the right to 'express views freely' (Article 12); 'the right to freedom of expression [...] to seek, receive and impart information and ideas of all kinds (Article 13) and to 'freedom of thought' (Article 14).

[3] Cam (2006) coined the term 'insocratic' (to be put alongside the terms illiterate and innumerate) to describe anyone who cannot adequately think for themselves in order to think effectively about life.

SOCRATIC PEDAGOGY: PHILOSOPHICAL INQUIRY THROUGH DIALOGUE

To most of us, conversation comes naturally. It is something we do every day; from fleeting exchanges at the supermarket, to inconsequential remarks aimed at filling up the routine morning greetings when we arrive at work, to convivial exchanges among guests at a dinner party. These conversations might touch on a topic, or, in the case of longer exchanges, move from one topic to another. On the other hand, we sometimes find ourselves engaged in more structured conversation. Unlike ordinary forms of conversation which are an everyday part of living, in structured conversations participants inquire into something, they seek an outcome, and make progress towards it. These are the sorts of conversations that we sometimes have with friends or family members that we are apt to call 'deep and meaningful', or when people come together in agreement, or when politicians seek genuine solutions, or professionals gather to deliberate over new ideas or hypotheses.

While a distinction can be made between these two very different kinds of conversation, it is not at all clear what distinguishes one from the other. Terms like 'conversation', 'discussion', 'inquiry' and 'dialogue' (and their many cognates) are often used interchangeably. For example, one way in which the term 'dialogue' is used is to describe a conversational interaction between at least two speakers regardless of the purpose. But sometimes we want to make a distinction between 'discussion' and 'dialogue'. In doing so, we are distinguishing between people talking to each other in everyday conversation and those engaged in an exchange of ideas or opinions. At other times, we need to make a further distinction between dialogue as the exchange of ideas and opinions, and dialogue as inquiry or as philosophical reflection.

Our task in this chapter is to consider some fundamental questions about dialogue to see what they reveal about dialogue itself. This is a necessary task for a comparison of the different models of dialogue that will unfold in subsequent chapters. Our concern in particular is with dialogue in relation to Socratic pedagogy, a form of reflective thinking or inquiry that requires a certain kind of communion between listener and speaker; an inquiry with the purpose of pursuing 'truth' or progressing toward understanding or meaningfulness. Note however, that this chapter should be read as an illustration of what takes place in dialogue, *not* as an attempt to formulate a precise definition that provides a directive for guiding educational theory and practice. Thus, we begin with an overview of dialogue, leading to a comparison of dialogue with other forms of communication. Dialogue is not just a mere conversation, nor is it a debate or series of monologues. It is a method of joint understanding rather than producing adversaries or winners. In the second part of this chapter we will explore the importance of identifying silence in dialogue. Silence plays a part in assisting dialogue but can also act to inhibit genuine dialogue. The term 'technologies of silence' illustrates the many ways in which people may be silenced. We will also look at silence as a time for critical reflection and lastly, review the importance of Socratic pedagogy as reflective education, specifically philosophy as a collaborative activity.

WHAT IS DIALOGUE?

Just as there is a time and place for everyday conversation, or for more focused discussion, there is also time for dialogue. But what is dialogue? A common misunderstanding is that dialogue simply means a discussion between two or more people, in which case it is often contrasted with monologue. The term *dia* is not derived from the Greek meaning 'two' but from the Greek meaning 'through'. The use of *logue* is derived from *logos,* which has multiple meanings from language to reason.

> In the fundamental sense, then, dialogue is a process of thinking or thinking through something. On the grounds of pure etymology, there is no requirement that there should be more than one person involved. Furthermore (and just as importantly), if the involvement of more than one person is not a necessary condition for dialogue, it is not a sufficient one either. Just because two people are talking to each other, that does not of itself mean that there is a dialogue, in the strict sense, going on. Dialogue and discussion are not the same thing. Unfortunately, everyday use tends to undermine this distinction. (Curnow, 2001, p.234)

This quote by Trevor Curnow raises a number of important questions about dialogue. Is dialogue the same as two people having a conversation? If not, then what distinguishes one from the other? If the involvement of another person is not a necessary or a sufficient condition for dialogue, then how does dialogue differ from monologue? To avoid the problem of vagueness over the term 'dialogue', let us now make some distinctions, in particular on different types of discussion that might be considered dialogue but are not.

Dialogue is Not Mere Conversation

We have all no doubt been party to a conversation or witnessed conversations between others. To illustrate my point, let us imagine three friends meeting at their favourite café, deeply immersed in each others' stories, which move from their relationships with family and friends in common, to their joys and sorrows, future employment prospects, and opinions on current affairs. There is, among other things, laughter, friendly banter, and occasional expressions of agreement and disagreement. As the purpose of their meeting is to share conversation over a cappuccino or Earl Grey tea, the mood is more likely to be one of offering support, encouragement, or a shoulder to cry on. This café conversation scenario, of course, does not discount the possibility of the friends engaging in more structured conversation, but it is unlikely to lead to an extended dialogue whereby assumptions are examined and disagreement is valued as a catalyst for further inquiry. These kinds of conversations usually seek equilibrium rather than engagement in dialogue. Nevertheless, it is possible to imagine that a conversation over what wedding flowers would suit a sage coloured wedding palette could shift to questions over independence and identity in marriage. The friends may still be inclined to journey along the conversation, offering helpful advice rather than, say, questioning assumptions on the meaning of marriage. But we can also imagine the friends engaged in dialogue together and relishing the opportunity to explore their disagreements to come to a greater understanding of each other and strengthen their friendship. In doing so, the friends have moved from having a mere conversation to engaging in dialogue.

Dialogue, as Susan Gardner (1995) puts it, is "no mere conversation." As the example of the three friends in the café illustrates, when kept to mere conversation the exchanges aim for equilibrium. However, as the conversation begins to explore disagreement and eventually becomes a dialogue, the aim is for disequilibrium, creating opportunities for a renewed understanding that comes from difference. Lipman (1991) identifies motivation for the talk itself as that which separates dialogue from mere conversation. A conversation, he argues, focuses on creating equilibrium between those engaged in it. A dialogue, however, aims at disequilibrium in order to bring new understanding to the topic under discussion, and perhaps at the conclusion of the dialogue equilibrium may again be restored (p.232). In an inquiry it is our disagreements as well as our agreements that shape the dialogue. What we are aiming for is a renewed understanding that comes from exploring ideas in disequilibrium. In this process, we reconstruct our previous knowledge. As the example illustrates, a conversation about marriage aimed at retaining equilibrium may revolve around the style of dress the bride will be wearing and the flowers in the church, but a dialogue about marriage will focus on issues such as the bride's identity in relation to changing her name or on the nature of marriage. Another way in which Lipman distinguishes between conversation and dialogue is that the former is an exchange being driven by a personal process of sharing information, and the latter follows a logical thread, whereby the participants are interested in the comments of others to further the inquiry, and to reaffirm or disprove their own argument (p.232).

An inquiry where participants are not engaging with the ideas of each other can be a series of monologues. When there is no internalisation of the process of dialogue, what we are left with is a series of interconnected monologues by individuals rather than a group moving towards a new understanding of the matter under discussion. I will have more to say on this later in this chapter, but for the moment it is suffice to say that the opposite situation can sometimes occur, whereby a dialogue may emerge out of other forms of discourse. For example, conversations that may not necessarily start with engagement may turn into a dialogue if there is genuine inquiry, as illustrated in the example of the friendly café conversation that may turn from talking about wedding dresses and flowers to more critical subjects such as identity and marriage.

According to Gardner (1995), it is the progress toward truth that "is vital to the practice of inquiry ... at least if such progress is possible" (p.38). For a dialogue to be productive the participants must in fact produce something of substance, which, in turn, would make that dialogue substantive. This product, according to Gardner, is truth. Without the necessity of trying to reach it, a dialogue would have no direction and there would be no motivation for its participants. Gardner is not advocating a Platonic conception of truth—one that is absolute and founded on certainty. In fact, she contends that truth may not, in fact, result at the conclusion of the dialogue. However, she stresses that having truth as a goal gives the inquiry purpose. Justus Buchler also identifies that the conclusion of the dialogue is not as important as the process itself. Although we may not come to a conclusion (or find 'truth' in the Platonic sense of the word) he argues that "a product is inevitably established in any given hour of discussion," and that participants "may have no right to demand final answers, but they certainly have the right to expect some sense of intellectual motion or some feeling of discernment" (in Lipman 1991, p.231). According to Clinton Golding (2005), the purpose of dialogue is not truth but to seek understanding or meaningfulness (p.1). This, of course, brings into question what truth is, especially with regard to the processes and procedures of inquiry. There is a longstanding controversy in philosophy, and to a lesser degree in education, over what ought to count as truth. As this wider exploration may distract us from our task, for the moment it is suffice to say that it is a regulative ideal (Gardner, 1995; Lipman, 1988).

Gardner's distinction between mere conversation and dialogue concurs with the view of Lydia Amir (2001) with regard to the dual meaning of dialogue as conversational interaction and as colloquy.

> In the formal sense, 'dialogue', 'talk' and 'conversation' denote spoken language or linguistic practice. This is a strictly observational definition of dialogue, adopted by, amongst others, ethno methodologists. Their preferred term—conversational interaction—refers to any sequence of oral utterances in which more than one speaker are engaged successively, regardless of purpose ... In the content-oriented sense, dialogue means 'colloquy' and won very early a status of its own: it was counted as a joint communicative activity with the goal of discovering truth. (p.239)

This conception of dialogue as colloquy has retained its currency among scholars who see dialogue as fundamentally important from a philosophical and educative perspective, and it looms large in the different models of dialogue explored in later chapters of this book.

Laurance Splitter and Ann Sharp (1995, pp.34–40) also point out the difference between ordinary conversation, in which there is either not much thinking or thinking which is not well-formed, and structured conversation or dialogue, in which participants engage in a kind of reflective inquiry. They recognise four conditions that define dialogue as different to conversation. First, the talk must focus on a topic that is either problematic or contestable insofar as the community must think reflectively about their viewpoints or perspectives. The tension present in this case is likened to the tension of a stringed instrument—it is only this tension that produces new music or in the case of dialogue, new perspectives. Splitter and Sharp note that some dialogues may concentrate on expression or creative discussion which is an important aspect of dialogue. Second, a dialogue is self-regulating and self-correcting. Students must have the ability to rethink their initial arguments but also be aware of why they have changed their minds. It is not enough to simply change the direction of thought for no good reason or through faulty reasoning. Third, the talk is of an egalitarian nature where individuals are valued as equal members of the community. Fourth, chosen topics are mutually interesting to each individual in the community. Splitter and Sharp warn that this may not be possible in the initial stages of dialogue. However, interest may evolve for those individuals for which interest is not sparked from the outset.

Dialogue is not mere conversation; however dialogue may come out of conversation in the illustration of the café conversation mentioned previously. In a conversation it is equilibrium that the friends strive for, however, in a genuine dialogue it is the balance between equilibrium and disequilibrium that gives the process its richness. By exploring both agreement and disagreement, a greater understanding may come about. There must be a genuine commitment and engagement between the individuals if it is to be considered dialogue, otherwise it may just reflect a series of monologues. Dialogue is also characterized by its progress towards truth, or what Amir (2001) terms 'colloquy'. Importantly it is also considered a form of reflective inquiry.

Dialogue and Debate

It is not at all unusual for the terms dialogue and debate to be used interchangeably to denote an exchange of words with an emphasis on talking through a problem. General usage aside, the two terms clearly can be distinguished from each other. Whereas dialogue is collaborative, debate is oppositional. Debate is something that occurs between antagonists and adversaries, and its goal is to win an argument (Lindop, 2002, p.36). An appeal to rhetoric, with emphasis usually on pathos or ethos, and little or no attention to the logic of argument, is not uncommon as a mechanism for persuasion in debates. Indeed, this is what Plato accused the Sophists of doing.[1] Dialogue, on the other hand, focuses on collaborative deliberation, with emphasis on reasoning and the logic of argument in order to gain an understanding of the matters under discussion.

Let us elaborate further in our comparison of dialogue and debate. As stated, dialogue is collaborative. The parties involved in dialogue work together as co-inquirers with the goal of finding both common and new ideas and improving on them. They listen to one another to understand and build agreement. It is a self-correcting process where ideas are considered and evaluated, which possibly could lead to a change of mind or a re-evaluation of points of view. Dialogue, therefore, has the capacity to promote open-mindedness to ideas and to being wrong. It invites keeping an issue open for further exploration even after the discussion has formally ended or reached closure. Debate, on the other hand, emphasises opposition. In a formal debate two sides oppose each other to prove each other wrong. The goal is clearly for one side to win with their ideas and for their point of view to emerge as victor. During this procedure each side contributes their ideas and defends them against any challenges by listening to the opposing side to find flaws and present only the opposing view. This gives no room for considering ideas or changing your mind, lest you lose. Debate encourages criticism of others, closed-mindedness to the ideas of others, and determination to be right. It creates a winner and a loser and is likely to discourage further discussion.[2]

Edward de Bono (1994), particularly, has misgivings over what he calls the adversarial model of thinking, which he argues was established over two thousand years ago with the 'Greek Gang of Three', his preferred term for Socrates, Plato and Aristotle. According to de Bono, with adversarial thinking each side takes an opposing position and attempts to attack the other side to prove them wrong with the aim of winning the argument. His view is shared by others such as Janice Moulton (1983), who describes it as aggressive but "often takes on positive associations" (p.149). However, unlike de Bono, Moulton argues that philosophical reasoning does not neatly fit into the adversary paradigm and that a misinterpretation of the history of philosophy and choice of philosophers has made it difficult to recast philosophy as anything but adversarial (pp.155–7). The Socratic Method, contrary to de Bono's attack, is often considered to be a prime example of philosophy which is dialogical in terms of its literal form and dialectic in structure, and thus does not lack a constructive or a creative element simply because its intended purpose is to discover 'truth'. Indeed, elements of de Bono's 'parallel thinking' which he contrasts to philosophical thinking can be found in the Socratic Method, particularly cooperative and coordinated thinking (Burgh et al, 2006, pp.36–41). Nevertheless, de Bono's criticisms apply wholeheartedly to debate.

Cam (2006) notes "that the dynamics of an inquiry differs from that of a debate" (p.44). By the term inquiry I take Cam to mean dialogical inquiry. According to Cam (pp.44–5) in a debate each speaker must be committed to sustain their given position. Unlike dialogue where the aim is to consider all arguments, the aim of debate is to win an argument—speakers are not responsible for considering other positions as that is the responsibility of the opposing side. Whereas a debate consists only of two sides (there is only agreement and disagreement on the issue), in an inquiry there may be various levels and shades of disagreement and agreement. Unlike debate, in an inquiry agreement may be contingent on certain points to be clarified. Students may both agree and disagree with a statement, agreeing with some points but not others. Cam argues against debate as being a type of dialogue insofar as the participants in a debate are not allowed to express their own opinions but must agree with their team's argument and disagree with the opponent's argument. He says that "debating points often do not depend on the soundness of the argument but on rhetorical devices designed to cut the ground from under the opposition and to sway the audience to one's side" (pp.44). This is not true of a dialogue, which allows for one's own opinions to be expressed as long as they are productive.

It is noteworthy that Cam raises the topic of playing devil's advocate whereby someone puts forth a proposition in order to explore an idea further by testing it against an opposing one (p.45). Playing the devil's advocate is a useful tool in an inquiry insofar as it may test propositions and thus deepen inquiry. Ross Phillips (1994), too, argues for the importance of the devil's advocate in inquiry in order to examine all aspects of the issue under discussion. He sees little trouble in voicing an alternative view in order to further examine the issue at hand. However, Cam warns that playing devil's advocate has its dangers with regard to creating an adversarial atmosphere; that students in an inquiry may use this technique to deliberately disagree and this may interfere with the progress of the dialogue. As Cam (2006) says:

> Students who delight in contradiction or who constantly play the sceptic, may bring a sense of fun to the proceedings, but their input needs to be tempered by recognition that inquiry is an attempt to make headway with the matters under discussion. (p.45)

The role of playing devil's advocate should be identified and discussed at the beginning of any inquiry to avoid producing disagreeable students (i.e., students who disagree for the sake of disagreement). Otherwise, dialogue could be in danger of becoming debate.

Unlike dialogical inquiry, in a debate there is no room for genuinely being devil's advocate, as each of the opposing teams presents arguments either for or against a proposition. It is easy to see why debate as a tactic is often used in legal argumentation and by politicians. But in both of these cases, it is the task of a third party (e.g., members of the jury or electors) to listen to the arguments of both sides in order to make judgments to overcome adversary (either by verdict or by casting a vote). There is, of course, no guarantee that the propositions both for and against will be given equal consideration. For this to happen it relies on the open-mindedness and deliberative capacities of the third party, including the ability to be the devil's advocate. But the role of devil's advocate has no place in the actual debate itself insofar as the terms of the debate are set out, i.e., agreement is expressed only to the assigned proposition and disagreement to that of the opposition (regardless of any doubt about one's own opinion). A genuine inquiry, on the other hand, can benefit from participants playing devil's advocate as its aim is not primarily adversarial.

We can sum up by saying that dialogue differs from debate because a debate is aimed at winning an argument whereas a dialogue aims at a greater understanding through collaboration. Dialogue emphasises collaboration while debate emphasises opposition. De Bono cautions against introducing debates into education for its promotion of adversary, a criticism that he also retains for doing philosophy in education. Cam, however, makes further distinctions between dialogue and debate for this reason when he notes that dialogue allows for multiple possibilities, in a sense promoting open-mindedness. The role of the devil's advocate in dialogue has been questioned for its reflection of debate, but it is nevertheless simply a way to explore all sides of an argument, and not just two arguments contained in a debate.

Monologue and Inner Dialogue

Earlier I mentioned that the common usage of the term dialogue as simply a discussion between two or more people can lead to it being contrasted with monologue. In this section I would like to explore this comparison further. So, let us for a moment imagine the unusually long speeches recited by Willy Loman in Arthur Miller's play *Death of a Salesman*, or the string of jokes flowing from the mouth of a stand-up comedian on a late-night talk show, or the endless minutes of talk by someone at an intimate dinner party who shows little or no concern for conversation with others who have fallen silent. These are typical examples of monologue—an extended, uninterrupted speech by a single person.[3]

Now imagine the sober but solitary figure of *The Thinker,* the bronze and marble statue by Auguste Rodin. The statue is often used to represent philosophy—a man in meditation battling with a powerful internal struggle. Whether or not this is an apt representation of philosophy is disputable.[4] Of immediate concern to our discussion is whether or not inner discourse, as represented by *The Thinker*, is a kind of monologue or dialogue. As mentioned previously, Amir (2001) defines dialogue as "a joint communicative activity with the goal of discovering truth" (p.239). She argues that a monologue is a kind of dialogue in that it uses the same processes, with the difference being that the discussion is with oneself rather than with others (p.240). Even when we engage with others in dialogue we do not discontinue the monologue, as we continue to formulate the ideas that contribute to the dialogue. Whereas Amir wishes to claim that monologue with oneself is a kind of dialogue, I make a distinction between a non-critical inner discourse or internal monologue and a critical inner discourse or internal dialogue.

An internal monologue can be similar to the monologues of Willy Loman in *Death of a Salesman,* with tendencies toward uncritical and unreflective monotonous speech, but differing only insofar as it is done in silence with oneself. One talks *to* oneself rather than *with* oneself. There is no exchange of ideas or opinions, no self-correction or no discursive interaction between listener and speaker. Only one voice is taking part and being heard. On the other hand, an internal dialogue, like its external counterpart, is a communicative activity with the goal of discovering truth, but rather than being a joint activity with others it is a kind of joint activity with oneself. Amir's description of monologue as a kind of dialogue is what I am calling internal dialogue. Unlike internal monologue, internal dialogue is critical and reflective. It is also a vital part of dialogue with others, as it would not be a dialogue proper if the inner discourse ceased—without an 'inner listener' there can be no dialogue in the content-oriented sense of dialogue as colloquy.

When the thinking and dialogue that occurs externally translates internally as inner speech, this process is described by Russian psychologist Lev Vygotsky as internalisation. In a dialogue we may become increasingly conversant at continuing the inner dialogue and the external dialogue at the same time, in effect multi-tasking our thoughts as we express them while concentrating on other perspectives in the dialogue. According to Vygotsky's (1987) process of internalisation the subject is engaged in internal dialogue, what he calls 'solo thinking'. His theory of solo thinking helps to clarify the distinction between internal dialogue (i.e., monologue as a form of dialogue) and monologue. Internal dialogue may be thought of as the very process of thinking; the voice in our head when we are thinking through a problem. In sum, dialogue cannot exist without internal dialogue, and no amount of monologue can act as a substitute.

Dialogue, Rhetoric and Dialectic

We now turn to dialogue as philosophical reflection and analysis. On the one hand, the term dialogue is often used to refer to the literary form of Plato's works and those other works that appeal to this literary form. On the other hand, and more importantly, dialogue can be described as dialectic insofar as it refers to its philosophical form or structure. To gain a better understanding of dialogue it is useful to make a comparison between dialectic and rhetoric. According to Curnow (2001), dialectic is concerned with the form or structure of dialogue. It is a specific type of dialogue insofar as it is a continual process that focuses on questioning and the answering of questions (p.234). The process is one of thesis, antithesis and synthesis and is distinctive by the resolution of tensions and contradictions over time (p.234). Curnow suggests that this process, as reflected in Plato's dialogues, is in general a positive one. Given the discussion in this chapter already, it is easy to see the links between dialectic and dialogue.

Rhetoric, on the other hand, is often cast off as inferior to dialectic. Historically, Plato's treatment of the Sophists in his dialogues is largely responsible for the modern view of rhetoric as confusing or illogical argument used for deceiving someone. The Sophists were depicted as selling rhetoric that mirrored dialectic, employing rhetorical sleight-of-hand and ambiguities and vagueness of language in order to support fallacious reasoning to achieve their purposes, which was to persuade or convince others. But to say that rhetoric is simply the 'art of persuasion' is misleading, as dialectic is also used to persuade. According to Aristotle, rhetoric is the counterpart of dialectic.[5] While both are proof-centred, and are used in persuasion, they have different purposes. Dialectic relies exclusively on argumentation and is used primarily within a discipline, which consists of experts who test for the truth of their claims and consistency of argument. Rhetoric is aimed at a general audience or target group whose members do not necessarily have expert knowledge, and therefore persuasion is *not only* a matter of arguments and proofs, but also of credibility and emotional attitudes. We can see from our earlier discussion on debate the links between rhetoric and debate, i.e., the intention of persuading the audience to adopt one point of view.

From our discussion in this first part of the chapter we can see that dialogue is not just mere conversation, nor is it debate or monologue. Dialogue can also be said to be necessarily dialectic, with the aim of resolving disagreement through rational discussion or to search for truth. Let us now turn to the role silence plays in dialogue, as both companion and inhibitor.

OUT OF THE SILENCE

Silence, simply put, is the absence of noise. In a world filled with all kinds of noises, it is very rare or not at all that we experience this kind of silence. We are, of course, not concerned with 'dead silence', but the ways in which silence functions in social interactions. As such, silence is the absence of speech. It plays a variety of roles in our everyday interactions and in the ways we communicate. For example, in designated 'quiet zones' such as those in libraries and cinemas, and increasingly public spaces where mobile phones are barred. Interpersonal relationships too are filled with moments of not speaking, not necessarily to seek quiet but also as necessary to our interactions with others in order to communicate, whether that is in conversation, purposeful discussion, or in dialogue. Silence, or not speaking, is sometimes a matter of choice and other times it is imposed upon us. This distinction highlights two notions of silence: 'being silent' and 'being silenced'. The connection between the two is not as straightforward as it may first appear when observed in the context of the kinds of communication where speech and silence are interwoven, specifically dialogue which is the matter of our direct concern. However, conceptually we can separate them by linking silence brought about by choice to the notion of *being silent* and linking imposed silence to the notion of *being silenced.*

Let us now look in more detail at the connections between being silent and being silenced. When we enter a public library we are usually expected to be silent so as to not disturb others. While it is an expectation, we *do* have a choice to do otherwise, albeit that by choosing to speak we may forfeit the privilege to use the library. A similar illustration can be found in Remembrance Day, a day on which it is not uncommon for people to commemorate fallen comrades with a moment of silence. Some people may even use this 'commemorative silence' to engage in reflection on the act of war—'lest we forget'. It is a voluntary action that gives the individual the opportunity to be with their own thoughts. There is nothing imposing about such a silence unless the person is not partaking in the silence willingly. On such occasions, the expectation of silence itself can be imposing for some people as not everybody necessarily wants to commemorate war heroes at that time and so are effectively being silenced during that time. Nevertheless, it can be argued in cases like this and the library, that we knowingly engage in activities where silence is required. Both cases can therefore be said to be illustrations of being silent.

Now let's look at another example which is much more problematic. In the broader context, we have, what many people in Western countries see as natural freedoms—freedom of speech and the right to remain silent. Free speech inextricably includes the right to remain silent, i.e., logically anyone who is genuinely free to speak must also be free to not speak. The logical relationship between speech and silence in this instance links the right to free speech to the freedom from self-incrimination. To act on silence in this context is to not allow control by an authority; to allow no one person to completely control discourse. However, this example also acts to highlight that choosing to be silent can also be an act of silencing, i.e., silence is imposed on another person without choice. That is to say, by exercising the right to remain silent others are silenced, not in the sense that they are unable to speak, but they are no longer able to interact with the other party.

Generally speaking, silencing is a way of wielding power over others; that is, those being silenced have little or no choice in the matter. Another example of this can be found in parent-child relationships. Parents of teenagers may occasionally be subject to the 'silent treatment' which serves as a form of control to manipulate or punish. Friends who resort to the 'cold shoulder' are doing similarly. Both of these acts silence individuals because of the enforced block to any further communication by the person imposing such a barrier to others. Moreover, the silence may be accompanied by visual signs such as body movement and gestures, which indicates that silence, while absent of speech, is not always absent of language. Splitter and Sharp (1995, p.47) also draw attention to a relationship between silence and language. However, their discussion is within the context of silence opening the way for meaningful dialogue and questioning. We will look at this in further detail later in the section on silence as reflection.

In the literature devoted to looking at theories of silencing, theorists such as Michel Foucault and Luce Irigaray offer theories of how silence occurs in different contexts. Foucault devoted his theories of power and silencing of the individual, ranging from coercive forms of silence, for example through surveillance, to the institutional silencing that occurs in the outdated modes of mental institutionalisation of individuals (Foucault, 1975). In the case of the latter, the technologies of silence are present both psychologically and physically. Individuals may be 'given a voice' but only insofar as being spoken for. But, silencing can also be a gender issue. For example, while men are able to discuss topics such as abortion, women's health, child-birth and menopause, their lived experiences in terms of gender/sex identity are not the same. In the case of abortion men may have informed opinions about women's choice or the right to life, but the impact of abortion laws are not experienced directly by men as these laws are to do with control over women's bodies. Irigaray looks at such issues through an exploration of dominant discourses, particularly male-centric language, which she says serve to marginalise or silence women (Irigaray, 1985). She adopts the term phallocentrism which refers to the advancement of the masculine as the source of power and meaning through cultural, ideological and social systems that effectively strips women of agency, i.e., female subjectivity is constituted as Other, or as marginal, displaced by discourses of phallocentrism. Women may be given opportunities to speak but the language that women speak through, and are understood by, is not the same language spoken by the opposite sex. Terms such as 'equality', 'freedom', 'rights' and so forth, have historically acquired their meaning through masculine discourse.[6]

These perspectives of silencing have made valuable contributions to the understanding of power, domination and the construction of knowledge in the context of language and communication. However, we are not directly concerned with theories of silence in the wider context that Foucault, Irigaray and others address, although in some respects this line of thought speaks to the issues of power and the construction of knowledge. Our concern here is more specific: to explore the extent to which speech and silence are interwoven in relation to the construction of knowledge through dialogue, especially in the context of education. Firstly, we will look at silence as inhibitor of dialogue. Our focus will be on technologies of silence as a way of exploring the notion of imposed silence or silencing. Later, we will explore silence as companion to dialogue, particularly the reciprocal relationship between speech and silence as they function in dialogue.

Technologies of Silencing

Broadly speaking, silencing happens due to coercive measures. This could be that someone is actually doing the silencing, or due to structural arrangements, such as the placing of classroom furniture as found in many traditional classroom settings, or the use of pedagogies that make little or no opportunities for inquiry. It should be noted that silencing can occur when participants in a dialogue bring with them certain patterns of power resulting from learned behaviour of which they themselves might not be consciously aware. The issue of power will be examined in more detail in Chapter 6, but for the moment it is suffice to say that participants who are prone to silence or who dominate discussion might not be receptive to changing their patterns of behaviour (Yorshansky, 2007; Burgh &Yorshansky, 2008). In this section, of main concern will be technologies of silence as a way of understanding the role of coercive measures or structural arrangements in obstructing progress in a dialogue.

Naomi Sunderland (2002) identifies seven different kinds of technologies that leave people silenced: (1) stereotypes, social roles, identity and reputation, (2) employment contracts and working conditions, (3) personal shared [in]security and attacks on self-esteem, (4) hierarchy and the phenomenon of the institutional voice, (5) discourse and public education/consultation, (6) resigned, passive waiting hope as opposed to healing, active, or revolutionary hope and (7) focus on the future. I will be directly concerned only with those technologies relevant to our exploration of how silence interacts with dialogue, specifically the first, fourth and fifth technologies of silence listed. The others are specifically related to dialogues on biotechnology, and so are not directly related to our discussion on dialogue and silence in general. However, the second technology she mentions, 'issues of personal security and self esteem', is significant to the discussion on power in Chapter 6.

The first technology of silence has to do with 'stereotypes, social roles, identity and reputation' (p. 6). For our current purposes, the term 'stereotypes' shall refer to simplified conceptions of groups based on prior assumptions that there are attributes which all members of a group have in common. Stereotypes can be either positive or negative, both of which could lead to biased opinions or prejudices. Of particular concern is that stereotyping could lead to unwillingness to rethink our attitudes and behaviour towards stereotyped groups, particularly in the case of negative stereotypes. Negative stereotypes coupled with prejudices can prevent some people of stereotyped groups from succeeding in life, e.g., in the development of their identity, social roles, and reputation.

Sunderland argues that when we are labelled as a particular type of person, there are certain values and opinions that may be linked to that stereotype, and in some cases these stereotypes lead to a degree of silencing. For instance, the assumption that children are sponges informs how they should be educated; as empty vessels awaiting a transferral of facts. Paulo Freire (1970) warns against such a view, what he calls the 'banking model' whereby the teacher-student relationship is one of depositing and collecting; where students are receptacles for receiving, filing and storing knowledge given to them by the teacher. Similarly, the assumption that children have nothing of worth to say or that they do not have the capacity for sophisticated thought could result in missed opportunities to develop their capacity to reason. For example, the activity of philosophy is considered by some to be inappropriate for children, or to be treated cautiously when being introduced into the classroom, particularly for those in the younger age-bracket. Plato tended to restrict philosophy to mature students on the ground that it made younger people excessively contentious. This view, though not popular amongst philosophers today is also reflected in the words of Tony Coady, who cautioned that "philosophy can easily create 'smart-arses' out of bright kids if introduced to children too early" (in Slattery, 1995, p.21). This common misconception has repercussions for the development of children and their way of thinking. Contrary to Coady, the literature in the field of doing philosophy with children suggests otherwise, that children can engage in philosophical inquiry provided it is offered in a way that is suitable for their interests (Cummings, 1981; Niklasson, Ohlsson & Ringborg, 1996; Imbrosciano, 1997). If teachers, parents, or communities assume that the level of capability in children is limited to only certain kinds of thinking, then children will not be encouraged to learn beyond their individual means. This stereotype leaves children unable to voice their ideas, effectively silencing them.

On the other hand, stereotyping children as *always* having ideas to contribute can be just as concerning, even though this concept of the child could be considered by some to be a positive one. This concept of the child should not be mistaken with the view of the child as typically having a natural sense of wonder or curiosity. A propensity to wonder is not the same as always having something to contribute. To stereotype children in this way could lead to expectations about every child's ability to contribute to dialogue, regardless of whether or not they actually feel like contributing or feel that they have something to contribute. Julie Dawid offers a caution based on her observations of six primary schools using stories to engage students in philosophical inquiry.

> Feedback from the children indicates that a reluctance to speak may not be caused by a lack of confidence in expressing thought; it may be due to a lack of cogent thoughts to express ... This is not commonly recognised by teachers, as expressed in the School Two Teachers' attempt to encourage a quiet member of the class: 'Everybody has thoughts—come on, tell us what your thoughts are.' This teacher had failed to recognize that the problem may be other than a lack of confidence and that everyone's ability to 'have thoughts' differs vastly. (Dawid, 2005, p. 63)

This highlights not what Coady cautions against, but that this kind of stereotyping silences the child insofar as their ability is being judged on the attributes associated with all children. This may have a negative impact on the child in terms of their identity, reputation, and interactions with their peers. Stereotyping in this way could even be self-fulfilling insofar as the child could identify with the judgments of their teacher or peers. This may have even further repercussions with regard to the classroom no longer being a safe environment for children to take risks or reflect in silence. While philosophy offers a forum for the expression of thought, questioning and problem-solving, it also requires paying attention to context and observing the interactions of the participants in relation to speech and silence. This does not deny the importance of other forms of expression, for example, philosophical expression through art.

To do what Dawid warns against is to fall into a form of cold-calling where people are forced to contribute when put on the spot. Reich (1998) points out that cold-calling is a common misconception of the Socratic Method put into practice. It has, he says, been interpreted at some American universities as a way to catch students out by asking questions that demand instant answers. Cold-calling, as Reich describes it, could disrupt the progress of inquiry, as participants also require silence to formulate and think through their ideas. It is similar with 'round-robin' exercises. While giving each student a turn to speak consecutively ensures everyone has the opportunity to contribute to the discussion, the flow of communication will be stifled making it difficult for meaningful dialogue and questioning to take place. Using classroom approaches such as these do not actually give students access to dialogue. To the contrary, they serve to silence rather than to liberate.

Stereotyping as an obstacle to inquiry extends to ethnicity and race, social class, religion, and gender, sex and sexual orientation. This kind of stereotyping has relevance to the current educational climate which places emphasis on pluralism in terms of knowledge and values. As teachers we must take seriously the possibility that some cultures do not place a premium on certain approaches to dialogue and may indeed be compromised by such a requirement, but we also must acknowledge that engaging students in philosophical inquiry can also assist them to function better in non-traditional settings (Laird, 1993; Field, 1995).[7]

Sensitivity to the contexts into which we are introducing philosophy is therefore paramount.

> Philosophical inquiry must find a balance between students having to be aware that they are acquiring knowledge from within a particular dominant discourse (i.e., a dominant way of thinking about or viewing the world) and letting them generate their own agenda. Otherwise it could be complicit in, or perhaps even unknowingly proliferating the values and concepts it wishes students to challenge. (Burgh, Field & Freakley, 2006, p.19)

What is required is a dialogue that is concerned with creating spaces to embrace such diversity rather than dismissing it through assuming that one model of dialogue is appropriate in every context. Miller (2005) cautions that if we are to introduce inquiry into any classroom then educators must aim to create an intellectually safe environment. Acknowledging the context in which dialogue takes place will help teachers to avoid the technologies of silence that come about through stereotyping.

What our discussion so far reveals is that generalized perceptions or preconceptions of children and their abilities, or of groups of people, can lead to unchallenged stereotypes which teachers bring into their classrooms. What I have said can apply also to issues of multiculturalism, gender, sex, and sexual orientation. Stereotyping can impede inquiry though representations that are hard to shake off, which if gone unchecked will contribute to the presence of dominant discourses that serve only to silence rather than liberate individuals and groups. This applies also to the ways in which Western philosophy has been stereotyped as being inherently masculine and therefore adversarial and with an overemphasis on the critical and rational aspects of inquiry to the detriment of creative and affective thinking. Briefly, Western philosophy has its roots in Ancient Greece, a historical turning point that owes much to Socrates. Through the influences of Plato and Aristotle, in terms of methodology derived largely from the Socratic Method and topics of interest, it developed into the predominant philosophical thinking of Europe, and later spread throughout what is now referred to as the Western world, to places such as America, Canada, Australia and New Zealand. Along the way Western philosophy has had influence on and was influenced by Western religion, science and politics. While the history of Western thought in itself should not been seen as a problem for education, this very history raises issues about the exclusion of other ways of approaching philosophy, and subsequently its influence on educational theory, aims and practice. The traditions of the East and the West are sometimes used to demarcate different ways of thinking or approaching life; religion, science, family, community, politics and so forth. There have also been moves to bring the traditions closer together by describing what they have in common. Similarly, but with different histories, the traditions of African, Hispanic and Indigenous peoples could be brought closer or further apart. Feminist philosophy has also contributed to these discussions in terms of its emphasis on caring approaches to society and the environment.

Philosophical education in the form discussed in this book has a line of history that can be described as traditional Western thinking, but what needs to be avoided is any generalised perception of philosophy as either a universal way of thinking applicable to all traditions or as adversarial thinking in the way de Bono describes. To define philosophy narrowly in these ways is to ignore the richness of both its history as a discipline and its methodology. Janice Moulton (1983) observes that the justification for philosophy is that "it shakes people up about their cherished convictions so that they can begin philosophical inquiries with a more open mind" (p.156). I will have more to say on this in later chapters, but for the moment it is enough to state that philosophy is characterised either as a universal way of thinking or as an adversarial method which fails to recognise the integral relationship between critical, creative and caring aspects of engaging in dialogue together.

Sunderland's second technology is 'hierarchy and the phenomenon of the institutional voice'. Her concern is mainly about the relationship between professionals and the organisations that employ them. She argues that there is pressure to conform to the 'institutional voice' which may compromise not only the professional's personal values, but also their professional values to conform to the common view or the prescribed view of the organisation. This may happen due to a number of reasons, such as fear of reprimand or needing to come to some kind of consensus over an issue. This technology of silence is a form of coercion and has application to education. I refer back to the conception of the child as a receptacle awaiting knowledge to be 'poured into their heads'. In the case of values education based on assumptions that universally shared values can be found, or that values can be prescriptively taught, or that students will accept certain guides to behaviour, both teacher and student are silenced in terms of developing an understanding about the relationship between values, ethical deliberation and decision-making. This is true of models that are underpinned by character education, prescriptive approaches, and values clarification. Thus, curriculum and pedagogical constraints act as technologies of silence, effectively acting as an obstacle to genuine dialogue.

Conformity through subtle forms of coercion is not limited to institutions such as education or other professions. Peer pressure in friendships in order to fit into a group is a common but subtle form of coercion. In friendships, individuals may be aware of pressure to conform to the views of others, and consequently find it difficult to speak honestly over disagreements. Fearnley-Sandler (1998) highlights the split loyalties that students experience within classroom inquiries between following an idea that contributes to an argument and going to the aid of a friend. While she notes that this adds an extra dimension to inquiry in terms of helping others, it can act to also inhibit the exploration of ideas (p.28). In the classroom, this is especially problematic as disagreement and agreement are at the heart of philosophical inquiry. Moreover, while friendships may be a motivation for individuals to conform to the ideas of others, coercion can be more covert in an inquiry. Mor Yorshansky (2007) argues that certain power relations in an inquiry can block or influence the direction of inquiry. She says "[w]hile ideas are explored among the members, some may try to influence the inquiry and its result in favor of their particular interests by monopolizing discussion time and by insisting to voice their ideas and understandings over other timid and less influential voices" (p.19). Such actions serve to silence other individuals in an inquiry and block the progression of ideas of the whole group. It is worthwhile to quote Yorshansky in full here.

> Such attempt can be conceptualized as the use of coercion and domination by individual members who are able to use their influence, gain more power and influence the inquiry in an unbalanced manner. Thus, coercion and domination are practices which jeopardize the development of a deliberative democracy in the classroom, and the community's attempts to identify solutions for amelioration based on a collective perception of the good. (pp.19–20)

However, she says that by emphasising equal participation, which is necessary for engagement in dialogue, that we may hamper the genuine emotions or opinions that are naturally expressed in an inquiry. Measures taken to share the power in inquiry equally to all members can, at the same time, silence individuals. For example, 'round-robin' exercises designed to distribute power evenly can silence ideas by stopping the flow of argument and the process of 'to-ing and fro-ing'. I mentioned earlier the concerns related to such exercises as they make the assumption that each student has something to contribute despite some students requiring further time for reflection.

The very structures underpinning certain kinds of inquiry can also be coercive or result in a kind of conformity. As we have seen, technologies of silence can aid conformity in both institutional practices and friendships. But conformity can also come about through the seeking of agreement by consensus. To some extent the models of dialogue that are the topic of this book appeal to some kind of consensus, or at least they do so in practice. Two that spring to mind are reaching a common definition through a rigorous process of inquiry, and setting the agenda for discussion. I will be addressing the issue of consensus later in this book, but for the moment I will concentrate on what all conceptions of consensus have in common—the convergence of ideas. If a dialogue has the aim of consensus, either through unanimity, general agreement, or group decision-making processes that seek agreement from most participants and the mitigation of minority objections, the ideal is that of a process of collaboration not compromise. Participants are brought together until a convergent decision has been developed. However, in practice, placing high value on consensus in order to make judgments or come to decisions may cause some students to feel the need to conform to the views of others, rather than reaching agreement through reasoned argument. Consensus acts as a procedural principle for coming to collective agreement, which in practice results from either the development of relationships among participants to reaching 'willing consent' or the sacrificing of opinions. As such, consensus almost always requires some kind of compromise of ideas or opinions. In pluralist communities particularly, where there is a high degree of variation, compromise becomes a matter of finding agreement through the mutual acceptance of terms often involving varying the original purpose or goal. But a compromise of this kind should not be seen as compromising the procedural aims of a genuine dialogue as this might be what 'following the argument where it leads' entails in a pluralist inquiry. The important point is that teachers need to be aware of the context in which consensus is required, e.g., reaching a common definition through analysis or making practical judgments for decision-making, and to be aware of any coercive practices that silence individuals or minority groups.

The way in which agendas are set in philosophical inquiry can also have the same effect. For example, the selection of questions by voting, which has become typical to how teachers approach agenda setting in the community of inquiry, allows students to reach agreement on what question to address first, but places an emphasis on the decision of the majority rather than on collective agreement.[8] By restricting the items on an agenda or restricting input regarding the formulation of questions the exploration of ideas is limited, therefore effectively silencing opinions that may have had the potential to facilitate discussion in another direction. If voting is seen as indicative of democratic decision-making then it is not surprising that this is perpetuated by political parties who are elected through democratic processes which require a vote rather than deliberation. While the majority of votes reveals the winner of an election, this may not indicate the better preference, especially in democratic countries where voting is not compulsory. The amount of votes may indicate only the preferences of those compelled to vote and therefore not necessarily representative of the whole community. Referendums have also been criticised, despite the view that they offer some degree of direct participation in policy-making. As an aside note, if education is to support democratic ways of life, then resorting to voting rather than collective agreement serves to justify current democratic practices. Needless to say, we will be discussing the notion of consensus further, regarding its contributions to dialogue and the nature of agenda setting and formulating questions.

The third form of silencing is 'discourse and public education/consultation'. Sunderland argues that by not providing forums for citizens to discuss topics of importance, free speech is impeded and individual voices silenced. She is correct to say that deliberative forums provide opportunities for citizens to develop solutions to problems collaboratively, but this applies not only to public decision-making in a democracy but also to the kinds of educational settings that support democracy. Classroom dialogue is integral to democratic education and has the potential to engage students in life-appropriate ways of learning and to reconstruct children's view of public discussion. By promoting classroom dialogue, children are actively involved in deliberative process aimed at developing the social and intellectual dispositions and capacities needed for active citizenship. To ignore this is to inhibit opportunities to develop the capacity for freedom of thought and to think for oneself, and therefore increase the risk of silencing children as future citizens.

In sum, we must be aware that in promoting classroom dialogue it is approached in ways that are conducive to reflective thinking. I have already acknowledged the concerns that arise from forcing students to contribute to inquiry through stereotypes and coercive classroom activities. If philosophy is a form of *freedom* then students should be exposed to philosophy in a way that liberates them from technologies of silence, i.e., centred on collaborative, inquiry-based practices that facilitates free speech, deliberation, and informed decision-making. The UNESCO study backs such a move, in order to expose students to democratic ways of life and to prepare them for active citizenship.

Dialogue, Philosophical Inquiry, Silence, and Reflection

According to Splitter and Sharp (1995), speech and silence in dialogue are interwoven; "the distinction between speaker and listener tends to disappear and the moments of silence become integral to the inquiry" (p.47). Put another way, silence and speech play a reciprocal role in balancing power in a dialogue. Silence, therefore, also has a positive role to play in inquiry—a chance for participants to listen, to consider the ideas of others, to be probing questioners, and to formulate their own opinions in order to contribute to the progress of the discussion. That is to say, participants are required to hear what others are saying to formulate opinions and to listen to their own thoughts to reflect on the meaning of their own words. Silence is, as Splitter and Sharp (1995) put it: "essential wait time that should accompany questioning and problem-solving activities" (p.47). Powell and Connor-Green (2004) concur, adding that silence is an essential part of a dialogue as it takes the emphasis off simply talking in order to listen and think before contributing. What is noticeable in a dialogue that progresses is that as thinking becomes more complex there may be more silences during an inquiry. Paulo Freire has argued along similar lines. Silence, according to Freire, opens up a space for participants in a dialogue to genuinely listen to what others have to say. It affords them the opportunity to appreciate questions and doubts and to "enter into the internal rhythm of the speaker's thought and experience that rhythm as language" (Freire, 1998, p.104). Participants must be sensitive to their own contributions in regard to silence and speech so as to not subvert the dialogical process, but to share time with others so that they may also make contributions.

Martha Nussbaum (1993) claims that "the real value of philosophizing [lies] in the responsive interaction of teacher and pupil, as the teacher guides the pupil by questioning ... to become more aware of his own beliefs and their relationship to one another" (p.298). Nussbaum's comment could sum up well the view that the strength of philosophising is in its uniqueness to elicit immediate and responsive interaction among participants and between participants and the teacher. Perhaps a good case study to illustrate this is 'Joan's story' as told by Lipman (1991, pp.209–10). Joan has two separate educational experiences; one in which she attends a lecture on philosophical theory and another in which she attends an inquiry-based philosophy tutorial. In the lecture Joan ponders her own thoughts in response to the professor's words. But in the tutorial, the professor acts only as facilitator to a classroom inquiry and Joan discovers that there are other, multiple perspectives that she could not have considered on her own. Initially she is reluctant to contribute but finds that she is compelled to test her ideas against others. The responsive interaction among participants, and between participants and the teacher, requires awareness of their own thoughts and those of others, which is a listening process, one that demands silence. On the other hand, expressing ideas requires language. What Lipman and Nussbaum are alluding to is that engaging in philosophical dialogue demands an interplay of speech and silence.

Both Nussbaum and Lipman could be read as referring to philosophical inquiry as primarily a face-to-face interaction. A commonality in much of the literature on Socratic influenced teaching methods is an assumption that face-to-face dialogue retains its 'liveliness' as it happens in a 'here-and-now' atmosphere of responsive interactions between participants. Even though face-to-face dialogue is fleeting and will inevitably contain irregularities, there is emphasis on a reciprocal relationship in face-to-face dialogue that purportedly is not found in other forums where dialogical interactions occur over time or are delayed. Although not directly relevant to our discussion on silence and speech in dialogue, I would like to point out that there are also benefits not present in face-to-face interactions, benefits that may have implications for reciprocal roles of silence and speech in dialogue. For example, web-based dialogue provides a forum for people who may have previously been denied access to central forums, for example, people in remote communities, international communities, and where time-constraints pose an obstacle to regular communications. The literature supports the view that delayed dialogue (a term used to describe web-based dialogue) offers education an effective tool for reflective thinking as it allows students time to think about their contributions and the ability to edit statements before posting. For example, Kirk and Orr (2003) note that delayed dialogue overcomes problems with access to dialogue for the following reasons: (1) users can engage in dialogue at different times and in different locations, (2) access to dialogue is available for twenty-four hours [per day], (3) small group discussion online overcomes the schedule coordination problems of face-to-face groups, and (4) time can be taken for reflection, data accumulation, and the gathering of references in order to substantiate their positions. Similarly Davis (2002, p.31) asserts that not only does delayed dialogue allow time for more reflection, but there is also more time for participants to develop their arguments, effectively making their recorded contributions more thoughtful. While the immediacy of face-to-face is lost in delayed interactions, also having access to web-based technologies enhances the opportunities for reflective thinking. This is also the view of Carol MacKnight (2000) who argues that online dialogue cannot replace face-to-face but acts as an additional dialogical tool. She cautions against introducing online dialogue without face-to-face dialogue. Students must already have "comprehension and knowledge of the elements of an argument and thus how to interact with ideas and each other in a meaningful way" (p.39). What we can extrapolate from this is that, while delayed dialogue gives greater opportunity for essential reflection, it is unlikely that students will succeed in substantive, reflective exchanges if they have not learnt to carry on similar conversations through face-to-face collaborative dialogue.

Some authors[9] argue that reading a written text is a form of dialogue; an engagement between the reader and the writer through the medium of the text. Turning to Nussbaum (1993) again, she argues that books are inflexible because the written word addresses "very different people, always in the same way" (p.298). Books don't interact with the people in the same way as other people do. If the author is not present to engage in direct dialogue, then there is no real engagement in philosophical thinking because the author cannot follow the reader's argument to where it leads but rather, delivers the same argument to each reader regardless of the person doing the reading.[10] In terms of reading philosophy texts to enhance the inquiry process, Nussbaum does say that philosophy books may be a useful substitute for those experienced in philosophical dialogue, but warns against the complacency that comes from reading *about* philosophy rather than the action of engaging in philosophical dialogue.

> Real philosophy by contrast, as Socrates saw it, is each person's committed search for wisdom, where what matters is not just the acceptance of certain conclusions, but also the following out of a certain path of them; not just correct content, but content achieved as the result of real understanding and self-understanding. Books are not this search and do not impart this self-understanding. (p.300)

She does admit to Plato's recorded dialogues being an exception. Karel van der Leeuw (2004) also highlights the importance of written dialogues as a form of written philosophy, adding that they can act as a guide to the Socratic Method.[11]

To avoid any contention regarding the reading of texts *as* dialogue per se, it is safer to say that reading texts is a form of listening to others whose ideas and arguments can be taken back to the dialogue, and therefore becomes integral to the process of dialogue as in intellectual pursuit. Maughn Gregory (2002) discusses the importance of bringing outside texts to the inquiry. He argues that if we are to have reflective inquiries, then we need to consult written texts for further information and to conduct our inquiries in the wider context of the community. Engaging with texts allows for greater reflection of ideas that may be explored further in the context of classroom inquiry. The teacher not only acts as the facilitator of classroom inquiry but also acts as a mediator between classroom dialogue and the written texts which are the result of professional dialogues conducted in intellectual communities of inquiry (as formulated by Peirce). The to-ing and fro-ing between actively listening not only to the other participants but also to the writer, while at the same time reflecting on your own thoughts and expressing your ideas to the group, can be seen as engaging in a greater dialogue of ideas. This process, which could also include web-based interactions and research, incorporates both face-to-face and delayed dialogue that demands interplay between silence and speech in a discourse that belongs to the participants.

A note of caution: it is not always easy to detect what is going on in the interplay between silence and speech, which essentially can be observed only as a group dynamic. But with the dynamics of groups silence also operates at the level of the individual, which may or may not have a positive effect on the progress of a dialogue. It may sometimes be obvious that silence on the part of one or more students is for reasons other than for reflection and active listening. Such silence can be "difficult to deal with precisely because of its essential ambiguity" (Splitter & Sharp, 1995, p.47). It may be the case that some students have a propensity to remain silent for most of the time. Aside from the obvious disadvantage suffered by those students who are not regularly engaging in dialogue, their behaviour may also have repercussion to the dynamic of the group. Wendy Turgeon (1998) refers to such students as 'reluctant philosophers'. She concedes that there are multiple reasons why students are reluctant to actively participate in inquiry: personal reasons related to social dynamics such as inter-personal conflict, or deep seated reasons, such as problems or crises at home (p.11). Recall that Dawid (2005) cautioned against assuming that every student is *able* to contribute to the inquiry. What this indicates is that there are causal reasons why these students are being silent, possibly as an indirect result of encountering technologies of silence or an inability for expression through speech; preconditions that have the potential to disrupt dialogue. Simply put, being silent may indeed be silence as wait time during a dialogue, but equally it could also be a form of silencing, effectively causing the whole group to be silenced.

While this book is concerned with approaches to philosophical inquiry through dialogue, there is often a mistaken view that when we argue for a model of philosophy as pedagogy, that it is necessarily appropriate for every educational experience. As Gregory (2002) suggests, there must also be time for reflection and engagement with outside texts to inform inquiry. There are indeed many situations in the educational context that require students to simply read a book to collect information. There may be times when students require quiet reflection—silence as the absence of speech but not of language. There are times when it will be necessary for students to engage with a text to access further research but also to engage in delayed dialogue when face-to-face interactions are not readily available. The UNESCO report suggests that students need to have access to philosophy and philosophical inquiry, but this must not imply that dialogue be the only teaching methodology used. Good classroom planning and practice "takes note of the students' needs for variety in classroom organization" (Sprod, 2001, p.155). Many practical skills need to be learned, such as research and library skills, computer skills, as well as skills in dialogue. Moreover, having these skills will be invaluable to the process of inquiry itself in a modern world driven by information and communications technology—an incomprehensible world to Socrates and the Ancient Greeks. Socratic pedagogy needs to be an adaptation of the Socratic Method for modern times. It is Socratic because it is characterised by a particular kind of dialogue; a dialogue with regard for cognitive growth and respect of persons. These two dimensions of dialogue, as we have seen, demand a similar respect for the interplay between silence and speech. It is with this in mind that we now turn to Socratic pedagogy.

DIALOGUE AS SOCRATIC ENGAGEMENT

I mentioned earlier Rodin's statue *The Thinker,* a solitary figure deep in his own thoughts of introspective reflection. Its popularity as symbolic of philosophy is undeniable. In contrast Raphael's *The School of Athens* portrays philosophy as a gathering of people who share ideas. At the centre of the image Plato and Aristotle declare their different views of knowledge. Plato gestures upward to where knowledge of the forms lies, while Aristotle's gesture stresses observation as the source of understanding. To the left of both of them Socrates addresses a group of bystanders. This image more closely represents the view of philosophy I present here; as a collaborative activity to stimulate rational thinking and illuminate ideas in the pursuit of knowledge or greater understanding of the world.

The Socratic Method

This idea of philosophy as an open-minded inquiry and collaborative activity can be traced back to Socrates and what has become known as the Socratic Method. Socrates spent most of his life attempting to engage his fellow Athenians in the activity of philosophy: a method of critical inquiry that had no obvious methodology like geometry or physics. He encouraged the idea that philosophy should be a process of argument and analysis, but with emphasis on dialogue. By engaging people in dialogue, Socrates could show that the answers to life's questions were not so easily attainable. Anyone who engaged in discussion with Socrates nearly always found that their answers to philosophical questions were either inadequate or unacceptable. In the excerpt below, from Plato's *Republic,* Socrates and Cephalus are engaged in a dialogue over what it means to be just.

Socrates:	But let us consider this further point: Is not he who can best strike a blow in a boxing match or in any kind of fighting best able to ward off a blow?
Cephalus:	Certainly.
Socrates:	And he who is most skilful in preventing or escaping from a disease is best able to create one?
Cephalus:	True.
Socrates:	And he is the best guard of a camp who is best able to steal a march upon the enemy?
Cephalus:	Certainly.
Socrates:	Then he who is a good keeper of anything is also a good thief?
Cephalus:	That, I suppose, is to be inferred.
Socrates:	Then if the just man is good at keeping money, he is good at stealing it.

Cephalus:	That is implied in the argument.
Socrates:	Then after all, the just man has turned out to be a thief. And this is a lesson which I suspect you must have learnt out of Homer; for he, speaking of Autolycus, the maternal grandfather of Odysseus, who is a favourite of his, affirms that.
Cephalus:	"He was excellent above all men in theft and perjury."
Socrates:	And so, you and Homer and Simonides are agreed that justice is an art of theft; to be practiced, however, "for the good of friends and for the harm of enemies"—that was what you were saying?
Cephalus:	No, certainly not that, though I do not now know what I did say; but I still stand by the latter words.

This short excerpt gives us an illustration of certain techniques that Socrates employed. Socrates was explicit in his demand for rigor when he used argument to uncover assumptions and fallacious reasoning; he showed arguments to be invalid by his questioning. In his dialogue with Cephalus, Socrates shows the flaws in Cephalus' reasoning by showing how his definition of justice would in fact lead to a contradiction if applied to a different situation. In a series of arguments being met with counter-arguments, the logic of the reasoning is shown to be deficient. This required Socrates' interlocutors to be sure of their reasoning before they entered into dialogue. However, in most cases, Socrates would still help his interlocutors to uncover their own faulty reasoning. In classroom dialogues, students must be aware of their own reasoning and that of others.

The type of questions posed by Socrates usually always led to the realisation that answers to such questions are much more difficult than initially thought. Below is a summary of the techniques that are central to the Socratic Method.

1. Socrates claims to have no knowledge to impart, and admitted ignorance at the end of discussions as strongly as he did at the outset.
2. In each step of the dialogue, Socrates poses a question to which his co-inquirers would supply answers, which in turn are met by further questions from Socrates. His clarifying questions lead to their answers nearly always being inadequate or unsuccessful.
3. Despite Socrates' admission of his own ignorance, he facilitates discussion in a subtle direction.

Nevertheless, there is contention over what it means to be Socratic. In Plato's dialogues Socrates is described variously as midwife, gadfly and stingray. Although he claims he is not himself a teacher, Socrates as a philosophical interlocutor leads his respondents to a clearer conception of wisdom. Claiming himself to be analogous to a midwife Socrates says he is himself barren of theories, but knows how to bring the theories of others to birth and determine whether they are worthy. He is also referred to as the gadfly of the state because he was "a persistent irritant whose questioning and reproaches aim at preventing the citizens of Athens from sleeping till the end of their days, from living and acting without genuine moral reflection" (Arendt, 1999, p.206). Just as the gadfly stings the horse into action, Socrates stung Athens. He has also been described as "a stinging fish who paralyzes and numbs all who it comes into contact with" (p.206). In effect, this metaphor alludes to Socrates' ability to draw his interlocutors into dialogue and then, through his questioning he "infects his listeners with his own perplexities, interrupting their everyday activities and paralyzing them with thought" (p.206). Once his interlocutors have interacted with Socrates they can no longer be content to go about their daily business without thinking through examination. This view of Socrates is important for our discussions on pedagogy as it pertains not only to education generally, and classroom practice specifically, but also to a way of life whereby students are encouraged to be reflective in their everyday activities and not just those activities in the classroom.

Socratic Pedagogy

While Socrates is an important figure in the history of Western philosophy and is responsible for the development of what we now refer to as the Socratic Method, I make no recommendations that schools should adopt the Socratic Method in the classroom, nor that students be expected to engage in Socratic practices in the way that Socrates did, especially in light of the ambiguities as to the precise nature of the Socratic Method. For example, Socrates is known for his relentless questioning of basic concepts, but in Plato's dialogues it becomes clear that he had certain cherished beliefs that underlie his questioning that sometimes led him to direct the conversation in subtle ways. He also had a specific kind of knowledge that he viewed necessary to discovering a good life. However, there is no denying that his principle of 'everything must be open to question' is fundamental to getting people to re-examine what they think they already know for certain. Recall that Socrates was considered a stinging fish for this reason, encouraging a way of life that is underpinned by constant questioning and re-questioning. What I am advocating is the development of Socratic classrooms through Socratic pedagogy, an approach influenced by Socratic methods but with further refinement. We need to identify those aspects of Socratic traditions that are applicable to classroom practice as this provides a focus for defining an approach to teaching and learning through collaborative, inquiry-based dialogue.

Socratic pedagogy calls for a specific relationship between teacher and learner, one in which the teacher understands the need for students to think for themselves in order to provide a practical means for students to improve their ability to think about problems and issues they are likely to encounter in their lives. Cam (2006) concurs that the Socratic Method itself may not always be ideal for the classroom, but that there is merit to being Socratic.

> Yet there can be no doubt that the ability to think about the issues and problems that we face in our lives, to explore life's possibilities, to appreciate

alternative points of view, to critically evaluate what we read and hear, to make appropriate distinctions and needful connections, and generally to make reasonable judgements are among the attributes of anyone who has learnt to think effectively in life. (p.1)

Socratic pedagogy is reflective education, in which thinking is understood as a process of inquiry. In an inquiry it is our disagreements as well as our agreements that shape the dialogue. Cam argues that this backward and forward motion of agreement and disagreement is what gives an inquiry its rigor, as it moves from convergent to divergent thinking through the course of the dialogue (p.44). It is important to note, however, that the aim of Socratic pedagogy is not to discover truth, at least not in the sense of discovering certainty. Rather Socratic pedagogy is an educational process, a regulative ideal which has as its foundations that all knowledge is fallible and stands open to future revision.

The idea of fallibility is central to our understanding of dialogue as expressed here. Its origins can be traced back to the philosophical works of Charles Peirce. Peirce rejected the idea of Cartesianism; that the mind is the key to unlocking knowledge, and therefore that truth and certainty are to be found in the individual consciousness (Pardales & Girod, 2006, p.300). He recognized the value of exploring disagreement and agreement with others, emphasizing collaborative thinking and knowledge derived from what he called communities of inquiry.

> In sciences in which men come to agreement, when a theory has been broached it is considered to be on probation until this agreement is reached. After it is reached, the question of certainty becomes an idle one, because there is no one left who doubts it. We individually cannot reasonably hope to attain the ultimate philosophy which we pursue, we can only seek it; for the *community* of philosophers. Hence, if disciplined and candid minds carefully examine a theory and refuse to accept it, this ought to create doubts in the mind of the author of the theory himself. (Peirce, 1955, p.229)

Peirce asserts that dialogue and thinking collaboratively is not only a positive way of thinking, but absolutely necessary to the acquisition of knowledge and understanding and hence essential if we are to arrive at 'truth' at all.

Fallibilism, Peirce thought, is central to the journey towards truth or reality. Ideas are under constant scrutiny by a community of inquirers, for it is constant examination and re-examination that can bring the group closer to knowing. Pardales and Girod (2006) refer to this process as people coming together to serve as a "jury to ideas and hypotheses" (p.301). Peirce's view of truth could be described as coming to know the world through rigorous analysis and re-analysis by the community. Once all ideas are tested against counter-arguments, the group may be confident that they have arrived at truth and reality: "The opinion which is fated to be ultimately agreed upon by all who investigate, is what we mean by the truth, and the object represented in this opinion is the real" (Peirce, 1955, p.38). However, it is only as a community of inquirers that truth may be uncovered.

Like Peirce, Lev Vygotsky also saw the necessity for collaborative thinking. A proponent of social constructivism, Vygotsky's theories align with that of Peirce. His *zone of proximal development* is a space in which children's natural capabilities can be furthered through their interaction with others. Vygotsky's notion of *scaffolding* means that, through both interaction with members of the wider community and with classroom peers, children's individual achievements can be enhanced (Berk, 2000, pp.259–69). Sprod (2001) argues that this "conceptual and reasoning space [is a space in which] children can operate with help from a group, but are not capable of operating in on their own" (p.148). This is not at odds with Peirce's view on collaborative inquiry. Vygotsky coined the term 'Community of Learners' which describes how different members of the wider community can contribute to student-learning (Berk, 2000, pp.259–69). If the contributions are from a diverse range of people, then learning can be broadened in much the same way as communities of inquiry use different ideas and views to shape the dialogue, in order to achieve better outcomes than inquiring alone would produce.

Vygotsky's theory of social-constructivist learning is strengthened by his theories on thought and language. Vygotsky (1962) was concerned with the relationship between thought and language, which he argued have distinct genetic roots. In Chapter 4 of *Thought and Language*, 'The genetic roots of thought and speech', he studied this connection at various stages of human development. While thought and language operate separately in early infancy, referred to as the pre-linguistic stage, they develop as the child uses the spoken word to reflect her intellect. Until this point, speech is present as a survival function only, for example, to express hunger. As the child develops, speech becomes more meaningful and has direct interaction with thought as the child realises the functionality of the spoken word. From approximately the age of two until preschool age, the child understands that everything has a corresponding word. From this stage forward thought and speech remain interlinked:

> The relation of thought to word is not a thing but a process, a continual movement back and forth from thought to word and from word to thought. In that process the relation of thought to word undergoes changes which themselves may not be regarded as developmental in the functional sense. *Thought is not merely expressed in words; it comes into existence through them.* Every thought tends to connect something with something else, to establish a relationship between things. (p.125, *italics* my own)

Vygotsky called the process of the interplay between thought and word a 'word meaning' (Medoca, 1997, p.30). He also argued that the process could never be complete as thought is continually enhanced by engaging in social speech. Vygotsky saw the value in thinking as a social process, and believed that thinking was enriched by social speech as opposed to thinking through solitary endeavours such as reading or writing or thinking alone. These skills come out of being guided beyond one's own individual capabilities. What happens, according to Vygotsky, is that the individuals involved in the collaboration have an *intersubjective* connection whereby the knowledge is a shared sense of understanding that comes from the contributions of different individuals (Berk, 2000, pp. 261). This cannot occur when inquiring alone. This is illustrated in Joan's two experiences of philosophy education mentioned earlier. In the first instance she was essentially inquiring alone, with the lecture as a text on which to reflect. However, in her second experience, the ideas that she had in the lecture were extended by the ideas of others that diverged from those introduced in the lecture. Intersubjectivity is, hence, the connection that occurs between individuals engaging in collaborative inquiry. We can suppose then that Vygotsky saw learning as dialogical and, like Peirce, that he rejected the Cartesian view of acquiring knowledge.

In sum, Socratic pedagogy is a process of reflective education through dialogue as a way to construct knowledge and create meaningfulness. The process is not an individual one, but a communal one in which the ability to think for oneself can be said to be one of its educational aims and practices. Moreover, Socratic pedagogy has the potential to contribute to the thinking curriculum, and clearly addresses the concerns outlined the UNESCO study in relation to 'thinking as freedom'.

Socratic Pedagogy and Democratic Education

Another reason for accepting truth as a regulative rather than as an attainable ideal, and thus to recognise the necessity of Socratic pedagogy in education, is pluralism. In a multicultural society there are many visions of the good, but "the diversity of society precludes us from identifying any one as the pinnacle of what it means to be human" (Reich, 1998, n.p). Socratic pedagogy, therefore, has a place in civics and citizenship education. It has the capacity to assist students in learning the skills and habits necessary for participation in democratic ways of life, especially for an understanding of pluralist democracy. This sentiment is reflected in the words of Nussbaum when she says "in order to foster a democracy that is reflective and deliberative, rather than simply a marketplace of competing interest groups, a democracy that genuinely takes thought for the common good, we must produce citizens who have the Socratic capacity to reason about their beliefs" (in Reich, 1998, n.p). To produce such citizens, we must start in the classroom. Socratic pedagogy has the capacity to help students to examine the world around them and to acknowledge that doing philosophy can improve their ability to think more effectively about problems and issues, and hence to reflect on democratic ways of life.

Cam (2000) claims that having access to dialogue is a basic freedom and an integral component of democracy and living a democratic life. The role of education is to develop a democratic citizenry, i.e., citizens with democratic dispositions and the capacity to reason and make judgments. What lies at the heart of a democratic society is the deliberative citizen. It is through dialogue that students can gain an understanding of the processes and procedures underlying deliberative inquiry, and learn to practice democracy and citizenship. Education and democratic citizenship become intertwined; a social and educative process of growth, not merely a preparation for life. Philosophy as freedom, simply put, means having the capacity to engage in dialogue with others, liberated from technologies of silence to pursue the question of: 'What constitutes a good life?' Practicing thinking in education that goes some way to solving society's issues, which is the first pillar of action for UNESCO, may just result in change at some level. Dewey (in Lipman, 1991) sees this as the basis of education.

> An educational system that does not encourage children to reflect—to think thoroughly and systematically about matters of importance to them—fails to prepare them to satisfy one criterion that must be satisfied if one is to be not merely a citizen of society, but a good citizen of democracy. (p.113)

A distinction can be made between 'educating for democracy' and 'democratic education'. Whereas education for democracy focuses on the acquisition of knowledge and skills as a means to improve the capacity of future citizens to exercise competent autonomy, democratic education recognises the social role of schooling as that of reconstruction and that children and young people have an integral role to play in shaping democracy (Burgh, 2003; Burgh, Field & Freakley, 2006). A commitment to Socratic pedagogy as a social and educative process of growth, not merely a preparation for life, is a form of democratic education not only because it is designed to bring about deliberative democracy, but it is in itself a form of deliberative democracy, where communicative and deliberative capabilities and attitudes are developed in order to nurture thoughtfulness and reflection to support democratic ways of life.

SUMMARY

Dialogue is a specific form of engagement whereby individuals can test ideas against others to create a better outcome than thinking alone can achieve. Dialogue is specifically for the purpose of travelling together to achieve a better understanding of the matter under discussion. It is a process of inquiry where individuals can explore agreements and disagreements to come to decisions based on the mutual search for truth. A genuine dialogue should aim to be as free as is practicable from technologies of silence that have the potential to impede inquiry. However, a genuine dialogue also welcomes silence because it "can function as a 'probing questioner' which grounds the speech of all participants" (Splitter & Sharp, 1995, p.47). As such, silence and speech work hand-in-glove in the interaction between thinking and dialogue. In the next chapter we will look at three models of dialogue that can contribute significantly to our understanding of philosophical education and the development of Socratic classrooms.

NOTES

[1] Sophists were rhetoricians who were skilled in rational argument. They taught people their craft for pay and this earned them the scorn of Socrates and Plato. See Rohmann (2000).

2 For more information on debating rules and formats, refer to Phillips (1994).

3 Strictly speaking, the term 'monologue' applies to a speech made by one person in the company of others, whereas the term 'soliloquy' is used for a speech spoken by one person who is alone. However, the distinction usually applies to dramatic or literary forms of discourse. In such cases the term 'dramatic monologue' is used to distinguish it from monologue generally. I shall use the term monologue to refer to both kinds of 'single speech' as well as any long speech delivered by one person who forgets or neglects the others who are there.

4 *The Thinker* has been used at times to represent *philosophy, especially modern philosophy since Descartes.* A cursory internet search reveals that this depiction is also a popular symbol for tertiary philosophy courses.

5 See Aristotle's *Rhetoric,* in Kolak (2000).

6 Moira Gatens has the best approach to silencing of 'different voices' in her idea of the 'body politic' where she says that marginalized voices can only be heard as hysterical, not as 'legitimate voices'.

7 Robert Laird (1993) has used philosophical inquiry with children in the Buranga Community in the Northern Territory, Australia. He found a noticeable improvement in their oral skills and in their confidence. On the one hand, this can be seen as a positive indicator because the children function better in non-traditional community. On the other hand, it draws attention to the complexities of language use and its relationship to cultural identity.

8 A variety of ways have been suggested to assemble questions or make connections between different kinds of questions (see Cam, 2006; Burgh, Field & Freakley, 2006). However, I mention voting for questions simply because it is still common practice among teachers. Arguably, this practice has limited value as way of structuring an agenda.

9 See La Caze (2008).

10 Nussbaum likens philosophy books to a manual whereas engaging in dialogue is action. Philosophy books that describe philosophical ideas are like tennis manuals; they can only take you so far in terms of instructing someone how to play tennis.

11 Karel van der Leeuw (2004) also highlights the importance of written dialogues as a form of written philosophy. She notes the benefit of written dialogues as our only record of what Socrates did and points to the fact that any guide to the Socratic Method comes from Plato's dialogues. While Socrates rejected the written word, it is because of it that his legacy remains. Hence, the 'Socratic dialogues', as recorded by Plato, have value insofar as they allow us to access that which Socrates does.

SOCRATIC PEDAGOGY AND CLASSROOM PRACTICE

As a result of current innovations and reforms in education, teachers are increasingly required to adopt new approaches to teaching and learning, with emphasis on curriculum integration and new pedagogies to facilitate student-learning. In connection with these reforms a growing number of theorists of education are advocating inquiry-based education with emphasis on integrating curriculum, pedagogy and assessment to improve teaching and learning. This is in stark contrast to traditional or direct teaching methods. Of particular importance is the increasing acceptance of the need for the teaching of philosophy and philosophical inquiry to children. This development is recognised in the UNESCO study as a response to cultural and political needs. This is one of the reasons why the teaching of philosophy and philosophical inquiry to children was given a privileged treatment in that study.

> The impact of philosophy on children may not be immediately appreciated, but its impact on the adults of tomorrow could be so considerable that it would certainly make us wonder why philosophy has until now been marginalized or refused to children. (UNESCO, 2007, p.4)

If more children are learning philosophy it is because more teachers are introducing it into their classrooms or more people are creating conditions that support the teaching of philosophy. Although still in its infancy, philosophical education represents a change in educational objectives and approaches to teaching. What is not clear is the ways in which different kinds of pedagogical approaches to philosophical education could develop that would be applicable to any curriculum.

This chapter explores three approaches to dialogue that have their roots in the Socratic Method or inform classroom pedagogy that is typically Socratic in form. They are Socratic insofar as they provide models that draw attention to different aspects of the Socratic Method. That is to say, they are methods of inquiry that have application to classroom practice but also have in common the cultivation of good thinking and its improvement. In particular, they have application to educational settings committed to thinking as a process of inquiry, especially for the development of intellectual dispositions and capacities needed for active citizenship. Simply put, these three approaches to inquiry can inform what a Socratic classroom might look like.

The three models of dialogue that share fundamental characteristics of the Socratic Method are: the Community of Inquiry, Socratic Dialogue, and Bohmian Dialogue. First, I introduce Matthew Lipman's Community of Inquiry, the teaching method that informs his Philosophy for Children program. His program includes a series of curriculum materials for children, consisting of novels and accompanying teachers' manuals, aimed at improving children's thinking skills, which he argued would improve the relationship between deliberative judgments and democratic decision-making. We shall explore Lipman's views on the importance of learning to think; a central theme in his educational theory and practice. To draw out the ties between Lipman's view on thinking, education, and democracy we examine the ideas of educationalist and philosopher John Dewey and his predecessor, pragmatist philosopher Charles Peirce, as well as Russian psychologist Lev Vygotsky, all of whom supply a theoretical basis for Lipman's theory and practice.

Next, we focus on Socratic Dialogue, a distinctly different approach to Socratic pedagogy but with similarities. Founder Leonard Nelson's aim was to educate children to want to seek truth, and to encourage self-esteem. Whereas Nelson gave few guidelines on how to employ his method of dialogue, his pupil Gustav Heckman developed guidelines for how discussion should be conducted. We explore the rules for Socratic Dialogue, the role of the facilitator, and the importance of reflecting on experiences common to all participants.

Finally, we examine dialogue as formulated by David Bohm. Bohmian Dialogue can assist in our understanding of the communal dimension of inquiry, and the role of care in the development of genuine engagement through dialogue. In particular we analyse Bohm's views on: listening as key to understanding, relationships in the dialogue, and the connection between these relationships and thought.

PHILOSOPHY FOR CHILDREN

Imagine a classroom full of children all focused on one joint activity. The children sit in a circle, facing one another, with legs crossed and furrowed brows, with visible signs of thinking processes shown on their faces as a teacher reads a story about two friends. The class pool ideas from the narrative just read and come up with a question that they are wondering about. The question 'What is a friend?' has been narrowed down by the class through careful facilitation by the teacher. One child draws a connection to the narrative and suggests that one of the characters was being a friend when he shared his sweets. Another child asks a clarification question and probes for further thinking; 'but is it only friends who share—can't you share with someone who is not your friend?' The teacher suggests that the class find an example of sharing that does not occur between friends. The class continues to dialogue together and to and fro between examples and counterexamples, asking for clarification and extending on the ideas of others. The teacher documents the exchanges until the paper clipped to the board is filled with the thinking processes of the class and the names of the children responsible for them. At the conclusion of the inquiry, the class has come to a collective understanding. They engage in a process of reflection, assessing their thinking together as a group.

This description is typical of classroom dialogue with students in what is referred to as a Community of Inquiry. Students put forward their views, describe, question and argue their points of view. As part of this process, they reason, justify and make sense of their experience. The Community of Inquiry is one approach to Socratic pedagogy. However, while this method could be said to have Socratic roots, its development in a social and educational context is more recent and can be traced back to Charles Peirce who originally sought to bring scientific inquiry to philosophy. He argued for the idea of science as an activity in which a community of scientific inquirers (or other scientifically based disciplinary communities) is engaged. John Dewey later broadened its application to the educational context generally. This was later extensively developed by Matthew Lipman as the pedagogical dimension for his Philosophy for Children program.

Background and History

Lipman initially began his journey of developing Philosophy for Children in the late 1960's as a lecturer at Columbia University, New York. While reflecting on the educational system in the United States, he found himself frustrated with the level of critical thinking that students had upon their arrival at university (Lipman, 2004, p.5). Eventually, with Ann Sharp and other colleagues, Lipman set about developing Philosophy for Children, an inquiry-based education program designed to integrate curriculum, teaching and learning through the practice of philosophy as the methodology of education. It consisted of a series of purpose-written philosophical novels and accompanying teacher manuals for early, middle, and senior phases of schooling. The novels, written in narrative form and containing characters that children could relate to, explored philosophical questions and issues, and provided a foundation for the development of philosophical thinking tools. The novels are intended to be read by students and teachers in teacher-facilitated communities of inquiry. Lipman's view is that the fostering of thinking rather than the transmission of knowledge is central to school education.

Since then Philosophy for Children has developed in various ways throughout the world, through training and publications. A variety of terms are used to discuss the teaching of philosophy to children from 'P4C' which has become an informal trademark for Lipman's program, to 'philosophy *with* children', which is not only the preferred British term, but distinguishes Lipman inspired programs that use specific written materials for British students. Another term used is 'philosophy in schools', which has been adopted in Australia to describe the direction of teaching philosophy as inquiry-based education. A large body of literature and classroom resources has also been developed in Australia, some of which have moved away from Lipman's original purpose-written material. Nonetheless, all of these attempts to develop or enhance ways of teaching though philosophy retain Lipman's original ideas that are characteristic of reflective inquiry-based education.

The Community of Inquiry

In the literature on Philosophy for Children, the phrase 'converting the classroom into a community of inquiry' is usually understood as the application of Lipman's educational philosophy to guide classroom discussion. In its broader application it means to convert the entire classroom or educational practices into a community of inquiry (Lipman 1991; Splitter & Sharp, 1995). The former is best described as the 'narrow-sense' Community of Inquiry and the latter the 'wide-sense' community of inquiry (Sprod, 2001, pp.152–56).[1] The literature on Philosophy for Children is vague as to what converting the classroom into a community of inquiry exactly means.

Peter Seixas (1993) makes a distinction between a classroom Community of Inquiry and an intellectual or professional, discipline-based community of inquiry. An intellectual community of inquiry retains its original meaning as formulated by Peirce and is grounded in the notion of communities of discipline-based inquiry engaged in the construction of knowledge. Seixas points out that these communities of inquiry (e.g., scientific inquirers, psychological inquirers) are the producers of knowledge, and that this knowledge informs specific subject areas within the curriculum. A classroom Community of Inquiry, on the other hand, is subject to the curriculum rather than being in a position to transform it. Any attempt to conflate the two, he argues, is not advisable for knowledge between communities is not unidirectional. Classroom communities of inquiry serve the purpose of developing an understanding of the skills, knowledge and methodologies of the disciplinary-based communities.

> As students are not in school voluntarily, and as they are usually subjected to a curriculum that is not of their making, forcing students to be part of a learning community at the beginning of a schooling experience is unreasonable. They do not, at the outset, represent the shared values of scholarship and participation that members of a professional, discipline-based, Community of Inquiry do. (Pardales & Girod, 2006, p.308)

Maughn Gregory (2002), on the other hand, maintains that a Community of Inquiry in the classroom should not be removed from the professional, discipline-based community of inquiry. He argues that an intellectual community of inquiry, or what he refers to as a community of experts, should be mediated by the classroom teacher as facilitator. It is the responsibility of the teacher to connect the students to the practices similar to those of expert communities of inquiry. This implies more than a classroom of students engaged in dialogue but also includes other teaching and learning strategies and activities are incorporated as part of a greater inquiry, for example, research, engaging with texts, experiments, field studies, and service learning. It was also Dewey's view that the classroom should be situated in the wider community and that the walls of the classroom should extend beyond the school to include the greater community.

Let's return to the Community of Inquiry as formulated by Lipman. Lipman's Philosophy for Children is an "attempt to reconstruct (not water down) the discipline of philosophy: to make it accessible and attractive to children who will then be able to appropriate it and thereby acquire the tools, skills and dispositions they need in order to think for themselves" (Splitter & Sharp, 1995, p. 99). Philosophy for Children is not simply a skills program but an approach to teaching and learning to enhance philosophical thinking. There are two basic principles to Philosophy for

Children: (1) an introduction to philosophical concepts and procedures through the process of reading and interpreting narratives, and (2) a methodology based on the Community of Inquiry through which philosophical dialogue can take place.

Classroom Practice

The Community of Inquiry follows a basic pattern of inquiry (Lipman, 1980; Sprod, 2001; Burgh, Field & Freakley, 2006; Cam, 2006). It has two distinct phases; a creative phase and a critical phase. The creative phase is marked by an initiating stage, consisting of the introduction of a problematic situation, asking questions, and agenda setting, as well as a suggesting stage which is the formulation of ideas, conjectures and hypothesis. The critical phase involves reasoning and conceptual exploration, evaluating evidence and criteria, and concluding.

Bearing in mind that the framework for the Community of Inquiry can be adapted to different classroom situations and needs, traditionally it is an inquiry that begins with the reading of a philosophically significant story. Students are asked to think of philosophical questions that arise out of the story. The group then decides on one question, perhaps the one most fundamental to the inquiry, to begin discussion. The inquiry then proceeds until either the group finds a natural end point or the lesson comes to an end. The final stage of inquiry is self and peer reflection, where the group must reflect on their own thinking in the inquiry and of the group as a community. This is only a brief overview of what a Community of Inquiry might look like, but let us now elaborate on the model further.

The Community of Inquiry can be adapted to a variety of classroom and educational settings; as a lesson in itself, and across subject areas in order to integrate curriculum, pedagogy and assessment as a way of improving or enhancing teaching and learning. The starting point for inquiry is the introduction of stimulus material. The type of stimulus used depends largely on the age of students in the class, the subject matter taught, the purpose of the activity, and other factors that teachers will usually be concerned with when developing lessons. Teachers may wish to introduce a purpose-written story wherein the philosophy is embedded within the story, or they may use existing children's literature, or any other stimulus materials, e.g., newspaper headlines, magazine articles, or movies which lend them to philosophical questioning, to initiate dialogue from the group.[2] For example, Susan Wilks (1995) shows how fairytales can be used to elicit dialogue about concepts, such as what it means to be good. Once the students have engaged with the stimulus, it is normal practice to give them time to digest the material. The teacher then asks students if they have any questions they would like to raise. This is a very important part of the process, as the interest must come from the students themselves. The questions that the students volunteer will determine the type of inquiry that will ensue.

Looking at Wilks' example of some questions that may result from exploring fairy tales, we have: (1) 'What makes a character good?' (2) 'What actions do characters perform that are good?' and (3) 'What actions do characters perform that are bad?' (p.83). From the list of questions raised by the group, students then decide on a question, or group of related or interconnected questions to focus on during classroom discussion. For example, the question selected may be, 'What makes a character good?' The students' questions set the agenda, and are vital for stimulating further discussion. Discussion may or may not stay on the original question, e.g., 'What makes a character good?' and can flow onto an array of issues. This is not necessarily a problem, provided that the inquiry focuses on an idea or issue, and the discussion builds around it. Lipman insists that the logic of the argument itself should lead the inquiry (2004). So after the agenda is set, the dialogue may go in many different directions depending on the requirements of the inquiry. It is worthwhile to quote him in full here as the idea of 'letting the argument lead' is central to our understandings of the Community of Inquiry.

> When the classroom has been converted into a community of inquiry, the moves that are made to follow the argument where it leads are logical moves, and it is for this reason that Dewey correctly identifies logic with the direction of inquiry. As a community of inquiry proceeds with its deliberations, every move engenders some new requiredness. The discovery of a piece of evidence throws light on the nature of the further evidence that is now needed. The disclosure of a claim makes it necessary to discover the reasons for that claim. The making of an inference compels the participants to explore what was being assumed or taken for granted that led to the selection of that particular inference. A contention that several things are different demands that the question be raised of how they are to be distinguished. Each move sets up a train of countering or supporting moves.

Under the guidance of the teacher, students will discover that discussion is more than simply expressing opinions, or eliciting a range of responses but is disciplined in its logic. They may be asked to give reasons for their views, and since reasons "may pull in different directions, and some are likely to be stronger than others, the [students] will find themselves in need of criteria by which to judge the outcome" (Cam 1995, p.42). The teacher's role is vital to successful inquiry. Whilst it is important that the students' questions set the agenda, the teacher must help students develop the habit of exploring disagreement, and to be mindful of the progress of the discussion. Divergent opinions must be explored, e.g., through considering alternatives, appealing to criteria, making appropriate distinctions, seeing implications, and giving reasons (pp.41–54).

The role of the teacher is that of facilitator and co-inquirer. This is paramount, as the teacher must model the procedures of inquiry in order for students to engage collaboratively and to "follow the inquiry where it leads" (Sharp 1993, p.59). Lipman represents the teacher as facilitator through metaphors like the captain of a ship or a conductor of an orchestra. It would be detrimental to inquiry if the teacher were seen as an expert or imparter of knowledge, as he or she is responsible for the form of discussion and not the content (Freakley & Burgh 2000, p.7). The teacher's role is to bring out the skills of others through coordinating "highly complex and varied activities" rather than holding knowledge as "contents to be doled out to students" (Lipman, 1991, p.212). The teacher is also a role-model for students in the inquiry. While the teacher should be wary of becoming heavily involved in the substantive content of the inquiry, they should model the procedural aspects. In the illustration of a Community of Inquiry at the beginning of this chapter, I illustrated how the teacher asked the class if they could think of any examples to further the ideas of one of the children. By asking procedural questions that facilitate discussion the teacher models the behaviour that is required in the inquiry (Howells & McArdle, 2007). The teacher also has the task of monitoring the discussion and to ensure that the rules of inquiry are followed. The most notable of these is that every participant must be self-reflective (Splitter & Sharp 1995, p.16). Being self-reflective means that participants should be willing to modify and adapt their arguments if they cannot adequately respond to an opposing argument or alternative perspective. This should not be seen as a competition. However, if a participant in a group has firmly held beliefs on a particular issue, then he or she should be allowed time to process and articulate a counterargument before agreeing with another argument (Thomas 1997, pp.42–8). The dialogue should be prevented from straying from philosophical inquiry into unfocused discussion or anecdotes.

The procedural aspect of inquiry, otherwise known as the process of inquiry, guides both the way in which the community interacts collaboratively, and the progress of the discussion. For example, the characteristics of an inquiring community include listening attentively to others, responding to ideas and not the person, openness to consider alternatives, being prepared to challenge ideas and have ideas challenged, as well as asking questions, exploring disagreements and making links between ideas. These characteristics refer to how the participants in an inquiry engage with each other as a community. This is different, but not separate to the substantive elements of the inquiry. The substantive dimension is the "subject matter, the content, things worth inquiring about" (Burgh et al, 2006, p.138).

The critical elements of inquiry include being able to reason critically and think conceptually. For example, participants can engage in self correction, identify weakness in premises, fallacious reasoning, and unwarranted generalisation, as well as develop the skills of categorisation, concept exploration, finding definitions, and classification. Critical thinking is integral to philosophical inquiry, as participants must learn the rules and skills that are at the heart of reflection and judgment. These rules and skills aid in making the discussion a dialogue, and not a mere conversation. For dialogue to be productive, it must produce something, which is what makes a dialogue substantive. Creative thinking makes an important contribution. Through engaging with ideas, such as exploring alternatives or building on the ideas of others, and developing a hypothesis, students gain a deeper understanding of what is being inquired into.

At the conclusion of the inquiry participants must value the process and not only the outcome of inquiry. Lipman (1991) argues that the inquiry is an end in itself. He says "[s]eldom have I seen children dissatisfied with the product they took from a philosophical discussion, even if it is only some modest philosophical distinction, for they recognize how before that acquisition they had even less" (p.231). Golding

(2002) adds that there must be progress made if the inquiry is to be worthwhile. Perhaps he puts it best when he says "When you do philosophy you end up more confused, but you are confused at a higher level" (p. 10). This raises the issue of how to assess the quality of the inquiry in relation to its educational aims and practice. However, because the Community of Inquiry emphasises both community and inquiry, assessment of both the cognitive and social behaviour of the class as a whole is required in to order give a practical indication of its progress for both teacher and students alike. It is, therefore, useful at the conclusion of the inquiry to allow time for students to engage in self- and peer-reflection to make qualitative judgments about the cognitive and interpersonal outcomes that occur during the dialogue. Usually this takes the form of reflection on procedural questions, which are aimed generally at social behaviour or interactive patterns of the community This will assist in an understanding of how students engaged with one another (e.g., 'How well did we listen?' 'Did we search for alternatives?'). Reflection on substantive questions considers the quality of the inquiry, how philosophical rich the discussion was (e.g., 'Have we made good progress towards answering the question?' 'Did we sufficiently examine the concepts used and reasons given?'). Arguably, this is the most important part of the inquiry as it allows for: (1) consolidation of thinking through self-realisation, and (2) room for growth as students come to realise where they need to work on some areas or continue with aspects that went well in the inquiry.

Questions for reflection are not intended as a checklist for students to simply tick one at a time. Rather, they are meant to elicit discussion on opinions about students' experiences of the inquiry process in similar ways that the inquiry itself is conducted. It is a kind of meta-dialogue which is both an individual reflection and a group reflection for which the teacher is a part. While careful observation of the inquiry itself will give an indication of such behaviours as listening and turn-taking, as well as more substantive aspects such as building on ideas and asking for clarification, self and peer assessment at the conclusion of a session is designed to assist students to reflect on their inquiry and encourage them to self-correct. The process of reflection and self-correction is vital for the progress of inquiry—as participants become more reflective about their behaviour during inquiry they are likely to learn to take more responsibility for the improvement of their thinking. This kind of reflection can gradually become more sophisticated, for example, questions for reflection could become more in-depth and complex and reflective journals can be used.

The Community of Inquiry as Ethical Inquiry

Engaging students in dialogue offers them the opportunity to explore ethical issues collaboratively. Dialogue is important in nurturing imagination in students, helping them gain a sense of community, as well as an understanding that trust and respect are integral to being a part of such a community. Understood in this way, Lipman's approach to integrating curriculum, teaching and learning offers more than a thinking skills program. Other proponents have noted that the Community of Inquiry is important for the development of dispositions ranging from democratic dispositions to multiple intelligences including emotional intelligence.[3]

Lipman (1991b, p.7) insists that philosophy is a way of cultivating reflective thinking rather than creating a classroom full of philosophers. The aim of the Community of Inquiry is "not to turn children into philosophers or decision-makers, but to help them become more thoughtful, more reflective, more considerate, more reasonable individuals" (1977, p.69–70). By developing these dispositions, Lipman thought that students would be better equipped to think ethically and consequently to become reflective and engaged citizens in a democracy. By being self-reflective, we are able to think about how to approach a situation, and to consider how we should act at any given moment to make informed decisions regarding our interactions with others, and with the environment. Cam (1994) interprets Lipman as saying that being reflective is in fact what being moral is all about; that "the alternative to moral instruction lies in developing children's reflective moral judgement" (p.23). Splitter and Sharp (1995) claim that "[w]hen it comes to ethical development—that is, the development of traits which make it possible to form good judgements about how to act and how to live—the reciprocal relations which link our self-directed thoughts, feelings and actions with those thoughts, feelings and actions directed towards others, are fundamental" (p. 165). They argue that this requires reflection in order to come to the realisation that others may have different desires, thoughts and opinions. Students will then make ethical decisions based not only on their self-interest, but on the interests of others also.

Lipman (1988) argues that philosophical inquiry and ethics go hand in hand, and should not be devoid of one another. Cam (1994) concurs with Lipman that philosophy has an ethical component, insofar as philosophical inquiry reflects an ethical process (pp.19–21). They contend that the very process of engaging in Community of Inquiry is exemplar of the behaviour required outside of inquiry that requires such dispositions as respect, tolerance and fair-mindedness. However, ethical inquiry is also a sub-discipline or branch of inquiry and has its own application. A philosophical inquiry should also be devoted to questions of ethical importance regarding what is the good life. Children must be concerned with moral issues throughout their inquiry.

What participants make in the discussion is an intersubjective connection, insofar as the process of inquiring and reflecting together can help participants gain a greater understanding of the topic at hand. By asserting and justifying one's own opinions, as well as taking on board or rejecting other opinions, a participant may arrive at a perspective that has been shaped by having the group as a sounding board (Thomas 1997, p.44). It is through this type of inquiry that participants are likely to achieve more than an individual working alone could possibly achieve. Intersubjectivity is the process by which participants develop understanding and create meaning through the exploration of ideas in collaboration with others. Splitter and Sharp (1995) use the following analogy to explain the connection between individual perspectives and the construction of knowledge.

Just as in physics we learn that the things we observe are affected by our observations, so the person who thinks for herself understands that the subject matter of her inquiry can never be completely severed from herself as an inquirer. This is not an argument in favour of subjectivism or relativism, but an *acknowledgement of the power of individual perspectives.* It is precisely for this reason that the person who thinks for herself is committed to the inquiry process, a process which involves self-correction and a coming together of different perspectives. (p.16, *emphasis* mine)

In terms of ethical education, I posit that Splitter and Sharp's notion of committing oneself personally to the inquiry is central to developing a greater understanding of the relationship between individual values and collective decision-making. If the inquiry is applicable to all individuals engaged in dialogue together, and they are each committed to the process of inquiry, it is more than likely that they will develop their own perspectives of world-views. As Lipman (1977) puts it, "every child should be encouraged to develop and articulate his or her own way of looking at things" (p.62). This goes to the heart of the Community of Inquiry, which Lipman (1988) says is an exemplar of democracy in action.

The idea of democracy is central to the Community of Inquiry and to ethical education (Vicuna Navarro 1998, pp.23–26). Lipman (1988), inspired by Dewey's notions of education in preparation for democracy, based his program around these values.[4] Democracy, in the case of the Community of Inquiry, allows all participants the opportunity to voice their opinion. The dialogue that is based on these principles is in itself democratic, and thus creates the potential to promote or foster democratic dispositions and behaviour. According to Lipman, the Community of Inquiry is an effective method not only for civics and citizenship education, but generally, for ethics education, and is more reflective of Socrates' attitude. The notion of following the argument to where it leads "has been a perplexing one ever since Socrates announced it as the guiding maxim of his own philosophical practice" (p.230), and hence is central to the question of "what is a good life?"

Philosophical Education and Constructivism

Lipman was certainly influenced by theorists who valued children as active constructors of knowledge. It is not surprising, therefore, to find that social constructivism underpins his theories on learning and teaching. Using Peirce's original conception of a community of inquirers, Dewey's manifestation of inquiry-based learning in the classroom, and Vygotsky's social constructivism, Lipman could build his idea of a Community of Inquiry.

Although we have already looked at Peirce briefly in Chapter 1, we will revisit him here. Peirce's ideas are integral to Dewey's theory, for his emphasis on fallibility is at the heart of inquiry. Lipman (2004), too, saw this as his guiding maxim.

Inquiry began with the failure of our key beliefs and ceased when that belief had been repaired or replaced. We were alerted to the realization that one of our beliefs wasn't working by the onset of doubt. It was doubt that caused us to reflect, to inquire. It was doubt that compelled our attitude to switch from an uncritical one to a critical one. It was doubt that forced us to begin thinking imaginatively, creatively, productively, so as to come up with a hypothesis of what could be done to make our doubt subside. (p.3)

Lipman says that fallibility is the basis of his Community of Inquiry which was borrowed directly from Peirce's idea of fallibility in scientific communities of inquiry. Therefore Peirce becomes important to Lipman's concept of inquiry as a community process. Recall that we explored Peirce's idea that knowledge can only be obtained if it is tested against other ideas. Peirce's pragmatist approach should not be confused with scepticism which is the train of thought that one should question everything.

Lipman was baffled by Dewey's dismissal of philosophy as purely a theoretical discipline and his failure to put it to practical use. While Lipman brought out the philosophy in Dewey, it was not recognised by Dewey that philosophy would have its place in the classroom despite his interest in philosophy as a discipline (Lipman, 2004, p.2).[5] Dewey was originally concerned with the notion of scientific inquiry. Scientific education, according to Lipman, seemed the easy connection for Dewey between inquiry and education. Lipman saw that the same connection could be made between philosophical inquiry and education and so he sought to make a practical philosophical model for education purposes. Dewey's most notable influence was his approach to democratic thinking as practiced in the classroom and reflected in the construction of his *Laboratory School* which turned the school into a miniature society. Lipman (1991) notes that Dewey's theories of reflective thinking which involves an awareness of one's own thinking and how this may impact on others is a framework for both democratic thinking and ethical thinking. Lipman says "To know the consequences of ideas is to know their meaning, for as Dewey, pragmatist and follower of Peirce, was convinced, their meaning lies in their practical bearings, the effects they have upon our practice and upon the world" (p.106).

Vygotsky's theories on social-constructivism can also be seen as an influence on Lipman. Lipman notes that Vygotsky's emphasis on thinking and cognitive skills and metacognition were becoming an important part of a new wave of education in the 1970s. Vygotsky can be traced in Lipman's theories of internalisation. It is Lipman's view that the process of inquiry, if it is successful in the classroom, will translate to behaviours adopted both inside and outside of a Community of Inquiry. The dispositions to think ethically, for example, if practiced in an inquiry will give students the disposition to use the same decision-making skills required in the inquiry to apply to situations outside (Lipman, 1991, p.242)

We now have an understanding of the Community of Inquiry as Lipman intended it to be implemented. We have explored the theoretical underpinnings in terms of Lipman's overall goal to engage students in active citizenship by thinking together. While the process of inquiry is important to Lipman in terms of letting the argument lead, this process of thinking collaboratively was a catalyst for the creation of democratic dispositions. Taking his lead from Dewey and Vygotsky, it was Lipman's view that engaging students in dialogue would naturally relate to dispositions outside of the classroom. Lipman's idea of thinking through inquiry is inherently creative while also retaining a balance of critical and caring thinking (the latter will be explored later). In contrast, Nelson's Socratic Dialogue focuses on critical philosophy. It is to Nelson and Socratic Dialogue that we shall now turn.

NELSON'S SOCRATIC DIALOGUE

Imagine a group of students philosophising in a classroom using personal experience as the primary building block for understanding issues. The process, due to its specific structure, can be likened to an hourglass. Facilitated by an experienced teacher, the students begin with a universal question. One by one the students offer examples, each of which undergoes analysis until one of them is chosen as the focus for rigorous discussion. Their only purpose at this stage of the inquiry is to determine where, in the example, the universal can be found. From the widest part of the hourglass they move toward its narrow waist. The group does this by trying to decide on a definition through consensual articulation, in an attempt to try to particularise the universal. From here the dialogue begins to broaden again. The working definition is again applied but this time to all of the other examples raised earlier by the students. They do this in an attempt to decide if the definition is truly universal—a continual process of modifying where necessary. At the final stage, now toward the bottom of the hourglass, they try to falsify the definition with counterexamples until the group has succeeded in its quest to find a conclusive definition. If such a definition cannot be found, they continue to undergo this process and modify the definition until they do so. Let us now look at the history and background of how such a process developed in educational settings.

Background and History

In the 1920s, German philosopher Leonard Nelson adapted and promoted the Socratic Method as a way of renewing education and politics. Nelson was not simply interested in philosophical education, he was also interested in mathematics and politics. These interests influenced his approach to education through an emphasis on logic and reason, and his inherent desire to create reflective and critical citizens. Following the thinking of Immanuel Kant and Jakob Fries, he believed that by working collaboratively in groups, participants could critically investigate their own beliefs by understanding how they came to their judgments and the assumptions that go unnoticed in their efforts to give meaning to their experiences. Identifying the Socratic Method as both critical dialogue and a means to awareness of the limits of human cognition, Nelson emphasised the Socratic search for the foundations of knowledge more prevalent in the later dialogues of Plato, and played down the Socratic claim of 'not knowing' or coming from a position of ignorance. This is significantly different to Lipman, who, through his pragmatist links, held onto the notion of fallibilism as a regulative ideal of the community of inquiry.

While acknowledged for having contributed significantly to political theory, Nelson's development of these theories was cut short by his early death at the age of forty-five. Similarly, his work on Socratic Dialogue was also incomplete. His adaptation of the Socratic Method may not have seen the light of day had it not been for one of his students, Gustav Heckmann, and later among others, Jos Kessels. Heckmann is particularly renowned for being responsible for its distribution in Europe. Because Nelson wrote primarily in German, his many contributions have not been translated into English and are, therefore, not widely accessible in the English-speaking world. Much of what we know about the success of his method of dialogue is the result of those practitioners who introduced it into educational and other settings.

Like Dewey, Nelson had an experimental school. The purpose of *Landeserziehungsheim Walkemuehle* was to "train its pupils in enlightened and liberal citizenship" (Blanshard in Nelson, 1965). Writing on the aims and purposes of the school, in the publication of Nelson's collected papers, *Socratic Method and Critical Philosophy,* Blanshard wrote the following in his foreword.

> Nelson developed in his own classrooms a method of teaching philosophy that seems to have been extraordinarily effective. He believed it to be derived from the nature of the subject itself. What is philosophy essentially? ... It is a special kind of mental activity directed toward a special end. If we can agree about this end, we can perhaps also agree about the activity, and about the best means by which one mind may induce it in others. (p.vi)

Proponents of this method agree that engagement in philosophical dialogue through striving for consensus leads to a close examination of arguments and hence a propensity for reason through a process of self-examination and self-criticism. The common view held by the proponents of Socratic Dialogue is that the model has an emphasis on collective agreement in which the group journeys together through dialogue to reach a consensus at the conclusion of the inquiry, and a group understanding of the topic under discussion. The group reaches this conclusion through a series of steps. Nelson proposed that the group proceed through seven steps that follow sequentially (the process we will address in more detail later). These steps, according to Nelson, must be followed rigorously in order to conclude the dialogue. Not everyone agreed with Nelson. For example, if there is not enough time to complete all of the steps then no conclusion can be reached. This led to a number of interpretations of Nelson's original formulation of Socratic Dialogue.[6] Nonetheless, Nelson was adamant that there may be a need for the modernisation of Socratic Dialogue, and hence it could be argued that Nelson may have agreed with the adaptation of his own method. Some proponents who have adapted Socratic Dialogue argue that, had Nelson been present today, his model may have followed a slightly different direction with regards to his interpretation of reaching consensus. Like Lipman who offered training in the

Community of Inquiry, training workshops are available for the purpose of educating facilitators in the process of dialogue. The 'Kopfwerk Berlin' is mainly responsible for training in Europe and has also engaged in training in the United Kingdom.

Nelson is startlingly similar to Lipman in his outcomes for education despite the years and continents that separated them. Both argue that philosophical dialogue in the classroom is for the cultivation of judgment. Like Lipman, Nelson argued that the Socratic Method is "the art of teaching not philosophy but philosophizing" (Nelson, 1965, p.1). However, unlike Lipman, who argued that the aim of philosophical education "is not to turn children into philosophers or decision-makers, but to help them become more thoughtful, more reflective, more considerate, more reliable individuals" (Lipman, Sharp & Oscanyan, 1980, p.15), Nelson placed more emphasis on "making philosophers of the students" (Nelson 1965, p.1). Whereas, Lipman does not intend to make philosophers of students but rather to cultivate the skills used in philosophising, Nelson's overriding aim was "for the education of responsible political leaders" which he argued could be achieved by thinking philosophically and ethically (Kraft in Nelson 1965, p. ix).We can make the distinction that while both theorists had a similar outcome in mind, for Lipman the focus was on the ethical individual whereas Nelson saw the ethical individual as the political individual.

Socratic Dialogue

Dieter Krohn (2004) points to four features that must be present if a dialogue is to be called a Socratic Dialogue. These are: (1) starting with the concrete and remaining in contact with concrete experience, (2) full understanding between participants, (3) adherence to a subsidiary question until it is answered, and (4) striving for consensus. These defining features of Socratic Dialogue are best explained in terms of their application to practice, which will be the topic of the next section. But I offer here a brief account of each to highlight their importance as defining features for practice.

In Socratic Dialogue, experience and concrete examples play a crucial role in testing universal claims. To Nelson, knowledge must remain connected to human experience. So, rather than considering hypothetical situations that draw on experiences 'out there' concrete examples allow the contentious concept being questioned to come out of lived experiences. This is where Krohn's second feature comes into play. Because the dialogue is concerned with finding a definition, in order to gain full understanding between participants, there must be continual reflection on the application of the concept to these concrete experiences. This process requires participants to adhere to the subsidiary question until it is answered. The subsidiary question in this case may have come out of initial questions that required narrowing down to what is central in the problematic situation. It is this question that holds the focus for the rest of the dialogue. These three features are driven by the most defining feature of Socratic Dialogue—striving for consensus. To come to conclusive definitions there must be a collective understanding in order to claim, at least provisionally, that there are no further counter arguments.

Socratic Dialogue, according to Boele (1998), is like sport.[7] Every sport has rules of play, which act as guidelines for the players, and helps spectators to understand how the game is played. Socratic Dialogue also has rules, which can be extrapolated from Krohn's four features. However, Boele notes that in order to follow these rules participants must have certain attitudes toward dialogue. These are more like dispositions than rules or guidelines, which he describes as Socratic virtues (p.52). If we take a closer look at Boele's analogy, we can also infer that while rules act as guidelines for both players and spectators, they also define a game as a particular kind of game, which ultimately sets one sport aside from another. The so-called rules of dialogue that Boele talks about also separate Socratic Dialogue from other forms of dialogue or inquiry. The six pedagogical measures described below, and the framework for inquiry discussed in the next section, illustrate this point further.

In Socratic dialogue, the role of the teacher as facilitator is more directive than participatory. While teachers may be "well acquainted with the finer points of the subject under discussion, they remain completely outside the argument itself" (Brune et al, 2004, p.161). The facilitator's task is not that of co-inquirer, rather, he or she has the responsibility of ensuring that the discussion remains focused and that the steps are followed until consensus is reached. Because the method of inquiry is rule-bound, the facilitation is integral to successful discussion. Rene Saran and Barbara Neisser (2004) note that the rules of facilitation will apply differently to school teachers than to adult educators. They assume that the school teacher would have more responsibility for behaviour management than would the adult educator. Whilst it is recognised that teachers are not imparters of knowledge, they must still be seen as figures of authority in order to remain in control of the dialogue, but at the same time being a gentle guide for the dialogue (Brune et al, 2004, p.165). This balance will be different depending on factors such as the age of the students or whether the education is compulsory or voluntary.

Heckmann (2004) gives us six 'pedagogical measures' that a facilitator should follow when conducting a Socratic Dialogue. These measures also give us a good insight into the very principles of Socratic Dialogue as they should be upheld by the facilitator. They are: (1) content impartiality, (2) working from the concrete, (3) mutual understanding, (4) focusing on the current question, (5) striving for consensus, and (6) facilitator interventions. The first measure, content impartiality, refers to the responsibility of the facilitator to remain impartial about the question being discussed (p.109). Because Socratic Dialogue is student-directed, to make substantive contributions would undermine the very purpose of the dialogue.

[I]t is an indispensable requirement to prevent teacher judgements from exercising any influence. Where such influence is not excluded, all further effort is to no avail. The teacher will have done his best to steal a march over the student's own judgement by offering his own prejudice. (Heckmann, 2004, p. 109)

Heckmann's second measure is 'working from the concrete'. Nelson saw practical experience as one of the defining features of his model, and by drawing back to a concrete example the question could be put into the context of a real-life experience. The facilitator has a responsibility to guide the group back to this experience throughout the process of dialogue. 'Mutual understanding', the third measure, has to do with the role of the facilitator as being imperative to productive thinking. It is the facilitator's responsibility to make sure that all students understand each other, which therefore demands that the facilitator be a step ahead of the students at all times. This can occur by modelling procedural questions, for example, by asking questions such as 'I'm not sure if I understand; what was the meaning of your statement' if a student has been unclear in getting their meaning across. The fourth measure is 'keeping focus on the current question'. The facilitator must keep the group focused on one question. However, Heckmann (2004, p.110) acknowledges that if the group notes that another question is needed for clarification before the original question can be addressed, they may make a digression. The fifth measure is 'striving for consensus', which, as I have stated, is the model's most defining feature. This is addressed in more detail later on in this chapter, suffice it to say that it is the role of the facilitator to demand consensus from the group. The final measure is 'facilitator interventions'. The facilitator is free to interrupt the dialogue in order to keep the group on track, but should be free from personal contributions in order to prevent influence on the substantive elements of the dialogue. These six measures give guidelines for how a Socratic Dialogue should be conducted by a facilitator and also give us an insight into the important aspects of dialogue.

Nelson's original view was that participation in Socratic Dialogue would generally be two or more days. It is this factor that makes it difficult to implement, so subsequently the model has been adapted in a variety of ways and for different settings. A standard variation of the original model now exists called a short Socratic Dialogue. In other modified forms it has made its way into education, consultancy, and educational workshop. The techniques have also found a place in philosophical counselling; the most visible proponent is Lou Marinoff in the USA.[8] Murris and Haynes (2001) point out that both Nelson's and Heckmann's ideas are not suitable for educational settings "because of the rigor involved in this kind of dialogue this is possible only when children are engaged on a *voluntary* basis, and therefore it is not suitable for mainstream education" (p.162). Due to its structure it is not only unsuitable in terms of fitting into the school curriculum, but it also cannot therefore be enforced.[9] While these concerns are understandable, Socratic Dialogue should not be dismissed so readily as not having any contribution to make in contemporary primary and secondary classrooms. It is a matter of finding ways to modify it to suit the particular educational setting. With this thought in mind we can move onto our next topic—classroom practice.

Classroom Practice

It is generally agreed that Socratic Dialogue can be described as a framework of inquiry consisting of seven steps. They are: (1) choose an appropriate question,

(2) choose a personal experience to apply to the question, (3) find a core statement, (4) identify the experience in the core statement, (5) formulate a definition, (6) test the validity of the core statement, and (7) find counterexamples. These steps must be rigorously followed in order to reach a conclusion at the end of the dialogue. So let us view them in more detail.

The question that the participants in the group are to pursue for the coming days is the first step in Socratic dialogue. For our purposes let us assume that this question is an ethical one. After putting forth suggestions, one question is chosen, whether this be an amalgamation of more than one question or a contribution from one member only. All other questions must be put aside to focus on the one at hand. These questions can be filed away for another session at a later date. This is the first instance in the process where consensus features. Again, I will use as examples the questions from Wilks' book used earlier. The original question, 'What makes a character good?' can be reformulated to, 'What do we mean by good?' so that the concept of 'good' can be defined. Arriving at a definition by consensual articulation is fundamental to reaching agreement on the question of good character. It should be noted that it is not always the case that the participants choose the question. It is also common practice for the facilitator to select a question, in which case they must follow the criteria for selecting a question to make it appropriate for inquiry. The question has to be a 'real' question, not a theoretical one. It should always be connected with one's own experiences, and it must not lead to moral condemnation of anyone in the group (Kessels in Murris & Haynes 2001, p.162). The process of arriving at an appropriate question is much more structured than the process outlined in the previous section on the Community of Inquiry, but it nonetheless needs to be an open-ended question. There are three different levels of questioning that lead to a philosophical question appropriate for a Socratic Dialogue. Students should move from a concrete question to a more abstract question. Brune et al (2004, p.155) pose these as first, second, and third order questions:

- First order question: What is the character doing that is good?
- Second order question: What is good behavior?
- Third order question: What is good?

Personal experience plays a major role in Socratic Dialogue, and is at the core of the second step in the proceedings. There are two reasons for this. Firstly, the 'lived experience' volunteered by one of the participants in the group can be unpacked and used to illustrate inadequacy of the definition of the concept being explored. Secondly, it helps not only the bearer of the experience but also all of the participants to relate to the experience in order to better articulate their perspectives or feelings in regard to the topic at hand. The experience must meet certain criteria: (1) it must be the bearer's own experience, (2) it must be an event which has concluded prior to the commencement of the dialogue, and (3) it must be one in which the member volunteering the information is willing to extend and share all facets of the story for investigation (Prawda, 2000, para.6).

The third step builds around deciding on a core statement. Once the experience has been chosen, based on its relevance to the topic and its relatedness to many of the lives of the participants, it "is then retold in much more detail and the group poses any clarifying questions they have" (Marinoff, 1999, p.263). Once the experience has been broken into details, a core statement can be formed that integrates both the experience and the topic on which the group has decided to focus (Boele 1998, p.50). If we turn again to our example, then the experience would be applied to the question 'What do we mean by good?'

In the fourth step, the group must identify precisely at what point the topic under discussion (i.e., in our example, the concept 'good') occurs in the experience. As Marinoff (1999, p.263) states, "once everyone agrees on where 'X' occurs, you can begin to decide what 'X' is." In the excerpt from Plato's *Republic*, Socrates demonstrates this when he inadvertently says, 'if you can give me an example of justice, then you must tacitly know what justice is'. This illustrates why personal experience is so important. Participants can relate to the experience, but they must also use the example to help formulate a concise definition of the concept being discussed. Boele (1998, p.56) argues that the experience is the touchstone. Because participants can relate to this experience, it becomes central to reaching consensus. In our example, the participants formulate a precise definition of the term 'good'. Boele says "without something comparable, there will be no mutual understanding and no consensus" (p.60).

The fifth step in the process of Socratic Dialogue is arguably the most difficult because of the extensive emphasis on consensus, more than in any of the other steps. The group must come to agreement on a definition, using the experience as an example. This requires a rigorous process of conceptual analysis and logical reasoning referred to as 'regressive abstraction'. This technical strategy develops a syllogistic structure of thought as its method of rigorous inquiry. It is an abstraction because the "conclusion is derived from the inquiry by a process of abstracting from the concreteness of the example so as to uncover the assumptions about [the concept] which are contained in it. It is called regressive because the group works back, as it were, from the concrete example to the general answer to its opening question" (Van Hooft, 1999). In this case, if the group were inquiring about what it means to be good, the definition would be informed by a concrete example of where 'good' may have occurred. By identifying what good is in this case may inform the definition and the process continues.

Reaching consensus over definitions is at the root of Socratic dialogue. Socrates also strived for consensus over definitions, but not as an end in itself. Rather, it was a way of achieving greater understanding of certain terms used in the discussion (Lindop, 2002, p.37). Because a word may carry with it different meanings, conceptual analysis for Socrates played an important role in defining or clarifying terms. For example, in Plato's *Protagoras*, Socrates shows the inter changeability of meaning when referring to the term 'beauty'. After engaging in dialogue with a fellow Athenian, Socrates determines that beauty may not necessarily refer to physical attributes, but also to mental attributes (pp.36–7). The purpose of this example is to illustrate that words can be ambiguous or vague, and hence, that it is imperative to be clear about what we mean when using terms. By finding examples and using personal experiences we can define our terms. This process, if done rigorously, will bring about a conclusive definition, which is what Socratic Dialogue sets out to achieve.

Although the experiences of the other participants may have been put aside, in the sixth step of the dialogue these may be recovered and examined. The definition which forms the core statement that has been agreed upon by the participants in step three must then be applied to each of the other experiences to test the validity of the core statement (Prawda, 2000). If the core statement, for example 'good is anything that is altruistic' is manifested in all of the experiences, then the group can move onto the next and final stage of the dialogue. However, if an experience either refutes or places doubt on the accuracy of the definition, then the participants must regroup and review their definition until it can no longer be contested. After this is done, the group is ready for the final stage.

All prior experiences that have been volunteered in the process of dialogue have been restricted to all of the members' own experiences. In the seventh step, however, the participants must think of other situations, hypothetical or real, which can act as counterexamples outside of those already presented in order to refute the definition that has been established (Marinoff 1999, p.264). For example, the group should find situations that illustrate what 'good' is that doesn't appear altruistic. If the definition is again proven incapable of accommodating these counterexamples, then the participants must go back to one of the previous steps. It is the task of the facilitator to ensure that this happens, and that the group is brought back to the appropriate steps. Once the group can find no more counterexamples, and a conclusive definition is established, only then can the dialogue be concluded.

In a Socratic Dialogue participants can also engage in meta-dialogue, which is a dialogue on the process and strategies of the dialogue itself. A meta-dialogue can take place at any time. When students find that they reach a point that needs resolving due to conflict or inquiry being blocked, they can ask to break into meta-dialogue free from the substantive dialogue (Saran & Neisser, 2004, p.33). For example, if the group is stuck on a definition because one member is closed to further suggestions, the whole group can address the situation of blocking directly before continuing on with the dialogue. Meta-dialogue can also occur before the dialogue to clear up any problems before the group begins, or in cases when there are "any disciplinary problems or difficult group dynamic tensions during the lesson, one can immediately interrupt the main dialogue to clear up these difficulties in a meta-dialogue" (p.33). This aspect of dialogue is an important learning process as it allows for the participants to concentrate on the topic in a disciplined way in the inquiry itself. It should be noted that this was added to Nelson's original model by Heckmann but is now widely accepted as an integral part of Socratic Dialogue.

Socratic Dialogue and Ethical Inquiry

Nelson was interested in cultivating ethical thinking in students. A large part of his theory was devoted to ethics within philosophy. Many proponents of Socratic

Dialogue have used the method for ethical inquiry, and in many of the papers translated into English, Socratic Dialogue is viewed as being most useful for the exploration of ethical concepts as well as being a model that cultivates ethical thinking through its very process.[10] In other words, as well as a concern for the cultivation of judgment, the process of Socratic Dialogue is in itself an ethical process (Saran & Neisser, 2004, p.39). Dieter Birnbacher (2005) argues that the aim of Socratic Dialogue is to create independent minds in a collaborative setting through developing reasoned judgment in students. It is this ability to reason in a group based on personal experiences that makes Socratic Dialogue an ethical dialogue. Students need to develop judgment ability without the necessity of theoretical knowledge of philosophy, religious education, ethics or values education. He argues that Socratic Dialogue is particularly appropriate for developing such dispositions in children. Philosophy itself is concrete, related to life, and hence the reason why we start with a concrete example in Socratic Dialogue. It is integral to the cultivation of ethical thinking and the purpose of Socratic Dialogue that students should be able to think for themselves, or cultivate what Birnbacher terms independent minds. Nelson (1965) asks:

> How is education at all possible? If the end of education is rational self determination, i.e., a condition in which the individual does not allow his behaviour to be determined by outside influences but judges and acts according to his own insight, the question arises: How can we affect a person by outside influences so that he will not permit himself to be affected by outside influence? We must resolve this paradox or abandon the task of education. (p.19)

This paradox, he argues is resolved by engaging in philosophy. Nelson is adamant that the thinking must occur naturally for the students, free from any teacher influence. Socratic Dialogue is also valued because it is integral to the cultivation of democratic thinking through its emphasis on consensus. Consensus is viewed as a tool to ensure that not only students are clear in their meanings but by requiring consensus, students must have a deep understanding of what the other is saying. Only when we truly understand what another is saying can we either agree or disagree (Kletschko & Siebert, 2004, p.119). This, the proponents of Socratic Dialogue argue, is at the heart of democratic thinking.

Truth, Knowledge and Striving for Consensus

Nelson was influenced by the tradition of critical philosophy, and is renowned as a philosopher for his rediscovery and expansion of Kant-Friesian philosophy (Wiegner, 2005). According to this tradition the primary task of philosophy is criticism rather than the justification of knowledge (Ross, 2006). Following Kant, the term criticism means making judgments about the possibilities of knowledge prior to advancing to knowledge itself. The task of philosophy is to subject all theories of knowledge, including those about philosophy itself, to critical review as a measure of their validity. In other words, philosophical inquiry is not about the establishment and demonstration of theories about reality, but rather about the character and foundations of experience. Philosophy must concern itself with how human reason works, and within what limits, in order to correctly apply it to sense experience, and to judge if it can be applied also to metaphysical objects.

From these basic considerations and his theory of Socratic Method, Nelson developed the epistemological foundations of his method of dialogue. Socratic Dialogue is guided by the idea of regressive abstraction, described as the process of "inquiring into people's concrete and abstract conceptions by exposing the basis of the more general truths upon which these conceptions are founded" (Schuster, 1999, p.60). It is the establishment of knowledge as true through a process of objective verification gained from concrete judgment and personal experience. Understood in this way, Nelson has come under criticism on the basis that his view of rational philosophical truth as too closely aligned with Plato's theory of knowledge. This confusion has followed Nelson even after his death, even though "it is now clearer, after the work of Karl Popper, that Socrates was using the logic of falsification rather than verification" (Brown, 1965).

Heckmann (2004) has attempted to clarify the confusion by drawing attention to Nelson's most central feature of Socratic Dialogue—striving for consensus. Central to Socratic Dialogue, he says, "is the search for meaning beyond the purely subjective, to strive for valid inter-subjective statements, for truth, *as we used to say*" (p.111, *italics* mine). He seems to be saying that valid truth claims can be arrived at only within inquiring communities whose purpose is truth-seeking. He then acknowledges that confidence in valid inter-subjective statements has been undermined and that "[s]triving after truth and claims to have recognised truth in respect of a particular question are often considered presumptuous" (p.111). Note that it is not only claims that recognise truth that are under question, but striving after truth is treated with equal suspicion. He overcomes these objections in the following passage.

> Whenever we reach consensus about a statement in a Socratic Dialogue it has a provisional character. For the moment there are no further doubts about the outcome of our effort. Yet a point of view not previously noted can come into our awareness and arouse new doubts. In such a case the proposition has to be tested anew. No statement that ever emerges can ever avoid the need for further revision. (p.111)

Heckmann's position seems to be that the purpose of Socratic Dialogue is striving for truth, but any claim to have recognised truth is only provisional. If we accept this about Socratic Dialogue, then its educative value is not in producing answers, but rather as a means of evaluating beliefs.

What Nelson treasured most about the method used by Socrates, was its effectiveness in getting people to think for themselves, and to realise their own ignorance of the knowledge that they had once thought they possessed. Put another way, he was interested in the process of unlearning and getting students to discover the presuppositions and principles underlying their own beliefs. This is the historical Socrates of the early Platonic dialogues who never gets an answer that holds up to scrutiny. The idea that the method used by Socrates can produce answers was held by Plato, which is demonstrated in some of the transitional dialogues and certainly the later dialogues where Socrates resorts to leading questions; the dialogue with the slave to demonstrate knowledge as recollection, as featured in *Meno,* being exemplary. But it is these sorts of leading questions that Nelson was opposed to, and said should not be used.

> We must bear in mind that instruction in philosophy is not concerned with heaping solution on solution, not indeed with establishing results, but solely with learning the method of reaching solutions. If we do this, we shall observe at once that the teacher's proper role cannot be that of a guide keeping his party from wrong paths and accidents. Nor yet is he a guide going in the lead while his party simply follows in the expectation that this will prepare them to find the same path later on by themselves. On the contrary, the essential thing is the skill with which the teacher puts the pupils on their own responsibility at the very beginning by teaching them to go by themselves—although they would not on that account go alone—and by so developing this independence that one day they may be able to venture forth alone, self-guidance having replaced the teacher's supervision. (Nelson, 1929, p.439)

This issue of consensus as a defining feature of Socratic Dialogue still remains. Heckmann and other contemporary theorists still retain the view that consensus is an important aspect of the dialogue insofar as it requires the group to have a full understanding of the other views and is important for understanding of the topic in general. Regardless of whether or not Heckmann has an accurate account of Nelson's position on truth and knowledge (although it seems it must be conceded that he is correct), consensus must still play a featured role in arriving at truth, otherwise the dialogue will have a different structure and will no longer be a Socratic Dialogue as Nelson intended. Recall Krohn's list of the non-negotiable features of Socratic Dialogue, one of which is 'striving for a consensus'. The provisional character of Socratic Dialogue does not discount the value of consensus. To the contrary, it demands of all participants in the group that they strive for rigor in terms of paying attention to the logic of the arguments presented, to the analysis of concepts, and to the necessity of finding counterexamples to falsify claims. The hourglass remains the metaphor for how to proceed through the seven steps of Socratic Dialogue. Consensus does not happen as a result of verification, but when all attempts at falsification by the group have been exhausted. The group can claim to have arrived at truth, but with the understanding that any claim to truth is provisional.

If Socratic Dialogue functions as a means of evaluating beliefs by examining contradictions among their implications, then the method is not one of verification of truth but it "shares the logic of falsification with Popper's philosophy of science" (Ross, 2006). It is noteworthy that there are similarities between Popper's theory of falsification and Peirce's theory of fallibilism. Both accepted that we can never be completely certain about knowledge. The more difficult question is whether or not we can be reasonable in increasing our confidence in the truth of a theory when it passes observational tests. Popper, who was concerned with the logic of science, said 'no' because logically no number of positive outcomes that result from observations or experimental testing can confirm a hypothesis with any positive degree of probability, but a single counterexample is logically decisive. Peirce, recall, argued that significant insights or reliable knowledge could be achieved through a form of rational inquiry bound by the rules of an interpersonal scientific method. Nelson's concern was Popper's concern, which is evident in his demand for rigor in the procedures of logic.[11] In sum, truth in Socratic Dialogue can only be provisional, for universal claims derived from observation cannot be conclusively verified even by consensus.

BOHMIAN DIALOGUE

Imagine a group of twenty-five people voluntarily sitting in a circle with no pre-set agenda engaged in dialogue together. All have agreed beforehand that no group-level decisions will be made in the dialogue. Their purpose for being there is to create an open and free space where no-one is obliged to reach any conclusions, nor to say anything or not say anything. Each person naturally brings assumptions to the group meeting. But these assumptions are not brought to bear by others nor suppressed in any way. Instead, assumptions are suspended, and as the session progresses these eventually unfold. No-one seems to be judging one another even though they are asked to be as honest and transparent as possible as they share their ideas, controversial or otherwise. The group meets regularly for an indefinite period of time. Gradually the members of the group become familiar with the process and with one another. They are not here to solve problems or to resolve conflict, but they are all concerned about exploring thought, which may eventually result in increased understanding of fellowship among the group. The group is surprised that they have indeed resolved problems along the way, and their new experiences have developed a new understanding of culture and how to contribute to its development.

This encounter with dialogue as free inquiry was David Bohm's vision. Individual and collective assumptions, ideas, beliefs, values, and emotions that subtly control human interactions are explored collectively as a group in the 'spirit of dialogue'.

> The spirit of Dialogue is one of free play, a sort of collective dance of the mind that, nevertheless, has immense power and reveals coherent purpose. Once begun it becomes continuing adventure that can open the way to significant and creative change. (Bohm, Factor & Garrett, 1991)

We will now explore the last of the three models of dialogue, namely Bohmian Dialogue (also called Bohm's Dialogue or simply Dialogue).

Background and History

Bohm was primarily a physicist, but made profound contributions to science and philosophy. He contributed significantly to theories on quantum physics, worked with J. Robert Oppenheimer at Berkeley in the early 1940s, enjoyed much scientific collaboration, was author and co-author of many scientific books in which his important ideas were presented in concise and simplified form, and at the time of his death was Emeritus Professor at Birkbeck College in London. He became acquainted with Albert Einstein and entered into a series of intensive conversations with him. He also paid close attention to Einstein's epistemological challenges to Danish physicist Niels Bohr's interpretation of quantum theory. Bohm noted that the pursuit of scientific knowledge was hindered by personal ambition, adversarial defence of theory, and tradition. These observations led him to believe that it was not just scientists but that humans generally were caught up with similar motivations and actions which led to personal and social fragmentation, which cut across cultural and geographical boundaries. Humans, he remarked, learned to accept such a fragmented state of affairs.

Bohm also searched beyond physics and maintained a long dialogue with the Indian philosopher Jiddhu Krishnamurti and the English psychiatrist Patrick de Mare. From these enduring dialogues, which probed deeply into various dimensions of human knowledge and experience, the limitations of human thought, and the nature of insight and intelligence beyond thought, Bohm's work in physics became unique for he built a spiritual foundation into his theories that gave them a philosophical significance while at the same time preserving their empirical and scientific basis. These dialogues also produced his views on dialogue itself as a path to greater understanding and learning, which culminated in a published book, entitled *On Dialogue*. To counter the fragmentation and breakdown in communication in our culture Bohm argued that people in dialogue can collaboratively create the possibility for new insights, which would not occur by merely thinking on their own.

During his lifetime Bohm's increasing interest in the connection between philosophy, science and cognition, with themes of wholeness and interconnectedness, meant that his conception of dialogue evolved. Interest in Bohm's techniques of dialogue continued after his death, and as a result the dialogue has evolved beyond what he intended. Several groups have been formed around the world to engage in Bohmian Dialogue, and The Massachusetts Institute of Technology initiated a Dialogue Project. His techniques have been widely used in the field of organisational development, and they have also been adapted in 'prison dialogues' for staff and inmates as a way of increasing communication between them and to come to collective understandings.

The Features of Dialogue According to Bohm

To illustrate the connection between thought and individual and social fragmentation, Bohm appealed to an analogy of a watch. When smashed into random pieces, the separate parts are disconnected and unable to function, whereas intact they share an integral relationship with one another as a functional whole. Analogously, human thought processes have a tendency toward perceiving the world in a fragmentary way, to break things up into discrete logical and ontological categories, which human selves believe to be actual representations of the way the world is, i.e., we assume automatically that our representations are true pictures of reality. This is due to the structure of our consciousness, formed over the whole of evolution. Our beliefs and values are grounded in assumptions that have their origins in many contributing factors; parenting, media, peers and so forth. But we fail to see them as guides for action, as unexamined beliefs and values, or unquestioned knowledge. Dialogue was Bohm's key to helping people understand one another and to understand the way they perceive the world.

> Dialogue is really aimed at going into the whole thought process and changing the way the thought process occurs collectively. We haven't really paid much attention to thought as a process. We have engaged in thoughts, but we have only paid attention to the content, not to the process. Why does thought require attention? Everything requires attention, really. If we ran machines without paying attention to them, they would break down. Our thought, too, is a process, and it requires attention, otherwise it's going to go wrong. (Bohm, 1996, p.9)

Simply put, the beliefs and values that we hold are the product of all of the environmental factors, social, political, technological and so forth, working in conjunction with one another. We should not be so arrogant to think that our beliefs and values are the product of individual thought that springs from within us, otherwise we become like the machines that break down due to lack of attention. If thought derives from collaboration, then we can examine and perhaps change our way of thinking through collaboration—through dialogue.

According to Bohm, dialogue is essentially a conversation between equals. It does not share the same meaning as 'discussion' and 'debate' which involves breaking things up. Both these forms of conversation, he says, "contain an implicit tendency to point toward a goal, to hammer out an agreement, to try to solve a problem or have one's opinion prevail" (Bohm, Factor & Garrett, 1991). It is also not an 'exchange' which is characterised by conversation aimed at friendship, gossip and other information. On these points he would find agreement with Lipman and Nelson. They would also agree with Bohm about his understanding of dialogue as educative, and as a way of exploring presuppositions, ideas, beliefs and feelings and the 'quest for truth'. However, the purpose of Bohm's model of dialogue is notably different. He was concerned *primarily* with the process of dialogue and the correlation between thinking and speech, rather than the content of the inquiry. This is not to say that Lipman and Nelson dismissed the importance of reflecting on and analysing what and how one thinks, feels and learns. Lipman, in particular, was conscious of the need for dialogue as a meta-cognitive process. However, they placed more emphasis on problem-solving, upon which meta-cognition is the medium to achieving that goal. Bohm is important because of his emphasis not on what we inquire into but *how* we engage in dialogue and the thought processes behind our interactions with others—what he understood as a kind of meta-dialogue aimed at clarifying the process of dialogue itself.

Bohm's method of dialogue could be said to capture the spirit of what he thought of as a non-purposive, free and open space. Peter Garrett[12] lists what he thinks are the main features for the creation of such a space.

– Listening/attentiveness: Hearing from a point of view as an outside listener, standing aside from our assumptions.

- Speaking/authoring: Speaking not from one's own perspective, but thinking about what needs to be said.
- Suspension/disassociation from ego/identity: Standing aside from your own beliefs as an observer. Thinking of thought as collective and the need to contribute to it. Also, suspending your feelings for the moment. Feelings of anger etc may still be felt, but think about why such feelings come about. Being aware.
- Respect for each other and the process: The group being a nucleus of thought. Forging a fellowship that goes together into inquiry.

Listening and being attentive have a major role to play in dialogue. To be engaged in dialogue together is more than simply coming together to talk—it may not be the case that they are actually actively listening and therefore not engaging in dialogue (Reeve, 2010, pp.97). The participants need to develop what Bohm calls an 'impersonal fellowship', which is a trust and openness, regardless of not sharing any history or experiences together (Bohm, 1996; Reeve, 2005). Participants should listen attentively and collaboratively create something new or innovative from the views shared by the group. Listening attentively is a prerequisite for mutual understanding and exploration of human thought. It affords the opportunity for participants to examine their preconceptions, prejudices and patterns of thought. To relate this back to our earlier discussion on silence, silence is used as wait-time and as a probing questioner (Splitter & Sharp, 1995, pp.47–48). According to Garrett listening attentively allows for each individual to stand away from their own viewpoints to 'really listen' to what is being said by others. In this listening situation, it is not listening from a personal viewpoint but in the role of an 'outside listener' where what is being received is not to be interpreted based on preconceptions, assumptions, unchallenged beliefs or values.

We have already noted the interconnectedness of silence and speech in a dialogue in the previous chapter. When silence is treated as an opportunity to listen, to consider the ideas of others, to be probing questioners, and to formulate opinions, participants are thinking about what needs to be said in terms of contributing to discussion; to *connect* with others in dialogue. To Bohm, speaking in dialogue is not to speak from one's own assumptions but to keep track of those assumptions. As Garrett says, the overall direction of the dialogue must come from the needs of the dialogue and group rather than an individual perspective. Particular attention must be paid to the direction of the dialogue and to what others are saying. Attention in this case is twofold: to the dialogue itself and to the contributions of the other participants (both verbal and nonverbal). They must work together in dialogue toward a shared understanding. The difficulty is that the dialogue has to deal with the assumptions of the participants, but not just the assumptions themselves but the thinking processes behind the assumptions. This usually manifests in feelings of frustration, anger, and other feelings and emotions, due to the different value systems and cultures in a group with large numbers. Moreover, participants are likely to be tied up in their own interests, or inclined to place more weight on their own opinions and values, and in all likelihood to defend their own positions. To work collectively as a group under such circumstances, the participants need to suspend their assumptions in order to consciously open themselves to listening and understanding each person's point of view.

The idea of listening attentively and keeping track of assumptions requires the suspension or disassociation from one's own beliefs and feelings. Bohm recommends that we don't suppress our assumptions, but to create a space between our judgments and our reactions so that we can listen to others in a new way. This can create opportunities for any ill feelings or frustration towards others or their ideas to be dealt with more reflectively. Dialogue, thus, becomes a way of freeing ourselves from assumptions rather than assumptions themselves becoming a technology of silence (e.g., assumptions based on stereotypes). Seen from this perspective, it is not a matter of suppressing assumptions, but rather they are merely suspended in terms of making judgments based on them. This has the potential to create reflective group practices which can act to counter adversarial interactions among participants. Garrett refers to this aspect of the dialogue as the principle of suspension or disassociation from ego or identity. By this he means that there must be a concentration on the progress of the dialogue in general and the attention to the group's direction rather than an individual argument. By disassociating from the self, there is chance for a greater collaboration that is free from adversary.

Lastly, but certainly not of any lesser importance, is the principle of respect for each other and the process. By this, Garrett means forming a relationship based on fellowship. There is a mutual respect for each individual that is connected through the dialogue and also a respect for the dialogue itself. Bohm uses the term impersonal fellowship to describe the experience of collaborative dialogue wherein the participants are engaged in the process not the content of thought in order to overcome their perceived blocks or limitations. They suspend their assumptions, judgments, and values, and enter into a dialogue and the flow of meaning so that the group can move away from an emphasis on the individual aspects of ego to a group process. To have respect for each other is to put aside our attachments to the content of thought and be involved in an exploration of common meaning from which a shared state of consciousness emerges—an internalisation of the inquiry process. Hester Reeve (2005) describes the relationship between participants in dialogue as analogous to spectators supporting the same team at a football match. While the football fans may not have any personal connection outside of the football match, they unite in their commitment to the game. Their connection in this space is their common interest in football. They have a sort of 'fellowship' rather than a friendship. This is similar to the relationship that individuals in a Bohmian Dialogue have with each other, however, Reeve notes that there is more trust involved in a dialogue because each person is required to contribute and essentially take on the role of the facilitator (p.9). In both of these instances, friendship may ensue from their connection over common interest and, as Bohm suggests, a friendship that results after dialogue is stronger because their initial relationship underwent an exploration of values and assumptions.

Let me briefly sum up what has been said so far. Bohm "insisted that sustained inquiry into the nature of consciousness and the 'ground of being' is essential if we are to have some prospect of bringing an end to fragmentation in the world" (Nichol, in Bohm, 1996, p.xvii). Bohm's techniques are intended to bring about connectedness. Like Bohm's metaphorical watch smashed into random pieces, which once had an integral relationship with one another as a functioning whole, thought gone unchecked can fragment things which are not meant to be separate. Bohm's overarching intention for dialogue was to shed light on the activity of fragmentation "not only as a theoretical analysis, but also as a concrete experiential process" (p.viii). Otherwise fragmentation of selves leads to social, cultural and political fragmentation. I will take up the matter of connectedness, and Bohm's ideas on this, briefly later in the chapter, and again in Chapter 6 on caring thinking. We will now take a brief look at what Bohm's techniques look like in practice.

Dialogue in Practice

In practice Bohmian Dialogue has no detailed organisational or procedural guidelines. Bohm found that a dialogue works best with a group of twenty to forty people gathered together facing one another in a circle. As a preliminary to the dialogue the group is introduced to the meaning of the activity. This might require the guidance of experienced facilitators so that everybody understands the difference between Bohm's method of dialogue and other group processes, including information on the suspension of assumptions, group expectations, duration and regularity of sessions, and the processes of collective inquiry without facilitation and a pre-set agenda. Their task is not like that of the facilitators described for the Community of Inquiry or Socratic Dialogue but to 'lead from behind' as Bohm puts it. Usually two hours is optimum for each session and the more regularly the group meets the more the participants become familiar with the idea of dialogue. But even the clearest introduction is likely to result in confusion, frustration, and self-consciousness. When the group finally commences there is still anxiety and concern as to whether or not the participants are engaging in dialogue. But this sort of behaviour is seen as encouraging, for the purpose of the dialogue is to explore the social constructs and inhibitions that affect communications, not to avoid them.

Once dialogue commences it is up to the group to find their own direction. This requires listening attentively and formulating questions. There is often a period of silence that precedes the dialogue before someone finds the words to begin discussion. This initial period can turn to awkwardness, but sometimes it is accompanied by a level of trust that someone *will* make the first comment and that others will then follow through with the dialogue. Garrett likens it to playing ball: if you throw it, you must be able to trust that it will in turn be thrown back to you. The absence of a facilitator means that during prolonged silences it is up to each participant to get the ball rolling, so to speak. Bohm and his colleagues have observed that some participants tend to talk more than others. Usually the less talkative ones will speak as they become more familiar with the experience and the more talkative ones will talk less and listen more. There is no limit on how long the group will continue its ongoing exploration. It would be contrary to Bohm's purpose of dialogue to become fixed or institutionalised. Dialogue must remain constantly open, which means constantly changing memberships and schedules to prevent rigidity. Alternatively, the group naturally dissolves on its own accord after a period of time.

Suspension of thoughts, impulses, judgments, and assumptions is crucial to the dialogue. Participants generally find this the most difficult element of the dialogue as mostly they are unfamiliar with this kind of activity. Suspension requires attentive listening and looking. It is necessary that participants speak for without it there would be no dialogue. But attentively listening to the group and to oneself is essential because this is where exposure to reactions, impulses, feelings and opinions can be given serious attention while they are actually being experienced. By sustaining attention on these experiences, the thought process can become more reflective, and the structures of thought that might otherwise go undetected could reveal their incoherence. This could have an impact on the overall process that flows from thought, to feeling and to acting within the group. This externalising and internalising of the process could lead to the reconstruction of thought both individually and collectively. The process has to be persistent for it to be successful.

The difficulties of initiating discussion notwithstanding, dialogue can begin with any topic that is of interest to the participants. The content should not be determined beforehand and no subject should be excluded. If some participants feel that certain exchanges or subjects are disturbing or inappropriate, it is vital that they express their thoughts or feelings during the dialogue. Otherwise participants might be inclined to complain or express their dissatisfactions or frustration afterwards. It is exactly these sorts of discussions that should be voiced inside the dialogue as it affords the opportunity for moving the dialogue into deeper realms of meaning and coherence beyond superficial conversation. Participants would be exploring the thoughts behind their assumptions, beliefs, and values as well as the feelings and emotions towards others.

At the end of a dialogue group session the participants may have developed a better understanding of some of their own presuppositions that underlie their convictions. Each participant has the further opportunity to individually reflect on what they learned before the commencement of the subsequent session. Indeed some of the participants may have already discovered that they have gained new insights through the process of collective creativity. However, Bohm hoped that these dialogue groups would continue to meet for the purposes of meeting collectively to explore the structure of fragmentation in order to create opportunities for fellowship and sharing.

Bohmian Dialogue and Ethics as Connected Selves

Dialogue as a free association conducted in groups to counter the fragmentation of selves emphasises its underpinning purpose of developing ethical persons. It is ethical not because it rests on any particular normative or meta-ethical claim.

Rather, the engagement in communal dialogue as a way of understanding the group as a whole reinforces certain behaviour through an awareness of the interpersonal relationship between the individual and the group. While Bohm's method of dialogue shares no ethical content necessarily, emphasis is on the creation of an ethical discourse. Engagement in dialogue is essential not for the sake of personal problems, but it is a matter of culture. The group is a microcosm of society, and the goal is to get the whole group to have a better understanding of it. Bohm's (1996) own words, I think, make this clear: "in a dialogue, each person does not attempt to *make common* certain ideas or items of information that are already known to him. Rather, it may be said that two people are making something *in common*, i.e., creating something new together" (p.2).

Due to the emphasis on collective thought, the relationships that are forged in the dialogue are intensified because of the reliance on each other. The forging of such relationships requires trust, especially because of the perpetual reliance on reciprocity in a dialogue that has no facilitator or no set agenda. There is also the reciprocal requirement that each of the individuals in the group will receive what is being said in an open manner. Not only are opinions, beliefs and values required to be considered by each of the participants in a respectful and considered way, but there must be genuine engagement, through a process of careful listening, reflection and contribution in order to create the opportunity to counter the fragmentation of selves and subsequent fragmentation of the social, cultural and political aspects of life. The challenge is to listen, and to create a new kind of association in which we listen deeply to all the views that people may express—a kind of wholeness. Given the emphasis that Bohm places on relationships, the ethic that underpins it could be described as an ethic of connectedness.

Connecting Science, Philosophy and Cognition

To recap, Bohmian dialogue is "a kind of collective proprioception or immediate mirroring back of both the content of thought and the less apparent, dynamic structures that govern it" (Bohm, Factor & Garrett, 1991). It creates an opportunity for each of the participants to reflect back to each other and to the whole group, the preconceptions, prejudices and the underlying patterns behind their thoughts, opinions, beliefs and feelings, and to examine them and to share their insights. Any number of people can engage in dialogue, including with oneself, revealing Bohm's recognition that internal dialogue is more that a monologue. However, he suggests the ideal is twenty to forty people seated in a circle talking together. The significance of this can be found in the reports from an anthropologist who lived with a group of North American hunter-gatherers. The group was typical of similar hunter-gather groups who ranged in size from twenty-five to forty people. The tribe met regularly, sat in a circle, and talked with no apparent purpose. There was no leader, everybody could participate, and no decisions were made. The meetings lasted until the group dispersed. Yet afterward the group seemed to know what to do as a result of knowing each other so well. Later in smaller groups they would make decisions and take action (Bohm, 1996, pp.16–17). From these observations he inferred the following conclusion.

[S]uch gatherings seemed to provide and reinforce a kind of cohesive bond or fellowship that allowed its participants to know what was required of them without the need for instruction or much further verbal interchange. In other words, what might be called a coherent culture of shared meaning emerged within the group. It is possible that this coherence existed in the past for human communities before technology began to mediate our experience of the living world. (Bohm, Factor & Garrett, 1991)

His friend the English psychiatrist, Patrick de Mare, a practitioner of Group Analysis, conducted research that reflected these practices but under modern conditions. Bohm adapted the theory of microculture and the idea of impersonal fellowship from de Mare. The theory of microculture proposes that groups containing a minimum of twenty and maximum of forty members (like those of the hunter-gatherer tribes) can act as a sample of the entire culture to which the group belonged, including multiple beliefs and value systems. The idea of a microculture came from de Mare's book *Koinonia*, which is about an operational approach to dialogue, culture, and the human mind, in the socio-cultural setting of a larger group. For Bohm the underlying cause of fragmentation can be located at the socio-cultural level, and therefore the dialogue groups "can serve as micro-cultures from which the source of the infirmity of our large civilization can be exposed" (Bohm, Factor & Garrett, 1991). On this view, dialogue is a form of 'sociotherapy' in which a caring regard can be extended to those outside of emotional connections through trying to understand "the dynamics of how thought conceives such connections" (Bohm, Factor & Garrett, 1991). From this kind of dialogue an impersonal fellowship can emerge. An impersonal fellowship implies that authentic trust and openness would emerge in a group context, even when the members of the group lack in any personal history whatsoever. Participants may form emotional attachments and want to continue meeting in order to maintain a sense of security and belonging. But the purpose is not to fall into what Bohm calls 'cozy adjustment' but to be persistent "in the process of inquiry and risking re-entry into areas of potentially chaotic or frustrating uncertainty" (Bohm, Factor & Garrett, 1991).

   Bohm's interest in the seemingly incoherent and fragmented human thought also led to his acquaintance with the Indian educator and philosopher Jiddhu Krishnamurti. He discovered that his ideas on quantum mechanics aligned with the philosophical ideas of Krishnamurti. They shared an interest in: (1) the idea that problems of thought are fundamentally collective, and not individual, and (2) the paradox of the observer and the observed, which implies that introspection and self-improvement are inadequate methods for understanding the nature of the mind and experiences of self. From his countless exchanges of ideas with Krishnamurti his idea of dialogue evolved. Listening was given a central place in his approach to group interaction. If groups of people listen attentively to one another and aspire to come to shared meanings then this would be the touchstone for effective communication which would have an impact on how humanity perceived itself and how they would conduct their personal, social and political lives.

What Bohm derived from his association with both men can be found in his book, *Thought as a System*, the title of which speaks for itself. Bohm claimed that if thought is a system and it is seen as an instrument for tackling a problem then thought itself is problematic. While Bohm didn't disagree that dialogue and other forms of group processes could be useful as a method for problem-solving, his concern was to develop a method of dialogue for the purpose of becoming aware of how thought works. In this sense Bohmian dialogue is a non-purposive dialogue.

> Whereas in Platonic dialogue thought is used as an instrument for tackling a problem, Bohm is of the view that too often thought uses us, and so could be seen as part of the problem. The aim of Bohmian dialogue is therefore not even to try to solve the problem, but to become aware of how thought works, and this is done through the medium of non-purposive discussion. For Bohm, wanting an answer, feeling the need to develop or defend a position, and treating the ideas of others in a judgemental way, are all instruments of obscuration. As soon as we try to accomplish a useful purpose or goal, we will have an assumption behind it as to what is useful, and that assumption is going to limit us. (Curnow, 2001, p.235)

Bohm stressed that non-purposive dialogue also had to be free flowing dialogue without a facilitator to guide discussion. Any guidance, no matter how carefully or sensitively applied, tends to inhibit the free flow of thought.

While Bohm's method of dialogue is not derived from the Socratic Method, his emphasis on the process of dialogue—on examining assumptions, self-reflection, listening and attentiveness, and impersonal fellowship—gives it a philosophical dimension. Curnow (2007), who has compared Bohm's method with other forms of dialogue, is of the same opinion.

> The technique of such a kind of dialogue rests much more heavily on listening. Does this have a philosophical dimension? Given that at least part of the exercise involves a bringing of underlying assumptions to the level of awareness, I believe it does. (para. 4)

Moreover, Bohm's techniques have particular implications for the development of Socratic classrooms, especially the cultivation of caring thinking in education. Unlike the Community of Inquiry or Socratic Dialogue, Bohm's main focus is on thought and collaboration. This makes his dialogue invaluable in giving us some insight into caring thinking which is manifest in communal dialogue; in the interpersonal relationships of the group, which is in a process of continual reconstruction, i.e., working together towards a renewed understanding. Bohm, like Krishnamurti and de Mare, shared in the desire to create a society that was self-reflective and dialogical. On this point, his goal was much the same as Lipman's and Nelson's; the cultivation of active citizenship through the practice of dialogue.

THINKING THROUGH DIALOGUE

We now have an understanding of the Community of Inquiry, Socratic Dialogue, and Bohmian Dialogue, three models of dialogue that to varying degrees are recognisably Socratic in their approach to teaching and learning. While not all are grounded in the tradition of the Socratic Method, each has something to contribute to pedagogy and the development of Socratic classrooms. Moreover, all three models go some way to satisfying the aims of the UNESCO study in regard to the liberation of the individual, freedom of thought, and developing and enhancing the social and intellectual abilities needed for active citizenship.

The notion of people coming together in a community of inquiry underpins Lipman's educational theory and practice. Taking his lead from Dewey, it was Lipman's view that engaging in the Community of Inquiry would naturally nurture the dispositions that he identified with democracy, such as social communication, mutual interest and respect for others. Nelson too shared many of Lipman's concerns regarding the education of children, and he believed that being 'partners-in-dialogue' would bring about the necessary dispositions for living a democratic life. Meanwhile, for Bohm, freedom meant becoming aware of how thought works and, like Lipman and Nelson, he had in mind the cultivation of active citizenship through the practice of dialogue.

The UNESCO study recommends that educators and philosophers should find ways to go about cultivating philosophical thinking. The three models of dialogue, although varying in their methods, can make a valuable contribution to the development and articulation of Socratic classrooms for the cultivation of philosophical thinking. The purpose of the next chapter is to explore further how their methods can be articulated in a framework for Socratic pedagogy. The intention is not to map out a detailed taxonomy, but rather to provide a starting point for defining an approach to teaching through dialogue as a collaborative, inquiry-based activity conceived of as multi-dimensional thinking, which is comprised of critical, creative and caring thinking. This will provide a framework for subsequent chapters.

NOTES

[1] Lipman's Community of Inquiry is indicated through the use of capital letters.
[2] Lipman developed a series of purpose-written novels with accompanying manuals. Since then other authors have developed materials ranging from children's stories, videos, and manuals to accompany existing children's stories. See de Haan *et al* (1995), Sprod (1993), Wilks (1995), Abbott and Wilks (1997), Cam (1993, 1994, 1997, 2006), Freakley, Burgh and Tilt-MacSporran (2008).
[3] See Golding (2004).
[4] Burgh (2003a,b) makes an important distinction between education for democracy and democratic education. I will not explore this further suffice it to say that the distinction cannot be ignored when it comes to the implementation of education reforms.
[5] Authors interested in the Deweyean aspects of Philosophy for Children have since attempted to 'put the Dewey back in Lipman' by placing an emphasis on democratic education and philosophical inquiry. See: Burgh (2003a), Cam (2000).
[6] For example, Lou Marinoff's Philosophical Counseling as well as Dilemma and Integrity Training.

[7] Boele's article offers a more detailed account than others written in English, and is commonly referred to in the literature on Socratic Dialogue.

[8] Marinoff uses Socratic Dialogue as a basis for his philosophical practice as it engenders clients with the ability to make meaning from their problems. Another proponent who uses a variant of Socratic dialogue is Oscar Brenifier. Brenifier has his own series of children's stories and conducts workshops in philosophy in education.

[9] Perhaps this factor explains (partially) why Socratic Dialogue has not been as successful in an educational setting in comparison to the Community of Inquiry.

[10] See various papers in Shipley and Mason (2004).

[11] Nelson's theory of knowledge deserves more attention that I can give it here. It is not a matter of brushing aside the logical and epistemological issues, but rather that the main concern and purpose of this book is with the practice of dialogue in educational settings. In other words, my interest is with the process of arriving at truth in dialogical inquiry; with its procedure as a regulative idea, rather than what might be said about the nature of truth when we have arrived at it.

[12] Some of the comments attributed to Peter Garrett were part of fruitful dialogue I had with him at *The Challenge of Dialogue Conference* in Berlin in 2005. Garrett, who is a main proponent of Dialogue, co-authored *On Dialogue: A Proposal* (1991) with David Bohm. He generously gave me his time to tell me about his discussions on Dialogue with Bohm.

DEVELOPING THE SOCRATIC CLASSROOM: METAPHORS OF ENGAGEMENT IN DIALOGUE

Much of education is focused on the achievement of certain basic skills and knowledge. This focus can be attributed to a commonly held view of education that raising the general level of IQ of children through the teaching and learning of thinking skills together with some knowledge of the world will assist them as future adult citizens. Beyond the '3Rs' literacy and numeracy are now the cornerstones of learning. The aim of many governments is to ensure that all students gain at least the minimum standard of literacy and numeracy so that they overcome educational disadvantage, and that it is crucial for children to develop these foundational skills at the earliest possible time in their school years. This picture of education draws attention to a comparable need to ensure that all students gain a minimum standard of being 'socratic'. My use of this term builds on Cam's (2006) observation that if school leavers were more-or-less illiterate and innumerate there would be an outcry, but in "contrast, students actually do leave our schools basically *insocratic*, and it is barely noticed" (p.1). As previously mentioned the merits of being socratic include: "the ability to think about the issues and problems that we face in our lives, to explore life's possibilities, to appreciate alternative points of view, to critically evaluate what we read and hear, to make appropriate distinctions and needful connections, and generally to make reasonable judgements" (p.1). What Cam is saying is that the education system has the responsibility to develop people's ability to engage in dialogue with the aim of developing their capacity to think for themselves. Put another way, schools need to promote *being socratic*.

This chapter extends on what we have previously outlined on Socratic pedagogy. To avoid nit-picking over what to include and what not to include in a list of identifying features that will inform us of the precise nature of the Socratic Method, this chapter will instead provide a focus for defining an approach to teaching through dialogue that has relevance to modern educational theory and practice. Dialogue is viewed in this way as multi-dimensional thinking, comprised of three interactive modes of thinking, which are critical, creative and caring. This will set the tone for the remainder of the book. In order to arrive at this point, we draw attention to the inter-relationship of *elenchus* and *aporia* inherent in the Socratic Method,[1] which we recognise as the interaction of critical and creative thinking. But all three modes of thinking need to be in play to be an effective Socratic pedagogy. In a multi-dimensional account of Socratic pedagogy there is more recognition of the interdependence in thinking collaboratively, which is one of the hallmarks of Socratic practice. Therefore, the metaphors used to describe the

Socratic dimensions of engaging in dialogue for each of the three models of dialogue are examined here. We begin by looking at the Community of Inquiry and the notion of letting the argument lead. In particular we pick up on Lipman's metaphor of a chamber orchestra as being analogous to how the Community of Inquiry works as it passes through the various stages in the pattern of inquiry from initiating, suggesting, reasoning and conceptually exploring, evaluating and concluding. His metaphor is best suited as a metaphor for creative thinking within a framework of multi-dimensional thinking. We then move onto Socratic Dialogue, which due to its specific structure, is depicted as an hourglass. That is: beginning at the top, where it is widest, with a universal question, toward the narrow waist to depict consensual articulation of a definition and the particularisation of the universal, to the bottom where it is wide again representing further dialogical analysis to undermine or falsify the definition. As a metaphor for critical thinking the hourglass is very effective. We then turn to Bohm who likens dialogue to a collective dance of the mind. Just like dancers who have awareness of their own movements and the movements of the other, dialogue is a collaborative activity that relies on such awareness. For Bohm, listening and self-reflection are the keys to dialogue and this is reflected in his metaphor. His analogy helps us to understand caring thinking better.

In the final part of this chapter we will point to the relationship between critical, creative and caring thinking in all three models of dialogue in order to provide a framework for discussions on Socratic pedagogy in the chapters to follow.

THE SOCRATIC CLASSROOM

Socrates' belief in understanding through dialogue is at the root of Socratic pedagogy and the creation of a Socratic classroom. Socratic pedagogy is defined by its emphasis on rigorous questioning and dialogue as a deliberative education tool. Robert Fisher (1995a) has this to say about educating Socratically.

> To educate, for Socrates, could not simply be a question of transfer of knowledge. Education was an activity of mind, not a curriculum to be delivered. To be involved in learning in a Socratic sense is to be involved in a personal drama, for it depends both on critical thinking and emotional commitment. It has both a rational and a moral purpose, it exists to engender intellectual virtue, a thinking that engages and develops the learner as an individual and as a member of a learning community. (p.25)

To appreciate Socratic education and pedagogy fully we need to take a look more closely at the Socratic Method.

The term critical thinking is often used to describe the Socratic Method. Some of the research into critical thinking describes it as primarily a rational skill for problem-solving (Catrambone & Holyoak, 1989; Needham & Begg, 1991). This view is held by Lindop (2002), who argues that the effectiveness of the Socratic Method is due to its concentration on conceptual exploration. He notes that "in any branch of philosophy, care for the meaning, for connecting concepts that should be connected, distinguishing what should be distinguished and realizing the role of context in appraising meaning are all preconditions for serious consideration of substantive philosophical questions" (p.37). Lindop is correct to point this out. However, it is not uncommon for philosophy to be mistakenly understood as exclusively an enterprise of conceptual development and analysis, and thus failing to see the richness of philosophy as pedagogy. We have already pointed to de Bono for his criticism of philosophy, which he makes synonymous with the Socratic Method, as overly critical in its approach. He warns that philosophy promotes adversarial thinking in the classroom and thus stifles creative thinking, while advocating for a creative and more effective approach to problem-solving "with emphasis on possibility and designing forward" (1994, p.vii). But de Bono fails entirely in acknowledging that philosophy is not "intrinsically fascist in nature, with rigid rules, harsh judgements, inclusion and exclusion, category boxes and judgements, and a high degree of righteousness" (p.6). What may appear to be embedded in the Socratic Method and hence philosophy itself, may be due to a misunderstanding of philosophy or misuse of philosophical pedagogy. He raises this point himself: "if a method is so easily abused and so rarely used 'properly' that method is faulty and there is little point in saying that it ought to be used 'properly'" (p.32). His admission is confusing. If understood in terms of multi-dimensional thinking philosophy can equally place emphasis on 'possibility and designing forward', as de Bono claims of his parallel thinking and lateral thinking. The assumptions that underpin de Bono's views of philosophy, which he himself fails to uncover, create misunderstanding that subsequently translates into teaching practices not in accord with Socratic practices.

Unlike de Bono, Lindop understands philosophy as the care for meaning and for connecting concepts, which broadens its application to include intellectual processes such as the setting of criteria, argument formation, making distinctions, categorizing, classifying, and their relationship to logic and reasoning. Nevertheless, Lindop's emphasis is still on critical thinking as primarily a rational skill for problem-solving, which some theorists argue is too narrow as it ignores the support of creative thinking (Duemler & Mayer, 1988; Slade, 1992). Extending on this, some researchers have shown that critical and creative thinking are inseparable and work simultaneously (Paul, 1994). Reich's view of the Socratic Method as essentially consisting of *elenchus* and *aporia* falls under this category. The *elenchus* is the process of questioning that Socrates engages with to elicit confusion from his fellow inquirers. Through his careful questioning, the respondents begin to cast doubt on the validity of their opinions, and eventually contradicting themselves, leaving them baffled as to their own ignorance on matters that they previously considered to have had knowledge. This state of confusion that results is the *aporia*. When the respondent has reached *aporia* both Socrates and his fellow inquirer can begin to search for truth from a position where previously held assumptions, mistaken for knowledge, have been exposed. The use of *elenchus* and *aporia* is a vital part of the dialogical process and inherently pedagogical (Reich, 1998). *Elenchus* encourages the exploration of assumptions, bringing participants to a position of doubt or wonder where certainty of judgment is suspended. *Aporia* provokes them to search for truth or meaningfulness through dialogue. In the classroom, the teacher takes on the role of Socratic facilitator, but the overall aim is that each participant takes on the role of Socrates as well as the role of his interlocutors.

The use of *elenchus* to bring about *aporia* illustrates also the inseparable interplay of critical and creative thinking in the dialogical process. *Elenchus* encourages us to be critical of our own thinking and the thinking of others. In turn, critical thinking gives rise to *aporia* and provokes creative thinking, which in turn encourages critical thinking and so forth. Engaging in this dialogical process provides opportunities for meaning to be created. This view, while still not fully encapsulating what is meant by Socratic practice does, nonetheless, recognise thinking critically as both convergent and divergent thinking. Convergent thinking is the process of assessing, evaluating, judging, concluding and implementing. Nelson's metaphor of the hourglass (described later) illustrates the process of problem-solving as convergent thinking. However, once through the narrow waist of the hourglass thought again becomes divergent. Divergent thinking defines creative thinking. It is that ability to modify, adapt and create ideas. Together, they produce an act of synthesis by putting thoughts together to *reconstruct* new ones.

Robert Fisher (1995a) highlights the importance of creative thinking to the Socratic Method. He notes that philosophical inquiry enlists multiple dimensions of thinking, which among other things enables the enhancement of creative thought. He draws parallels between the creative thinking required in philosophical inquiry and Albert Einstein's view that "[t]o raise new questions, new problems, to regard old problems from a new angle requires creative imagination, and makes real advances" (p.23). The collective generation of new ideas from a situation that the group has found to be problematic is inherently a creative process that facilitates the reconstruction of ideas; from previous assumptions to the exploration and development of ideas to a renewed understanding of the initial problem. The generation of ideas, therefore plays a vital role in the reconstruction of thinking which is central to philosophical inquiry. Oliver Wendell aptly describes the process as: "[t]he mind once stretched by a new idea, never regains its original dimensions" (in Fisher, 1995, p.24). The UNESCO study proposes that education should allow for approaches to pedagogy that create thoughtful students. If we can agree with Fisher and Wendell that philosophy is, among other things, an inherently creative endeavour with the purpose of 'stretching the minds' of students, then Socratic pedagogy cannot be overlooked as a prerequisite for good thinking and its improvement.

Talk of critical and creative thinking as crucial to engaging in philosophy and philosophical inquiry can eclipse discussion on the importance of community, which cannot be overlooked when considering philosophy as first and foremost dialogical. While there are phases of inquiry, both critical and creative, these are underpinned by the connections that each participant has to others in an inquiry. A large amount of the literature devoted to Socratic practices fail to fully appreciate the connections between people in inquiry, but instead focuses on the connection between the critical and creative phases of inquiry. If we agree that inquiry is to occur in a community, then it is remiss to simply make assumptions concerning the connections between inquirers. It is for this reason that I share the perspective of philosophical thinking as multi-dimensional thinking. There is still much to learn about multi-dimensional thinking. A substantial amount of research on thinking and meta-cognition comes from the field of psychology where definitions are substantiated by experimental methods. It is hardly surprising to see thinking as characteristically a rational skill for solving problems—with emphasis on the cognitive over the affective and social components. Philosophers, on the other hand, while not ignoring the empirical research, verify their definitions through theoretical analysis. My view of Socratic pedagogy as multi-dimensional thinking is based on such an analysis. Lipman (1991) is foremost as a scholar in this area, although alongside him there are others who have contributed to a greater understanding of the multi-dimensionality of thinking (Siegel, 1988; Ennis, 1993; Paul, 1993; Costa, 2001). Lipman (2003) reformulated his theory of multi-dimensional thinking (which prior to then he called higher-order thinking) as the interaction of three modes of thinking, which now includes caring thinking.

Note that in the chapters that follow we will explore in more detail critical, creative and caring thinking as interdependent components of multi-dimensional thinking necessary to Socratic pedagogy. As a preface to these chapters, the remaining sections will give an overview of the pedagogical dimensions of each of the three models of dialogue, and their relationship to the critical, creative, and caring components of multi-dimensional thinking.

ENGAGING IN DIALOGUE

To understand what makes each of the models of dialogue Socratic we need to identify the features that they have in common and what makes them distinct in terms of engaging in dialogue. This will allow us to draw some conclusions about where they may be useful for the enhancement of multi-dimensional thinking and hence Socratic pedagogy. By looking at the metaphors used to describe each model of dialogue this will allow us to discern the most significant aspects of inquiry. But before we proceed with our inquiry we need to clarify what engagement means when we use the term in regard to the phrase: 'engaging in dialogue together'. Simply put, it is where the learning happens. Daniel Shephard (2005) tells us that engagement is 'remarkable interaction'; it is where we can identify what is most remarkable in a process. A brief view of the synonyms for engagement reveals it to be an appointment, assignation, date, rendezvous, or tryst. These words denote a commitment to appear at a certain time and place. It can also mean a promise to do something in the future; the act of sharing in the activities of a group, to involve oneself, or to become occupied, to participate; to attract or hold attention, to draw into; to interlock or cause to interlock; to assume an obligation. In the context of engaging in dialogue nearly all of the meanings of the word are appropriate. Literally, engaging in dialogue means being 'committed to appear at a certain time and place' where we all come together to 'share in the activities of the group' for the sole purpose of 'participating' in inquiry. Figuratively, engagement as participation is to be 'drawn into' or 'interlocked' in a shared activity. Engagement can be cognitive or affective, and happens at a personal, psychological and social level. Indicators of successful engagement in dialogue include: the interweaving of speech and silence that accompanies questioning and problem-solving activities; the exploration of agreement and disagreement marked by self-correction; the use of analysis and reasoning to evaluate arguments; and the inter-psychological practices that are progressively internalised by the participants as described by Vygotsky's theory of social construction. Engagement in dialogue is what we strive for in Socratic classrooms. It is *the commitment to finding meaning and to progress towards truth in collaboration with others*.

Integral to engagement in dialogue is reconstruction, which I will briefly mention here as an introduction to later chapters. When students are genuinely engaged in collaborative dialogue they are effectively undergoing a process of questioning, self-correcting, and rebuilding—also described as reconstruction. Golding (2002) talks about the confusion that sometimes comes with a process such as this. It is an illustration of the rebuilding of thoughts through a 'to-ing and fro-ing' of *elenchus* and *aporia;* a process of openness to renewed meanings, of replacing or modifying previous ways of thinking and knowing. Put another way, when we are engaged in collaborative dialogue we are making connections between what we are learning and the people with whom we are learning, which leads us to reconstruct the way that we think. All three theorists, Lipman, Nelson and Bohm, have foremost in their minds the reconstruction of thinking. Underpinning this challenge is the development of intellectual and social dispositions and capacities necessary for active citizenship. Again, we can see the relevance to the UNESCO study, which stresses the importance of reconstruction in bringing about individual and social change.

THE PEDAGOGICAL DIMENSIONS OF DIALOGUE

In this part we will explore some of the metaphors that have played a significant role in shaping our understanding of what is typical of Socratic practices. I refer specifically to engagement in dialogue and its facilitation. First, we will revisit the metaphors used to describe Socrates' questioning techniques. Second, in order to locate the pedagogical dimension of each of the models of dialogue we will explore the metaphors used by Lipman, Nelson, and Bohm, all of whom emphasised various pedagogical components that could be described as typically Socratic. These differences have important practical implications for the practice of Socratic pedagogy.

Socratic Facilitation: Midwife, Gadfly or Stingray?

Chapter 1 gave a very brief description of the images used to illustrate Socrates' questioning techniques and ways of philosophising: as a kind of gadfly, a self-stinging ray, and intellectual midwife. Let us firstly address Socrates as gadfly. This term was used by Plato in the *Apology* for Socrates who upset the status quo by posing unsettling questions in an attempt to stimulate provocation. It fits well Socrates' own maxim that 'The unexamined life is not worth living'. He proved to be an irritant to unreflective citizens who, unlike Socrates who had no pretensions to knowledge, believed they knew and understood things that they did not really know or understand; "*to sting people and whip them into a fury, all in the service of truth.*" It draws attention to the close critical analysis that is required in the Socratic Method. In effect, what the metaphor alludes to is Socrates' ability to draw his interlocutors into dialogue where they are no longer able to go about their everyday lives without thought. But it also makes other more far-reaching assertions; that by beginning the process of examining life our lives will be disrupted so that we continually ask questions about social reality and accepted moral and political opinion. Once a person seeks truth in their life it is not so easy to return to ignorance. This is illustrated wonderfully in the film *The Matrix*. Keanu Reeves' character Neo takes a red pill in order to discover the truth about his own existence. Once the pill is taken he cannot but open his eyes to the truth. He can no longer turn a blind eye to the source of his own existence; that reality is an illusion designed to placate humans while they are actually agents of slavery and deception. Despite the actions of his fellow crusader, Cypher, who takes the blue pill to return to a state of ignorance, Neo remains committed to truth despite the fact that it is a far more difficult life that he's chosen, affirming the idea that the unexamined life is not worth living. In a contemporary setting the gadfly can describe someone who persistently challenges people in positions of power, the status quo or popular opinion.

Historically, references to the gadfly have been used in both an honourable and pejorative sense. The term was used by Plato to describe the relationship of Socrates as a provoker of the Athenian political scene, which he compared to a slow and dim-witted horse. Similarly, in *The Bible* there are references to the gadfly also in terms of political influence. The Book of Jeremiah states "Egypt is a very fair heifer; the gad-fly cometh, it cometh from the north." The term continues to be used to describe people, such as social commentators and investigative reporters, who ask provocative questions aimed at politicians and other public figures. The most common interpretation of this kind of provocative questioning is 'fault finding'. But this is misleading. To illustrate this we need to look no further than what Reich (1998) calls 'notorious American college law classes'. Lecturers who claim to use the Socratic Method are actually using a 'cold-calling' technique of questioning, i.e., asking questions to put students on-the-spot or for the sake of catching students out without an answer. In terms of educational aims and practices the use of the gadfly should be in a positive light. This is so because as classroom pedagogy it stands as metaphor for liberating students to lead a thoughtful, reflective life.

In *Meno* Socrates is called a stingray (or torpedo fish). This image sets out to show that Socrates makes his articulate interlocutors numb. They are left speechless that they could not answer his challenge on an issue that they had previously thought they knew or understood very well. Socrates himself is also left perplexed that he had no answer to such a seemingly simple question about something so basic. This image extends beyond that of the gadfly, and is much more powerful as a metaphor for Socratic questioning as peculiarly philosophical. The numbness from the self-stinging ray represents a person's speechlessness at being genuinely philosophically perplexed, even though they may have engaged in many discussions over the same issue with many others before. Unlike the gadfly image which represents the questioning of social and political realities, the self-stinging ray is an image of philosophy as inquiry into matters so basic as the meaning of common words where consensual articulation of a definition seem elusive so that even everyday words and expressions may be undermined. Philosophical questioning, like the self-stinging ray, leaves us perplexed, but we must be persistent in our questioning—to 'sting' us out of complacency. In terms of Socratic pedagogy, the educational aim of engaging in philosophical inquiry is so that students don't choose complacency over reflection and thoughtfulness. In terms of life-long learning, it is even more applicable as persistence for reflection and a commitment to having an inquiring mind.

Now, onto the image of Socrates as midwife "whose dissolution of the prejudices and prejudgements of his interlocutors helps them towards the revelation of their own thoughts" (Arendt, in Villa, 1999, p.206). The midwife image illustrates the inducement of perplexity which is portrayed as the labour of philosophical childbirth (Matthews, 1999, p.91). This view of Socratic Method is particularly important to Socratic pedagogy as it represents inquiry as a specific kind of questioning technique, that of a philosophical midwife to aid philosophical childbirth, which is "presumably the delivery of a viable philosophical theory, doctrine, or analysis" (p.91). While it is not the task of the philosophical midwife to produce knowledge (Socrates is ignorant, represented by the midwife as barren), the result of facilitative questioning is the birth of productive ideas. In other words, the interlocutor develops the capacity to seek truth through the facilitation of philosophical questioning. This is reflected in the Platonic dialogues when Socrates brings his interlocutors through a series of stages of inquiry. Initially the inquirer cannot give rise to a definition of a particular concept, but through Socrates' careful guidance, tacit knowledge of the concept is uncovered.

A midwife in the literal sense of the word is a person responsible for the prenatal care, support and eventual assistance to the birthing procedure. The mother, of course, is the one who gives birth. The midwife in most cases is a traditional 'birth attendant'. Socrates makes the connection between the role of midwife and facilitating a dialogue as the ideas come from the inquirer themselves and cannot be transferred as knowledge, in the same way that a birthing practitioner can aid in the delivery of the baby but is there in the role of *attendant* as opposed to the role of the mother, who is essentially responsible for the birth itself. This is arguably the most referred to metaphor to describe the Socratic Method which originally featured in Plato's *Theatetus*. In the Socratic classroom, the metaphor of the midwife is integral for identifying how we should facilitate inquiry. However, it is, as we have seen, not the only metaphor used to depict the process of inquiry. The gadfly and the stinging ray, which are often interpreted as adversarial aspects of the method, are important for our interpretation of Socratic pedagogy. For example, when we are 'giving birth' to new ideas, this must be balanced with a critical rigor that is reflected in the self-stinging ray image. After all, as Gardner (1995) says, dialogue is not mere conversation, it is hard work! It is not enough to generate ideas without balancing this with critical reflection and evaluation. The metaphor of the gadfly as a persistent irritant is similarly important here as this pertains to the commitment required in inquiry and the persistence that is sometimes required in order to explore disagreements as well as agreements.

The images of philosophical midwife, a kind of gadfly, and a self-stinging ray are not the only metaphors used to describe philosophical inquiry that is typically Socratic. For Lipman, the images of an orchestra and chamber music are what he considers best describes how the Community of Inquiry works. For Nelson's Socratic Dialogue, the hourglass represents the consensual articulation of a definition through rigorous conceptual analysis, evaluation and judgment. For Bohm, his method of dialogue is represented as a dance. It is to these metaphors that I shall now turn, keeping in mind that the metaphors of Socrates, particularly that of the midwife, as illustrative of the facilitation inherent in Socratic pedagogy.

The Pedagogical Dimensions of the Community of Inquiry

The Community of Inquiry has been variously described by drawing attention to the role of the teacher in running classroom discussion as a 'facilitator of inquiry'. Included in some of the descriptions are a number of metaphors to illustrate this role: provoker, motivator, facilitator, coach, and some even reminiscent of Socrates the gadfly and midwife.[2] Take the following example by Felicity Haynes.

> The children are the musicians, making the music, providing the content as they develop and refine their musical expertise. The teacher facilitates and guides, providing form to the piece or offering philosophical direction by the provision of open questions. (Haynes, 1997, p.17)

Reed also uses the theme of making music, but emphasises more heavily the role of the teacher as conductor.

> The teacher who is running a classroom discussion might view herself or himself as an apprentice conductor of an orchestra of skilled musicians. As conductor, she or he leads, but that leading is always based upon cues received from the members of the orchestra. (Reed, 1991, p.152)

These images aid as illustrations of the role of the teacher in guiding philosophical progress in open inquiry. The teacher is the conductor, the participants the musicians, and the community of inquiry the orchestra. However, upon closer inspection, the two metaphors vary slightly as to what is being guided by the conductor. As Lipman himself uses the making of music as a metaphor, this seems like an obvious place to explore the relationship between teacher and attending to the procedures of inquiry further.

It is noteworthy that Lipman uses a number of metaphors to describe the Community of Inquiry. However, his likening the thinking necessary in a Community of Inquiry to chamber music is most interesting in light of Goethe's description of chamber music as 'four rational people conversing', which recurs in descriptions and analyses of chamber music compositions.[3] Playing chamber music requires both musical and social skills which are different from the skills required in an orchestra of playing solo. Of particular relevance is that chamber music is not led by a conductor, so the musicians are responsible for embellishing on the music script, taking the lead from others and contributing when appropriate. Turning to Lipman (1991), he says that the thinking process that underpins the Community of Inquiry "is like a piece of chamber music where all involved must play at the same time judging whether to embellish on the music of the composer" (p.95). The significance of likening the Community of Inquiry to chamber music is not that there is no conductor, and analogously that the teacher has no role to play in the Community of Inquiry, but rather that dialogical inquiry is not aimless conversation for "the process has a sense of direction; it moves where the argument takes it" (Lipman, 2003, p.83). Moreover, it has practical implications when we consider Lipman's broader educational aims of getting people to think for themselves about the central issue in life, and that engaging in open-minded inquiry is an exemplar of democracy in action. Lipman, like Dewey, understood democracy as an associated form of life, and thus emphasised the social dimension of democracy—a kind of deliberative democracy. The Community of Inquiry represents what he describes as "the social dimension of democracy in practice, for it both paves the way for the implementation of such practice and is emblematic of what such practice has the potential to become" (Lipman, 1991, p.249).[4] In other words, "the community of inquiry provides a model of democracy as inquiry, as well as being an educative process in itself" (Burgh, 2003a, p.25). If education is to fit with democracy and support it, what both discourses need to have in common is an interchange of ideas in conversation, and from an educational standpoint, an interchange in which children bring their experiences to the inquiry. But as pointed out previously, this interchange is not merely conversation or discussion, it is dialogical. Dialogical inquiry has procedural rules which are largely logical in nature, but it is also substantive where subject matter is an exchange of ideas and experiences of one mind upon another, and therefore participants must follow the argument where it leads in the dialogue.

Recall in the previous chapter that we looked at the idea of letting the argument lead; there is no one person 'in charge' of the direction of the dialogue but the logic of the argument itself leads the community. While there is a facilitator present (just like there is a composer in an orchestra), the participants must be taken where the argument, or the music, is naturally heading. The idea of letting the argument lead and letting the music lead are intrinsically similar because they are based on the ideas of the participants themselves, hence why the metaphor is so important in highlighting this aspect of the Community of Inquiry. But let us unpack this idea a little further in order to avoid confusion. When Lipman says 'letting the argument lead' he does not mean that a facilitator should completely 'let go of the reigns'. Rather, the argument *is* the facilitator of the direction and students need to attend to what is required by the argument. For example, if inquiry reaches a point where the group needs to clarify a term, they need to attend to this aspect of the inquiry rather than continue. The argument, in this case, requires that in order to continue the group needs to digress for a moment into conceptual analysis. The teacher as facilitator may also be required to point to this need. Hence, Gardner's fear that Lipman's principle of 'letting the argument lead' could be misunderstood to mean that students pursue any or all ideas that come into their heads. While creative thought, or the generation of ideas, should be valued in an inquiry, it must be balanced by a level of rigor and self-reflection. The teacher must facilitate a level of quality from the students in terms of philosophical progress, rather than simply exploring ideas. Again, this highlights the difference between dialogue and mere conversation.

A chamber orchestra aims at performing and interpreting a piece of music and so inevitably creates something new with each performance. Similarly, no two inquiries are likely be the same as the participants may generate different ideas that would require analysis. In chamber music, the musicians have the ability to embellish on the written music based on the contributions of others. When one musician feels the need to embellish on the melody, the other musicians follows as if they are in a musical dialogue, which could lead to further embellishment. Goethe describes the process of producing chamber music as 'rational people conversing' (Stowell, 2003). Keeping this aspect of chamber music in mind, the metaphor becomes useful for emphasising community, through its focus on a collaborative approach to thinking, or performing a piece of music. Because each musician in the production of chamber music must work together closely, this is an inherently collaborative activity. This also illustrates that the different dimensions of thinking are not easily separated; an element of inquiry that reflects a creative process of letting the argument lead is also reliant on the participants to take the lead from each other, which requires making musical judgment collaboratively but keeping in mind the original score.

While Lipman uses the production of music as a means to illustrate the very process of community of inquiry, interestingly two researchers, Nigel Morgan and John Cook (2008), have explicitly used Lipman's community of inquiry as a framework for teaching undergraduate music in their tertiary tutorials. They claim that Lipman's model of dialogue reflects the way that music is constructed; that is, the characteristics of Lipman's community of inquiry are like those required in composing and playing music collaboratively. They are:

- listening to one another with respect
- building on each other's ideas
- challenging one another to supply reasons for otherwise unsupported opinions (and musical statements – interpretative or composed)
- assisting each other in drawing inferences from what has been said (and played)
- seeking to identify one another's assumptions

The effective use of the principles of the Community of Inquiry as an approach to teaching music further strengthens Lipman's analogy.

Letting the argument lead is at the very heart of divergent thinking. It allows for the generation of new ideas, where the dialogue requires it. I acknowledge, like Lipman did, that this also includes the application of critical judgment. However, letting the argument lead is inherently a creative process because participants scaffold on one another's ideas, and its facilitation requires an understanding of when to bring critical rigor to the inquiry. I will address the idea of creative thinking as generative thinking in the following chapter. For the moment I reiterate that creative thinking concentrates on the generation of ideas and meaning making, and that creative thinking and critical thinking are inseparable insofar as critical thinking is necessary to and brings forth the production of creative ideas. Creative thinking would ensue unbridled without critical thinking to instil some rigor to keep the inquiry on task, and to not unnecessarily diverge from the initial focus of the inquiry.

Lipman stresses that the Community of Inquiry is an ideal educational setting for multi-dimensional thinking. His analogy clearly points to both the social and cognitive aspects of thinking, and therefore could be said to be exemplary of multi-dimensional thinking. However, while it does act as a general description of multi-dimensional thinking, specifically it draws attention to the creative component of inquiry. Put another way, the analogy is indicative of creative thinking as an interconnected component of multi-dimensional thinking.

The Pedagogical Dimensions of Socratic Dialogue

The hourglass is the most frequently used metaphor to describe the process of Socratic Dialogue. In a process of refining and abstracting, the dialogue moves in a direction aimed at narrowing the question and definition down to then apply it in a general context. As Boele (1998) explains the dialogue begins wide with a general question, then it is narrowed down to find a core statement which focuses the relevant part of the example. This is the point of the hourglass that then may be widened through the application of criteria and other suppositions. This narrowing down of the question to a specific definition to be applied to the general is seen by the proponents of Socratic Dialogue as the source of great understanding between participants. They stress that it is not compromise that is strived for in this instance, but consensus, where all understand each other and find agreement.

Let us look at the hourglass as it is represented in Socratic Dialogue (Kessels, 2001, p.67):

_____*Question*_____

_____*Example*_____

_____*Judgments*_____

_____*Rules*_____

_____*Principles*_____

You can see that process of dialogue reflects directly the shape of an hourglass. Through the use of regressive abstraction participants use a specific personal experience to explore a philosophical concept where the hourglass gets narrowed down to a core statement. In order to test its soundness, the group then moves from narrowing the concept down to applying it to a wider range of examples where we see the hourglass widen.

The group begins in the widest part of the hourglass with a general question being asked. It is the widest point of the hourglass because it is from here that the question is narrowed down to a conclusive definition. Kessels (2001) notes that this is the process of *elenchus*, where 'breaking down' previous conceptions is paramount in order to reach a core statement. This occurs in a process of narrowing down towards the waist of the hourglass. Deciding on a concrete example is the next step down in the hourglass, which is where the concept is narrowed down further by drawing it to one particular example. The hourglass narrows as a concrete example is taken, and we "dig into it, go 'back' to the concept that is presupposed, and try to analyse this concept" (Boele, 1998, p.51). This leads to the general formulation of statements. We now enter into the narrowest part of the hourglass wherein "these statements are 'abstracted' from the concrete example" (p.51). At the very narrowest part of the hourglass, the group can find a core statement that sums up their explorations of the concept thus far. The rule is then tested through various other unused examples and then the group must think of further counter-examples to refute their definition. This process sees the hourglass moving from narrowing down to a process of broadening in order to come to as close as a universal statement as possible by testing it against multiple examples. The hourglass returns to its widest point again after narrowing and then expanding when the group has found a principle to apply to the concept in question. At this point the group should have reached consensus and the hourglass can, for the time being, go no wider.

The hourglass can also be applied in a literal sense as a timekeeper to indicate Socratic Dialogue as a careful process that takes time. The sessions are most useful over a day or a couple of days, but have successfully been modified to run over one session, or most conducive, over a couple of sessions involving one topic. This time enables the group to take care to examine all arguments and to make sure that each person truly understands the others. This period of time is necessary for the arrival at consensus. Boele (1998) points out that difference of opinion is the key to deeper understanding, but if we consider these differences "only as an annoying delay, we have the wrong expectations with regard to a Socratic Dialogue" (p.51). Students, he says, are surprised to find that consensus is possible if the time and care is given to truly understand each other; a "real consensus in a heterogeneous group of people" (p.57), whereby the group come to a new understanding.

The pedagogical dimensions are clearly illustrated in Nelson's analogy; as an analogy for the pattern of inquiry, and for the period of time and patience that is required in a Socratic Dialogue. While there is undoubtedly a concentration on critical thinking there is also a concentration on the interplay between listening and speaking in regard to questions and answers. Thus, the experience of participating in Socratic Dialogue as a method for reaching solutions is at the same time a learning process and a way of understanding thinking as inquiry.

The Pedagogical Dimensions of Bohmian Dialogue

Garrett draws parallels between the beginning of the Bohmian dialogue and a cocktail party. As the cocktail party begins people stand idly together and gradually conversations begin that engages them. There is no set agenda at a cocktail party, and likewise in the dialogue. In the kind of setting that Bohm recommended such conversations will eventually lead to genuine dialogue. Garrett also describes the process of dialogue as a game of ball that one might play with a dog. If the ball is thrown, the dog brings it back in much the same way as a person contributes an idea in a dialogue; it is the assumption that others will engage with that contribution. But it is Bohm's metaphor of a collective dance of the mind that is most insightful. As Bohm (1991) puts it, "The spirit of Dialogue is one of free play, a sort of collective dance of the mind that, nevertheless, has immense power and reveals coherent purpose." The free flowing movement of such a dance is meant to illustrate a movement between the mind and body, thought and feeling, in order to open the way to creative change. Just like dancing, in a dialogue participants become aware of their own movement in relation to others (in this case, their own thinking in relation to the group).

The metaphor of dialogue as a collective dance of the mind illustrates also an awakened awareness not just of cognition but its connection to bodily awareness. As Bohm (1991) puts it:

> We can be aware of our body's actions while they are actually occurring but we generally lack this sort of skill in the realm of thought. For example, we do not notice that our attitude toward another person may be profoundly affected by the way we think and feel about someone else who might share certain aspects of his behavior or even of his appearance. Instead, we assume that our attitude toward her arises directly from her actual conduct. The problem of thought is that the kind of attention required to notice this incoherence seems seldom to be available when it is most needed.

So the physical awareness of a dance is analogous to the mental awareness that participants need to have when engaging in dialogue together. If we engage in self-reflection we may be able to better understand how our thought acts as a system. If we do this, we can uncover some of the assumptions that we hold as belief. But this must occur in a dialogical setting where we can be self-reflecting by genuinely listening to others. As in a dance, we can make contributions and also understand the contributions of others. By listening to one another, we will sustain a dialogue in much the same way as being aware of the movement and 'togetherness' of dancing.

In sum, by giving attention to the overall process that flows from thought and feeling and how they play out within the group, Bohmian Dialogue can lead to a new kind of coherent, collective intelligence. As pedagogy Bohm offers a conception of dialogue as an active multi-layered and complex process of interaction between participants that enables the exploration of assumptions and communication in a joint quest for meaning.

DIALOGUE AS CRITICAL, CREATIVE AND CARING THINKING

Dialogue requires thinking. But what is thinking? As mentioned, there is a substantial amount of research on thinking that comes from the disciplines of philosophy and psychology. Philosophers generally have regarded the mind as the place where reasoning happens, and that the cultivation of reason is essential for critical thinking and the generation of ideas in order to solve problems that take place in a social context. Studies on the mind are by-and-large the domain of psychologists, particularly cognitive psychologists. While there is much room for error with regards to understanding children's development and thinking, philosophers and psychologists generally agree that thinking involves critical and creative aspects of the mind and that language has a central role to play in developing a child's understanding. To what degree and to how it might be explained is the cause for further empirical investigations. What is clear, however, is that intellectual abilities derive not only from what we have inherited biologically but that they are activated by social experience, education, and family and cultural environment. The scientific debates on social (or inter-personal) intelligence and the effects of argumentation on intellectual and social development notwithstanding, the theories of Peirce, Dewey and Vygotsky (discussed previously) together offer a plausible account of the central role of language to thinking, knowledge as socially constructed through an interactive process of intra-personal and inter-personal relationships, and the role of communal engagement in inquiry in making meaning from the world. To that effect we need to concentrate on the relationship between the critical and creative dimensions of thinking and the social context within which it occurs, which requires, among other things, the ability to think ethically, affectively, normatively, appreciatively and to participate in society. That is to say, the role of caring thinking needs to be put into the equation alongside critical thinking and creative thinking. Therefore, in this final section I will point to the relationship between critical, creative and caring thinking in all three models of dialogue in order to provide a framework for discussions in the chapters to follow.

The Community of Inquiry: Multi-dimensional Thinking

Multi-dimensional thinking or complex thinking are terms used to describe the Community of Inquiry, conceived of as having three dimensions: critical, creative and caring thinking (Lipman, 2003; Splitter & Sharp, 1995; Burgh, Field & Freakley, 2006). Creative thinking is seen as the generating and building of ideas, critical thinking as exploring concepts, reasoning, evaluating and concluding, and caring thinking as the skills required for being a member of the learning community and the process of inquiry. To explain the relationship between critical thinking and creative thinking, Lipman uses the analogy of a pilot controlling a plane. Creative thinking is like the acceleration and critical thinking is the careful application of the brakes. While the plane requires acceleration to move forward, in order to keep on course and have an element of control, the pilot must apply the brakes every so often to keep the plane balanced. This analogy is supposed to show that critical and creative thinking work in concert together. In addition Lipman (2004) concedes to the importance of caring thinking as a prerequisite to higher-order thinking which he views as not solely limited to the cognitive domain but as a cognitive-affective relationship. Without emotions thinking would be devoid of a values component, and without this component genuine inquiry would not be possible, for "inquiry is generally social or communal in nature because it rests on a foundation of language, of scientific operations, of symbolic systems, of measurements and so on, all of which are uncompromisingly social" (p.83). Thus, for Lipman inquiry is thinking in a community which requires not only discovering, inventing, and connecting, but also *experiencing relationships*. This necessitates caring thinking. Caring thinking, he says, allows us to focus on that "which we respect, to appreciate its worth, to value its value" (p.262). However, according to Sharp (2004), Lipman does not emphasise caring thinking to the extent of the other dimensions. She points out that while he does explore the nature of caring thinking in relation to critical and creative thinking, it is not given the same focus throughout his curriculum. Perhaps if he did give as much attention to caring thinking his analogy may have been extended to include the pilot's care for the passengers on the plane and for the process of flying itself that may motivate the process of acceleration or braking. I will deal with caring thinking in more detail on Chapter 6, where I will argue for a conception of caring thinking as *connective thinking*.

Lipman cannot be accused of not giving prominence to creative thinking, as it is a vital component of the Community of Inquiry. The idea that the argument should dictate the direction of inquiry is itself a creative process as it enlists multiple dimensions of thinking, as well as requiring a level of inventiveness and innovation. Because the outcome of the inquiry cannot be predetermined, no two inquiries can be the same. The teacher has a responsibility to allow for the natural progression to unfold which requires a balance between enlisting both creative thought in order to explore new ideas and generate alternatives, and critical rigor to avoid faulty reasoning and to develop criteria. A level of autonomy is required on the students' part; the thoughts must come from their own interests, which is an inherently a creative process. This leads us back to Lipman's analogy of the Community of Inquiry as chamber music. Each musician must work together, but it is the music (or the argument) that must be facilitated by the musicians (or participants in dialogue).

Lipman's emphasis on creative thinking cannot be overestimated. This is evident in his understanding of the Community of Inquiry as a productive pedagogy. It requires participants, guided by the teacher as facilitator and co-inquirer, to generate their own ideas and thinking. It is also evident in the epistemology of the Community of Inquiry as reflective equilibrium. Its outcome is the reconstruction or production of knowledge. By engaging in dialogue, the participants are engaged in a collaborative and cooperative mutual inquiry working together in creating meaning, where "disequilibrium is enforced in order to compel forward movement" (Lipman, 2004, p.87). Like chamber music, the dialogue is guided by the contributions of each of the participants and therefore involves the interchange of ideas to give it a sense of direction, rather than conforming to the formal structures of existing disciplines which have their own assumptions.

> A dialogue that tries to conform to logic, it moves forward indirectly like a boat tacking into the wind, but in the process its progress comes to resemble that of thinking itself. Consequently, when this process is internalized or introjected by the participants, they come to think in *moves* that resemble its *procedures*. They come to think as the process thinks. (p.21)

This passage suggests that a Community of Inquiry is more than following the dictates of critical thinking or logic and reason. Lipman, as we have seen, emphasises the Community of Inquiry, and by implication a dialogue, as multi-dimensional thinking. However, the productive element of inquiry cannot be ignored; that is, it requires imagination and the generation of ideas. These are fundamental components of creative thinking, which, as I have already noted, are given much greater attention in Lipman's writing than in Nelson's or Bohm's. It could, therefore, be said that Lipman's analogy illustrates the creative component of guiding inquiry, which brings together in harmony all three dimensions of thinking.

In sum, the epistemology of the Community of Inquiry is reflective equilibrium, understood as fallilbilistic, not absolute. This is why self-correction (critical thinking) and the maintenance of the equilibrium (caring thinking) are integral component of inquiry. In turn, emphasis on self-correction and maintaining equilibrium demands constant remaking, improving, revising, and looking for new ways of maintaining the equilibrium (creative thinking).

Socratic Dialogue: Thinking Critically

Socratic Dialogue, depicted as an hourglass, clearly indicates critical thinking, a process of coming to consensus about a definition or conclusion and the application of that definition or conclusion to the wider context. Bernard Roy (2001) says of Socratic Dialogue:

> The graphic representation of an hourglass is often used to represent the structure of these [Socratic] dialogues: through various stages of consent and dissent, as many individual stories as there are participants are condensed and funneled down to a core statement, the comprehension of which is expanded so as to yield as close to a universal definition as it is possible to reach. (p.232)

As discussed previously, the various steps in Socratic Dialogue represented in the hourglass, and described by Nelson as an epistemology of regressive abstraction, bring participants through a process of narrowing down and applying criteria. Boele (1998) argues that the rigor required by the process of narrowing down to consensus is where the dialogue gains its depth. If participants have arrived at a definition, then they will all have come to agreement based on a common understanding.

By putting regressive abstraction at the core of Socratic Dialogue, it could be construed that Nelson and his followers were concerned less with the multi-dimensional aspects of thinking or with thinking as situated within a community. However, Socratic Dialogue unavoidably enlists creative and caring thinking, simply because it encourages ordinary human reflection in a dialogue setting. For example, the generation of counterexamples or making distinctions requires creative thinking. Also, being a participant in the dialogue makes the process a social one, and therefore employs caring thinking. It is a cooperative activity seeking to explore philosophical questions and to gain understanding through the exploration of concrete experiences chosen by the group for detailed analysis. By engaging in the inquiry process together through thoughtful and reasonable conduct, participants are afforded the opportunity to improve their reasoning skills and enhance self-confidence, as well as grasp the moral perplexities of everyday life. Nevertheless, all of these are outcomes of regressive abstraction, which makes Socratic Dialogue by-and-large a dialogue governed by the rules of logic, and therefore a model of dialogue as critical thinking.

Bohmian Dialogue: Awakened Attentiveness

Bohm's approach to dialogue is multi-dimensional, but foremost his concern is not with the improvement of thinking, but with inquiry as socio-therapy. Firstly, the idea of dialogue as meeting without an agenda in order to create a free space for the generation of ideas or for something new to happen identifies the dialogue as a creative space. Secondly, the process of uncovering assumptions through suspension of judgment makes the dialogue self-reflecting and self-correcting, which can be identified as the critical dimension. Thirdly, and I think what defines Bohmian Dialogue, his concern with connectivity and the integral relationships of parts to the functional whole attests to caring thinking. Bohm proposed that in the collective free space created by dialogue, participants could learn about thought through suspending their habit of defining and solving problems, and instead attending to thought itself—a process he called collective proprioception or awakened awareness. Through an awakened awareness participants gain insight experienced as mirroring back of the content of thought and of the not so apparent, dynamic structures that govern it. Put another way, participants in a group come to understand that thinking is a complex systemic process, which includes cognition, body, emotions, feelings, and reflexes, and that by paying attention to thought the fragmentation of our socially conditioned thinking is revealed, creating opportunities for making new psychological (intra-personal) and social (inter-personal) connections. The notion of connectivity is nowhere more clearly illustrated than in Bohm's metaphor of the dialogue as a dance of minds. The dance illustrates the movement that is inherent in an inquiry process. Whereas in a dance people must be mindful of the way their movements impact on others, in the dialogue the process is self-reflective with awareness on the collaborative nature of thought. Due to the dialogue being dependent on the contributions of the participants to engage in meta-dialogue, caring for the process of the dialogue is of paramount importance. Further evidence of Bohm's attention to caring thinking is evidenced by his emphasis on the relationship between participants in the dialogue as having an impersonal fellowship. While he does not make this explicit, it is caring thinking insofar as the participants share an authentic trust and openness in the process of the dialogue (socio-therapy) rather than an emotional connection or typical conventions of familiarity (psychotherapy).

In addition to concentrating on connectivity, caring thinking is also displayed in the reliance on trust shared by the participants. For example, Bohm understood that in order to sustain group dialogue participants inevitably will encounter varied stages of inquiry that bring moments of dissonance, anxiety and conflict, especially upon their first encounter with a problematic situation. At the outset of the dialogue, which has neither a presupposed goal nor an agenda, participants must attend to 'that which needs to be said', which requires them to be open to their own prejudices and habituated thought as well as that of others (Reeve, 2005). It is Bohm's view that the topic of inquiry needs to be relevant and applicable to the participants' own lives, and therefore must come from the whole group. Put another way, finding 'that which is meaningful' first, before the actual dialogue, is as important as the dialogue itself. Group experience gradually leads to increasing coherence, whereupon a level of collegiality is attained (as an impersonal fellowship).

SUMMARY

We have now begun our exploration into the development of Socratic pedagogy. For Bohm it is the recognition that the experience of dialogue is more important than the content being discussed that distinguishes his experiment with communication from the more Socratic oriented dialogues favoured by Lipman and Nelson. However, implicit in Bohm's dialogue is the Socratic notion of scholarly ignorance. By suspending judgments and assumptions Bohm's intention was for the participants to experience that their previous claims to knowledge are grounded in assumptions, unwarranted assertions and contestable beliefs and values. So, while Lipman's and Nelson's dialogues emphasis the relationship between *elenchus* and *aporia*, Bohm adds the missing ingredient necessary for Socratic pedagogy. Put another way, Bohm highlights the importance of the metaphorical self-stinging ray in dialogue.

Critical, creative and caring thinking are important dimensions crucial to successful dialogue. In the next three chapters we will address all three types of thinking and how they contribute to Socratic pedagogy. I identify what is central to each of these dimensions of thinking, using the terms generative, evaluative and connective thinking to illustrate the multi-layered and complex process of interaction in multi-dimensional thinking and their relationship to my framework for Socratic pedagogy, which has a distinct pattern of inquiry that moves between critical and creative phases.

NOTES

[1]   Scholars have tried to identify the early Platonic dialogues as containing *elenchus* and *aporia* and the later as largely dogmatic. However, my purpose is not to advance Platonic scholarship on the nature of the Socratic Method, nor is it to produce a true account of what is true of the historical Socrates.

[2]   See Splitter and Sharp (1995); Portelli (1989); Johnson (1984); Santi (1993).

[3]   See Bashford (2003).

[4]   See also Lipman, Sharp & Oscanyan (1980), Lipman (1988, 1991).

CHAPTER 4

CREATIVE ENGAGEMENT: GENERATIVE THINKING

The idiom, 'philosophy begins in wonder', attributed to Socrates, does not mean idle curiosity but the seriousness of purpose of a puzzled mind as it sets out on a philosophical journey; a life of questioning and searching for truths. As Alfred North Whitehead put it, "Philosophy begins in wonder. And, at the end, when philosophic thought has done its best, the wonder remains" (1934, p.46). The idea that philosophy is based on the ability to wonder suggests that philosophy is inherently creative (Splitter & Sharp, 1995, p.31). The ability to question what is time, what is right, what is number, requires a level of creativity in order to look at everyday concepts differently and to generate ideas through the asking of such questions. But as Lipman points out this ability is not always taken seriously, nor treated as necessary to teaching and learning and the development of thinking and its improvement.

> Many adults have ceased to wonder, because they feel that there is no time for wondering, or because they have come to the conclusion that it is simply unprofitable and unproductive to engage in reflection about things that cannot be changed anyhow. Many adults have never had the experience of engaging in wondering and reflecting that somehow made a difference in their lives. The result is that such adults, having ceased to question and to reach for the meanings of their experience, eventually become examples of passive acceptance that children take to be models for their own conduct. (Lipman, Sharp & Oscanyan, 1980, p.31)

This passage points to the dangers of neglecting wonder in children. Lipman's use of the term 'wonder' means a natural sense of wonder; an inherent ability in children, which, if not attended to or nurtured, will be lost as we enter adulthood. By ceasing to wonder as adults, we inadvertently contribute to the diminishing of natural wonder in children, who eventually grow to become adults who place little or no priority on wondering, and on and on the cycle repeats. Wonder is, therefore, not only necessary for children's intellectual and moral development, but it is also a prerequisite for lifelong learning. The need to ask questions about the environment that surrounds us and to continually seek meaning as lifelong learners is at the heart of finding things wonderful because they cannot be immediately explained until we inquire into them. For Lipman, engagement in dialogue creates opportunities to develop and maintain the capacity to wonder.

Wonderment is at the core of creative thinking for problem-solving. Because humans require the skills of problem-solving to survive, the teaching of creative thinking is vital. According to Lipman (2004):

> Our doubts cause us to suspend our working beliefs, it is our creative thought that reformulates the problematic situation, entertains alternative hypotheses as a way to attack the problem, considers possible consequences, and organizes experiments until the problematic character of the situation is provisionally vanquished and a new set of working beliefs is put into place. (p.249)

Creative thinking, therefore, is pre requisted on the ability to wonder and assists in our ability to solve problems. If children's attempts to wonder, question, speculate and invent answers are constantly thwarted or rejected by adults, they cease to make connections from their own observations or to explore the world in different ways. Consequently, they become passive in their attempts to seek answers and eventually depend on the authority of adults. The more they rely in their formative years on parents and teachers the more they steadily lose opportunities for increasing their abilities to retrieve, connect, compare and transform information. Ultimately, when they do not fully understand an observation they wait for explanations from others (Fisher, 1990, p.30).

It is important to acknowledge here the interplay between critical, creative and caring thinking and in particular the relationship between critical and creative thinking in philosophical dialogue. This is acknowledged by various authors including Richard Paul (1994), Lipman (1991), and Splitter and Sharp (1995). While they note the differences between the dimensions of thinking, they acknowledge that they work in concert together. As Splitter and Sharp (1995) suggest:

> Because philosophy both encourages and relies upon those who can think for themselves, it involves a dimension of freedom; a capacity to take what one has learnt and relate it to one's experience in new ways. Children who think for themselves are both critical thinkers and creative thinkers. They value logical and conceptual thinking, but they also enjoy speculating, imagining, inventing, discovering and wondering.(p.97)

The balance between the two dimensions of thinking cannot be denied. The other dimension of thinking, caring thinking is also vital to dialogue, in particular for the idea of suspending our working beliefs and for enhancing the communal aspects of dialogue. We will deal with these connections in Chapters 5 and 6 when we look further at evaluative and connective thinking. For this chapter I will be concentrating on creative thinking even though it should be noted that the concepts cannot in practice be separated when applied to everyday practices. Practitioners should, however, be clear about how creative thinking interacts in dialogue and need to understand it by its unique characteristics.

This chapter will explore creative thinking. As this book focuses on the development of thinking and its improvement through Socratic pedagogy, I will be concentrating only on the aspects of creative thinking that underpin dialogue.[1] In the last few decades there has been a proliferation of literature and research on creative thinking coming out of the disciplines of philosophy, psychology and education, especially in relation to higher-order thinking skills and problem solving aimed at students at all levels of education. Simultaneously, this has led to the development of creative thinking programs and classroom strategies for developing students' creative capacities, the most widely used being Edward de Bono's CoRT Thinking Program which consists of a variety of creative thinking tools or 'attention direction devices' as he prefers to call them.[2] However, the term 'creative thinking' is used very broadly, and has spawned a plethora of buzzwords intended to capture its meaning; the most familiar being divergent thinking, lateral thinking, thinking outside the box or the square, and smart or novel thinking. Despite these efforts to elucidate the meaning of creative thinking the term remains vague to say the very least. Our first task, therefore, will be to identify the characteristics or general features of multi-dimensional thinking that are more typical of creative thinking than of critical or caring thinking. What is common to these characteristics or central to their meanings is *generative thinking*. By generative thinking I mean the production, development and extension of ideas that can in some way be applied to the world to situations or problems. We shall see where generative thinking features in each of the models of dialogue to show its practical application.

WHAT IS CREATIVE THINKING?

Much has been said about the nature of creative thinking and its role in developing children's ability to think well. It is not unusual for writers to describe what they consider to be qualities of creative thinking or what makes a good critical thinker. Lipman (2004a), for example, appeals to a cluster of value terms he thinks draws out its meaning. Included in his list are: wondering, inventive, questioning, generating, constructing, and composing. Fisher (1995c) refers to creativity in practice as fluency, flexibility, originality and elaboration, and making the familiar strange. Splitter and Sharp (1995), on the other hand, list the thinking strategies they consider necessary for creative thinking: problem seeking, anticipating, predicting and exploring consequences, and being imaginative. Burgh, Field and Freakley (2006) offer an inventory of qualities they think are common to the literature on creative thinking in a community of inquiry as generating and building on ideas, exploring and developing innovative ideas, and exploring alternatives and different perspectives, and elaborating on and clarifying meanings. Cam (2006) illustrates in his framework for philosophical inquiry that the stages of initiating and suggesting are inherently creative. While these authors have contributed to a greater understanding of the role of creative thinking in inquiry, in order to understand where creative thinking fits into Socratic pedagogy we need to investigate further what is common to the conceptions of creative thinking that appear in the literature on philosophical inquiry.

In this part of the chapter we shall see the characteristics that are common to the conceptions of creative thinking found in the literature on philosophical education. To start, we pay attention to two distinctions: (1) between being creative and being a creative thinker, and (2) between creative thinking in relation to dialogue and creativity in literature, art and other imaginative works. Next a comparison is made between the notions of construction and reconstruction in education. What is required is a level of divergent thinking in the inquiry, giving rise to ideas that diverge from established thought in order to, among other things, find new solutions to problems. However, what is inherent in divergent thinking is that there is a level of risk. Students are required to explore their ideas in a community which, for some, is a confronting task. We cannot forget also the connections between creative and critical thinking and in this section we address the relationship between them. We shall see the importance of caring thinking to creative thinking as creative ideas must be received in the community. While creative thinking is explored in isolation, it should be viewed as a process of multi-dimensional thinking; that is, in concert with critical and caring thinking. We will be elaborating on and exploring these ideas in the following sections which will inform what is meant by generative thinking.

Creativity and Creative Thinking

Let's begin by making a distinction between being creative and being a creative thinker. Lipman (1991, pp.193–212) notes that there is a difference between a creative teacher and a teacher who teaches for creative thinking. Some educators teach in a creative manner, giving lively and inspiring lectures using creative means by which to transfer knowledge. But this is different to teaching *for* creative thinking. Creative thinking can be promoted through dialogue, whereby learners encounter problematic situations for which there are multiple interpretations and experiences. In order to find innovative solutions, we need to develop the capacity to generate ideas and to make new connections to gain insights. Creative thinking is a learned process, requiring the guidance of the teacher as facilitator to encourage the exploration and development of innovative ideas through generating hypotheses and conjectures, exploring alternatives and different perspectives, and elaborating and clarifying meanings (Lipman, 1991, p.198; Burgh, Field & Freakley, 2006, p.113). A further distinction can be made between the creative process in the narrow sense as 'creative thinking in relation to dialogue' and in the broader sense when referring to 'creativity in literature, art and other imaginative works'. Briefly, creative thinking in dialogue provides a creative space for the emergence of new ways of thinking, acting, and relating to others, and is usually applied to finding innovative solutions to problematic situations. Creativity in literature, performance, music, visual art, and other imaginative works usually refers to the freedom of expression in response to an aesthetic experience. The distinction notwithstanding, there is certainly interplay between both, and nowhere is this more apparent in education than in the key learning area of the Arts. Engagement in aesthetic experiences and art responses to them is a way of expressing 'sensory knowing' or personal meaning, but students also engage their senses cognitively (i.e., thinking creatively, as well as critically) by responding as complex thinkers to enable them to develop an understanding of aesthetic values in relation to the environment and human creation in the Arts. However, while it is important to understand the relationship between creative thinking and the Arts, it is also equally important to address where it fits also in the other areas of the school curriculum. But as my concern is specifically with creative thinking in dialogue, which is much more general, I mention this only to clarify the intersection between these two creative processes.

So what is a creative thinker? Laura Berk (2000) argues that the ability for creative thinking is an aspect of one's personality. A creative thinker is an innovative style of thinker who has a tolerance of ambiguity and perseverance, and who characteristically has courage of their own convictions and a willingness to take risks (p.352). Robert and Michele Root-Bernstein identify the following as necessary characteristics of creative thinking.

Observing, Imaging, Abstracting, Pattern Recognizing, Pattern Forming, Analogizing, Bodily Kinaesthetic Thinking, Empathizing, Dimensional Thinking, Modelling, Playing, Transforming, Synthesizing. (in Lee, 2005, p.9)

Sharon Lee (2005) notes that the first nine characteristics are non-verbal characteristics that stimulate the thinker to transcend the normal cognitive boundaries and that the final four allow the individual to transfer the ideas into socially accessible ideas with which to interact with others. As previously stated, Lipman also offers a list of characteristics related to creative thinking, or as he calls them clusters of value terms. Some examples are: wondering, inventive, questioning, generating, constructing, and composing. These lists go some way to offering an insight, mainly by serving as cluster concepts to characterise, rather than to sharpen the vocabulary of, creative thinking. A more fruitful way, as I will show in the second part of this chapter, is to identify what underlies creative thinking, which I argue is generative thinking.

Construction and Reconstruction

What can be said so far about creative thinking? Creative thinking involves the learner in the construction or production of ideas. It is, therefore, at the core of constructivist theories of learning. In constructivist theories of learning emphasis is placed on the learner rather than on the instructor. Learners interact with situations in collaboration with others in the learning community and thereby gain an understanding of the features of those situations by trying out ideas and hypotheses, and fitting new information together with what is previously known. To become a creative thinker is to look at situations from a different perspective, and to explore them prior to making judgments—which requires to some extent the suspension of judgment. Constructive thinking is inventive thinking according to Piaget who posits that "to understand is to invent" (in Fisher 1995a, p.24). Inventive thinking is what Fisher (1995a) terms 'skillful thinking', which is the exploration and ability to expand on our original ideas. He notes that philosophical inquiry can open up multiple paths of exploration and is conducive to enhancing such thinking. It is the ability to look at something from new perspectives (p.23). This concurs with Shephard's (2005) notion of creative thinking as producing something new. We can conclude that creative thinking is inherently a constructivist enterprise, which relies on innovation, inventiveness, the suspension of judgment, and the production and expansion of ideas.

Constructivist thinking shares a relationship with the notion of reconstruction. It is telling when looking not only at the differences between construction and reconstruction but also at where they intersect. Looking at the differences, construction is the application of certain skills to produce new knowledge, whereas reconstruction involves bringing down old structures of knowledge to create new ones. What both have in common is that they are generative; that is, they are concerned with the generation of ideas. But it seems that embedded in the notion of construction is some kind of reconstruction, as ideas must come out of old structures. It could be inferred then that creativity also relies on a conception of reconstruction. Lee (2005) concurs with this view. According to Lee creativity is the ability to alter or change the space, the functionality, or the knowledge that preceded it. It is "the ability to construct new understanding or to establish a new skill or product" (p.7). This has ties with our previous discussion on the elenchus and the aporia. The elenchus is the process of examining assumptions about that which we take for granted and the aporia is the ability to build new ideas from the empty space that is left (which is analogous to the building of physical structures). Lipman (2004) makes a similar claim. He argues that creativity comes out of 'breaking through' existing theories. He acknowledges Kuhn's assertions that paradigm shifts only occur because there is an existing scientific system which other scientists aim to dispel. Creativity, therefore, is the ability produce something new but only insofar is it arises out of a framework already present that has been evaluated. Like renovating an old home, the structure must be in place for the new renovations to commence.

> It is unprofitable to think of creativity as a process of emergence out of nowhere. It is rather a transformation of the given into something radically different—not a rabbit produced by magic out of a silk hat, but a silk purse produced by art out of a sow's ear. (Lipman, 1991, p.202)

The analogy of Socrates as the midwife is particularly important here; as the teacher who helps people give birth to their ideas (or in other words, helps them to think creatively). It is questionable from this discussion and from Lipman's quote above if construction can occur on its own in terms of creative thinking or if it is always reliant on *re*construction whereby we create new ideas based on the breaking down of assumed or taken for granted knowledge. We will discuss this further in the next part of the chapter on generative thinking.

Divergence and Convergence

Creative thinking is tied to the notion of divergent thinking which has a reciprocal relationship with convergent thinking. According to Berk (2000) divergent thinking is the "generation of multiple and unusual possibilities when faced with a task or problem", whereas convergent thinking is "arriving at a single and correct answer" (p.351). Both of these aspects are required for thinking Socratically as we seek to understand each other through coming to shared meanings as well as extending our thinking by searching for alternatives that leads to divergent ideas, and hence to further dialogue. Divergent thinking is primarily based on the ability to both identify a problem and then go towards finding solutions to these problems. Given our present discussion on creative thinking our discussion will be limited to divergent thinking only. The purpose of raising convergent thinking was only to point out the context within with divergent thinking operates.

Divergent thinking, which requires participants in an inquiry to go out on a limb and come up with new possibilities to problems, is essentially 'thinking for oneself'. Thinking for ourselves is inherently creative and requires a level of divergence. Gilbert Ryle (1971) argues that creativity is present when we ponder because we must act as the teacher, helping our ideas to form. Essentially, we become the facilitator of our own ideas when we engage in divergent thinking because it requires ideas that are new and that extend on the previous ideas of others. It could be said that when we think *for* ourselves in order to generate ideas that this is an inherently dialogical activity because our ideas are also extended by the ideas of others. This is critical to the notion of following the argument where it leads inherent in the Socratic Method because we must facilitate our own ideas in collaboration with others. To follow the argument where it leads is to follow the logic of inquiry, but it is the *creative* ideas of the participants and their individual thoughts that shape it.

Let us reflect for a moment on what it means to adopt divergent thinking in the first place. To think something that is new and different from established thought requires an individual to go 'out on a limb' and to extend on the ideas presented in the argument. For some students this may be a confronting task. Creative thinking, therefore, requires participants in an inquiry to take risks. This brings up to the topic of our next discussion.

Creative Thinking and Risk

Lee (2005) describes creativity as a process of taking risks. In dialogue creative thinking does not only require participants to produce innovative ideas, but it also requires that the ideas are communicated to the group, which in itself may be a daunting process, especially if the group is a large and diverse one. Thus, having the confidence to display creativity is one of the very aspects of creativity itself. Jerome Kagan (1989) confirms this when he says that "an idea we call creative requires the reaction of another, not just the judgment of the inventor or of history" (p.206). Because dialogue is situated in a *community* of inquirers, it requires that others engage with our ideas for them to be truly received. This requires the ability to take risks and have confidence in one's own ability. Whereas children display a natural curiosity, which in itself is a creative process, the more aware they become of social norms, the more the step into the unknown becomes a daunting process.

Lee (2005) suggests that the "result of taking such risks is social stigma, alienation, uncertainty, censure, or disapproval" because it "is generally accepted that the domain of creativity is one of detachment or difference" (p.7).

Csikszentmihalyi (1997) reported on case studies that he conducted with various individuals who he considered to be successful creative thinkers. He assessed their dedication to their creative activities as opposed to succumbing to fear associated with taking creative risks, and found that most people believed that the result of engaging in creative activity far outweighed the risks involved. He called it *flow*; where the creative endeavour and the 'novelty of discovery' took over. This is reminiscent of Lipman's (1991) story about Joan who found that once she was exposed to the inquiry process, she felt the need to contribute to ideas and was swept up with the argument. This anecdote goes some way to showing the inherent level of fear and then reward that comes from engaging in the creative inquiry process where 'flow' takes over from any self-consciousness. Lee (2005) draws attention to the idea of flow in Dewey's thinking on the creation of an environment where flow is possible (p.8). Dewey argued that humans have the ability of creative thinking and that creativity comes from social stimuli coupled with our initial sense of wonder. With this ability in mind, he claimed that by placing the learner and not the teacher at the centre, that problem solving abilities would be present rather than just a transfer of knowledge. Both Dewey and Csikszentmihalyi found that the only way to enhance creativity is through a change in environment and not simply by encouraging a learner to be creative. Both also note that creativity can be best allowed to progress and 'ripen' if it is not just personal but social. This is particularly important to this book because this is the type of creativity to which I am referring. It is not an individual endeavour, but one that is able to grow through social interaction (Lee, 2005, p.8). Miller (2005) argues that creative thinking requires an environment that is 'intellectually safe' insofar as students are free to develop ideas within a supportive community. I explore this notion further in Chapter 6 with reference to caring thinking as a condition for an intellectually safe environment. The relationship between creative and caring thinking is something I look at in depth later on but the links should be noted here as well as the links to critical thinking which I will turn to now.

The Role of Creative Thinking in Multi-dimensional Thinking

It cannot be overstressed that the generation of ideas also requires a level of critical thinking. Lipman's analogy of the plane that needs both accelerator and brakes to fly is indicative of the need to accelerate creatively with ideas before applying the brakes of critical judgment. If we think of creative thinking as acceleration, then applying critical thinking is applying the brakes, lest we have a creative dialogue that is not balanced by evaluation and judgment. In other words, effective creative thinking is generally a free form of thought but it is not without judgment. While it is not restricted by criteria, Lipman (1991) claims creative thinking must be sensitive to criteria and must go through levels of critical thinking (p.194). He recognises two aspects of criteria-making as creative thinking—both the application of criteria to subjects and the criteria that are applied in creative thinking. This is where the divide between creative and critical thinking becomes blurred. Lipman discusses the interchange between rational and creative thinking. He sees these as being on a continuum or an axis whereby thought can be mapped.[3] Sometimes thought can be largely creative and free-flowing with little rational thought, and at other times creativity is diminished when thought becomes more rational (p.196). I will be paying more attention to critical thinking in the next chapter. Suffice it to say that Lipman suggests that creative thinking also comes from making judgments and conceptual analysis, and thus any philosophical inquiry is intrinsically creative. We cannot, as Lipman suggests, separate creative thinking from critical thinking as both are intrinsically linked in their process but we can show where some aspects of thinking are emphasised. For example, conceptual analysis is primarily a critical thinking process. However, to make links between certain concepts requires a certain inventiveness and creativity.

In terms of the relationship between creative thinking and caring thinking, Splitter and Sharp (1995) recognise that thinking creatively happens in the community between inquirers (p.16) which reflects a caring element of inquiry. Phillip Guin seems to concur with this when he argues that "[t]he non-intimidating character of the community [of inquiry], where all serious beliefs and proposals are entertained, encourages children to generate a rich variety of original ideas" (in Splitter & Sharp, 1995, p.16). As we discussed at the beginning of the book, thinking collaboratively allows for a greater exploration of ideas when suggestions are made by others beyond those we can suppose on our own. I would like to reiterate again that creative thinking must have a balance of critical rigor and must be situated in the community to allow also for a balance of caring thinking if it is to contribute to Socratic pedagogy.

GENERATIVE THINKING: A WAY OF THINKING CREATIVELY

Let us just take a moment to sum up what we have said about creative thinking. Creative thinking may be viewed in two different ways: (1) exploring and developing innovative ideas, which includes maintaining the capacity to wonder, applying divergent thinking, and looking at familiar situations differently, and (2) elaborating and building on ideas which includes the production, extension and development of those ideas, generating hypotheses and conjectures, and exploring alternatives and different perspectives. Inherent in creative thinking is a reviewing process that consists of reviewing what we've already done, deciding whether further exploration is required or if it is time to move on to critical thinking. Now that we have identified the characteristics or general features of multi-dimensional thinking that are typical of creative thinking, in this part we shall see that common to these characteristics or central to their meanings is *generative thinking*. Generative thinking is the production, development and extension of ideas that can in some way be applied to the world, to situations or problems. Generative thinking is comprised of four interrelated components: (1) wonder (2) production, (3) synectics, and (4) fluency.

Wonder is essential to generative thinking. It enables a situation to be encountered as problematic and enables the generation of hypothesis in response to it. This is central to Socratic pedagogy because teachers must educate in ways that allow for wonder in their students. Dewey suggests that inquiry should come from real-life problematic situations. A teacher who is open to allowing students to follow up on their wonder and to encourage wonder will encourage generative thinking. Wonder is generative because this is the initial starting point for creating and building on ideas.

The second component for generative thinking is production. Ruggiero (2007) claims that we must engage in thinking that allows for the production of ideas. Whitehead argues that there must be structures in place that allow us to explore multiple ideas.

> The probability is that nine hundred and ninety-nine of [our ideas] will come to nothing, either because they are worthless in themselves or because we shall not know how to elicit their value; but we had better entertain them all, however skeptically, for the *thousandth* idea may be the one that will change the world. (in Ruggiero, 2007, p.153)

As the aim of philosophical inquiry partly is to provide opportunities to discuss societal problems, then the focus on generative thinking in terms of its practical application to the classroom is essential. In order to produce ideas we need to engage in questioning. When we choose to look further into taken-for-granted claims through asking questions, we begin to generate new ideas. This requires a level of questioning that is heightened in a collaborative dialogue because we can test our ideas against others; that is, the production, development, scaffolding, and extension of our ideas through the process of inquiring together. For example, when we ask 'what is the good life' this requires an exploration into meaning and alternatives of what might constitute right and wrong. This requires innovation. Innovation comes about when we look at something from a new point of view after wondering (or asking questions), through "the application of an idea that results in a valuable improvement" (Rabe, 2006, p.12). If this is so, then developing the capacity for the generation of ideas can provide opportunities for supporting democratic ways of life. Certainly, the ability to think in such ways represents a microcosm of the social aspects required for democratic communities, and as such has application to what Dewey called the greater community.

Synectics is the third component of generative thinking. There is interplay between synectics and production. According to Fisher (1995b), synectics is making the familiar strange, to see the familiar in new ways (p.84). The process can be described as the reconstruction of an already trodden pathway. Ideas in this sense aren't new, but a reconstruction of old ideas. This is central to generative thinking. When we talk about generative thinking this involves both the generation of ideas but also the regeneration of ideas. Generating refers to the production of something. However, when we are producing something new these ideas arise from an old structure, whether this occurs through the exploration of an old concept or gaining new meanings. This is regeneration. Synectics has also been described as an approach to solving problems based on the creative thinking of a group of people from different areas of experience and knowledge. What is implicit in this is that it is focused on the collective process of generating and regenerating ideas. Synectics, therefore, describes the process of production and reproduction of ideas, as well as the way in which people in a dialogue collectively engage in communal dialogue in order to generate ideas through a process of collaborative reconstruction. In practice it relates directly to the creation of metaphor as a way of assisting to see the familiar in different ways. In terms of reasoning skills it appeals to analogous reasoning, rather than to inductive or deductive reasoning. Reasoning analogously draws connections between things or joins together concepts that normally would not be seen as connected in terms of similarities, and thus creates opportunities for making creative conceptual links between ideas in order to achieve new ways of looking at things.

Fluency of thinking is the fourth component of generative thinking. Fluency of thinking, according to Fisher (1995c), is the "ease with which we use stored information when we need it" (p.44). The more children generate "ideas in play and in formal settings the more fluent [they] will be in generating solutions to the real and important problems of life" (p.45). Fluency, therefore, can be described as flowing effortlessly, flowing or moving smoothly, to-ing and fro-ing, which are all inherent in the process of thinking creatively. Flow, the concept that underpins fluency, means to move or run smoothly with unbroken continuity as in the manner characteristic of a fluid. It also means to circulate, to move with a continual shift, to proceed steadily and easily and to arise or derive. Fluency is undeniably a central characteristic of generative thinking because it is a way of provoking us out of habitual thought patterns, and finding new ways of looking. We can apply the idea of fluency to Lipman's metaphor of chamber music. There is a level of fluency (and flow) inherent in the to-ing and fro-ing between the musicians as the music is developed. Because chamber music involves the regeneration of a central piece of music there is a level of reconstruction that occurs when the orchestra interprets a piece of music by embellishing on the ideas of one another. There is also a level of fluency that takes over as each musician embellishes on the ideas of others. However, none of this would be possible if there was not the sense of wonder to think 'outside of the box'.

Links can also be made between fluency and Vygotsky's Zone of Proximal Development. The difference between what students can do unaided and what they can achieve with scaffolding provided by the teacher can be achieved though extending on what may be considered as taken-for-granted knowledge and capabilities through the generation of new ideas. Generative thinking affords opportunities for risk-taking and divergent thinking, but through the process of scaffolding from a familiar place. By focusing on students' potential they are able to proceed ahead of their actual level of development or previous achievement, drawing on other participants in the dialogue in order to maintain fluency. The level of risk is also reduced as students initially come from a familiar place developmentally, conceptually and socially. This also allows for fluency between the interpersonal and intrapersonal practices within a constructivist learning environment.

GENERATIVE THINKING IN DIALOGUE

We will now explore where generative thinking features in each of the models of dialogue to show its practical application. Given that we have already identified the characteristics of generative thinking, let us now see where generative thinking features in classroom practice to further understand how it will inform our framework for Socratic pedagogy. We will look firstly at the Community of Inquiry and the idea of following the argument where it leads as indicative of fluency. We will also readdress the reconstructive nature of dialogue. Lipman's analogy is useful insofar as it illustrates the role of generative thinking within a multi-dimensional framework for dialogue, specifically in the Community of Inquiry. Socratic Dialogue also employs generative thinking as it requires, among other things, divergent thinking though the generation of questions and the production of counterexamples as a way of refuting or strengthening definitions. Finally, Bohmian Dialogue shows the interplay between generative and connective thinking through the collective aspects of synectic thinking and fluency. Let us now turn to Lipman's Community of Inquiry to understand the process of creative thinking within a framework of multi-dimensional thinking. It is with Lipman's emphasis on both critical and creative thinking that we should be mindful.

The Community of Inquiry

If we want a model of dialogue that is illustrative of generative thinking within a framework of multi-dimensional thinking, then Lipman's Community of Inquiry is an exemplary model for generative thinking in Socratic pedagogy. In this section I will show how following the argument where it leads is an inherently creative process, by which I mean it is characterised by generative thinking. We have already touched on this notion in this chapter but I will take this opportunity to draw together some further connections.

The Community of Inquiry is founded on the notion of following the argument where it leads to determine the direction of the dialogue. So, an obvious starting point for our discussion is to be clear about what we mean when we say 'following the argument where it leads'. For Socrates, the notion of following an argument where it leads is the guiding maxim for his own philosophical practice. While there is disagreement among scholars over what determines an argument's direction, Socrates, and certainly Lipman, did not intend it to mean that we follow arguments passively. For our purposes we could say that an argument must follow the logic of inquiry. But what does it mean to follow the logic of inquiry? It could be said that to follow the logic of inquiry is to follow the dictates of reasoning. To understand this notion only in terms of critical thinking restricts the role of generative thinking to working within a narrow framework of logic and reasoning so let us look at how it relates to generative thinking and the Community of Inquiry. According to Paul (1994),

> The words 'reasoning' and 'logic' each have both a narrow and a broad use. In the narrow sense, 'reasoning' is drawing conclusions on the basis of reasons, and in the narrow sense, 'logic' refers simply to the principles that

apply to the assessment of that process. But in the broad sense, 'reason' and 'reasoning' refer to the total process of figuring things out, and hence to every intellectual standard relevant to that. And parallel to this sense is a broad sense of 'logic' which refers to the basic structure that one is, in fact, figuring out (when engaged in reasoning something through). (p.105)

To clarify what he means by logic and reasoning in relation to generative thinking and dialogue, let us turn again to Lipman's analogy of a pilot flying a plane. Lipman's notion of following the argument where it leads suggests a broader sense of logic and reason, i.e., the total sense of figuring things out. This is necessarily generative because, while flying the plane, the pilot is accelerating toward a particular logical pathway that is essentially unknown until the plane passes by each point. Every move forward is a step in the direction of 'figuring things out'. There is a logical progression. What is central to this analogy is that even though the plane may journey in multiple directions, the very process of acceleration denotes a logical forward motion. In dialogue, while ideas may be generated, they follow the logical progression of generation.

On the other hand, Paul points to the narrower sense of logic and reasoning which entails drawing conclusions on the basis of reasons, and the principles that apply to the assessment of that process. In Lipman's plane metaphor, this would be the process of carefully applying the brakes to slow the plane down. We will touch upon this again in the following chapter, but for the moment, let us say that this view of reasoning and logic is concerned with critical thinking and convergence. In the broad sense what makes good reasoning good reasoning? It requires us to bring out what is implicit in our thinking, which is an inherently a generative process. Drawing conclusions is sometimes mistakenly seen as only working within the narrow sense of reasoning, but for Paul, this is just the tip of the iceberg.

> Becoming adept at drawing justifiable conclusions on the basis of good reasons is more complex than it appears. This is because drawing a conclusion is always the tip of an intellectual iceberg. It is not just a matter of avoiding a fallacy in logic (in the narrow sense). There is much more that is implicit in reasoning than is explicit, there are more components, more 'logical structures' that we do not express than those we do. To become skilled in reasoning things through we must become practiced in making what is implicit explicit so that we can 'check out' what is going on 'beneath the surface' of our thought. (pp.105–106)

When we are thinking in the broad sense of reasoning and logic there is a logical pattern of generation as thinking is extended on or expanded. Let us take another of Lipman's analogies to further understand how this fits into the Community of Inquiry. Lipman's analogy of chamber music is telling, for it depicts the generative thinking inherent in inquiry, which is analogous in the generation of music. He likens the Community of Inquiry to chamber music where all the musicians must play at the same time judging whether to embellish on the music of the composer (Lipman, 1991, p.95). This is analogous to following the argument where it leads;

when each musician is capable of contributing to the music set out in front of them (like the stimulus material presented at the start of the Community of Inquiry). The participants must work together, building on the ideas of each other, but essentially the music (or in Lipman's case the argument) is being constructed collaboratively by the musicians (or participants in the dialogue). Lipman's analogy when applied to generative thinking is illuminating insofar as it gives a sense that the musicians are directed in some way even though that direction is unfamiliar. The following quote by Paul could offer a possible explanation.

> [W]hen we are thinking something through for the first time, to some extent, we create the logic we are using. We bring into being new articulations of our purposes and of our reasons. We make new assumptions. We form new concepts. We ask new questions. We make new inferences. Our point of view is worked out in a new direction, one in which it has never been worked out before. (p.106)

When applied to chamber music the musicians 'figure things out along the way' but they do not do this without the skills required of a chamber orchestra musician. They work with what they know or are familiar with to guide them to figure the rest out anew. Similarly with inquiry in a dialogue; participants create new understandings and recreate old ones. This interplay is at the core of reconstruction.

Reconstruction in classroom practice means that teachers must allow for, and encourage, thinking that is divergent. The role of the facilitator in the inquiry is, hence, particularly important in letting the natural process of argument unfold. The facilitator must retain a firm balance between the discussion being guided by the students' own contributions of their thoughts, and knowing when to intervene when procedural or substantive error has occurred. In this way, students have to think for themselves as a group. Let me iterate here that Lipman promoted thinking for oneself not thinking by oneself. The argument that leads the discussion must come from the students and their own abilities to invent and follow the logic of their generative thinking, but this is also coupled with a critical process of reasoning and logic in the narrow sense. Engaging in classroom inquiry and engaging with arguments of others requires critical consideration of the argument that they present as well as looking critically at the arguments of others to identify errors in their reasoning. This approach means that the participants themselves, and not the teacher, shape the dialogue—even though the teacher is both facilitator and co-inquirer. Lipman (1991) says "I suspect it is, that thinking for ourselves is the most appropriate paradigm of creative thought …" (p.204). Perhaps Lipman describes it best when he points to 'invention' as being at the heart of creative thinking (p.193). Invention requires some kind of generation of ideas. The dialogue is based on the ideas of the students and the argument that logically leads from it. Generating those ideas does require inventiveness on the students' part, which includes elements such as "originality, novelty, generativity, uniqueness, breakthrough, capacity, surprisingness … liberating quality, productivity, freshness, imaginativeness, inspiredness, capacity to synthesize" (p.205).

Socratic Dialogue

While Socratic Dialogue has a primary emphasis on critical thinking, inherent in Nelson's analogy of the hourglass is the interplay with generative thinking. Most specifically, generative thinking is paramount in Socratic Dialogue when students are required to think of counterexamples to refute their definition. This is seen in the hourglass analogy where the funnel gets wider as different contexts are explored, which requires divergent thinking for the generation of different perspectives. In the broad sense, the hourglass follows a logical thread of figuring things out through the widening of dialogue. While the aim of the dialogue is to adopt convergent thinking through exploring arguments that will involve a to-ing and fro-ing between agreement and disagreement, in this stage of the dialogue students need to generate examples that can test the consensus that was previously reached. This stage of the dialogue is the most explicit display of generative thinking. Philosophy uses a number of generative thinking and inquiry tools such as: questioning, producing an agenda, creating hypothesis, making analogies, and seeing things from different perspectives. These processes are inherent in Socratic Dialogue as they are in the Community of Inquiry, but there is less emphasis on these than there is on evaluative thinking and inquiry tools in Socratic Dialogue. However, Nelson and his followers are adamant that Socratic Dialogue is for the cultivation of thinking dispositions and not just a way of acquiring critical thinking skills.

Bohmian Dialogue

Bohm refined dialogue to a creative art, and therefore it is inherently a generative process. To reiterate, Bohmian Dialogue has no facilitator and no agenda. It is solely up to the participants in the dialogue to construct their own agenda and to generate their own ideas. This makes Bohmian Dialogue a naturally generative process, as participation through a 'collective dance of minds' is all that the group has to prevent the discussion from wondering aimlessly. Because there is no starting point and no agenda, the creative process rests in the group's ability to generate a topic. It is a careful process of 'saying what needs to be said' and finding the balance between participants exploring their own ideas, but also paying attention to the ideas that are shared by the rest of the group. Clearly, Bohmian Dialogue relies on the goodwill of the participants for discussion to take place. It is not compatible with adversarial thinking, i.e., competitive, contentious, or aggressive behaviour. This is why Bohm emphasised the notion of an impersonal fellowship. This is not a recommendation to detach oneself, but rather to pay attention to what is going on, particularly to one's own thoughts and the assumptions underpinning those thoughts in order to prevent them from becoming obstacles to effective dialogue.

It should be noted that Bohm himself wrote extensively on creativity in his 1996 publication, *On Creativity,* but because its application is to creativity in science and not directly to the cultivation of creative thinking through dialogue I have not drawn on it here. However, Bohm's theoretical framework offers an effective means for facilitating transformative learning. In this sense, Bohmian Dialogue also has an emphasis on reconstruction. Bohmian Dialogue is a generative dialogue as it supports transformative learning processes within the context of collaborative, inquiry-based learning. But, as Bohm stressed, it is not the content of dialogue that is important, but dialogue itself is a path to greater wisdom and learning.

WHERE TO FROM HERE?

Let us review where we are at this moment before moving to the next chapter. What have we said so far about creative thinking? There are four characteristics: (1) wonder, (2) production, (3) synectics, and (4) fluency that are common to creative thinking. Generative thinking is central to the meaning of these four characteristics. Therefore, generative thinking is necessary for effective creative thinking. We have also identified where generative thinking fits into a multi-dimensional framework for Socratic pedagogy by demonstrating how it can be applied to each of the models of dialogue in order to gain a better understanding of its practical application.

We can extrapolate from the analysis in this chapter that generative thinking, in relation to multi-dimensional thinking, is best described by Lipman's model of dialogue. The Community of Inquiry, which embeds the principle of following the argument where it leads, illustrated by the analogy of chamber music, makes an important contribution to the development of generative thinking. This, in turn, informs the framework for Socratic pedagogy discussed in our concluding chapter. It is suffice to say that by recognising generative thinking as the pulse of creative thinking what we are indeed doing is showing both in theory and in practice what teachers will need to concentrate on when it comes to classroom practice. While it is important to note that teachers are developing creative thinkers, what the creative thinker has to bear in mind is that not only is their primary task the generation of ideas, but through engaging in the process they are also developing and improving their own thinking.

In the final chapter we will talk more about generative thinking in relation to multi-dimensional thinking as it sits in the framework of Socratic pedagogy. But to do this we also need to look at critical thinking in relation to evaluative thinking and caring thinking in relation to connective thinking. Let us now turn to Chapter 5, critical thinking and evaluative thinking.

NOTES

[1] Interest in creative thinking extends beyond education, and has received renewed attention in the current context of new media technologies and globalisation. There has been a growth in what is now referred to as the 'creative industries' or the 'creative economy', best described as the conceptual and practical convergence of the creative arts, cultural industries, and information and communication technologies, to develop a new knowledge economy with the interactive citizen-consumer in mind. For more information on creative industries and innovation, see Plesk (1997); Barton Rabe (2006).

[2] CoRT stands for Cognitive Research Trust. The program was designed for schools and is used internationally, but most widely used in Australia, Canada, New Zealand, Japan, Malaysia, Malta,

Singapore, South Africa, Italy, UK, Ireland, U.S.A., Venezuela, Philippines, and Russia. The CoRT Thinking Program is divided into six parts of ten lessons, and uses a number of attention-directing devices, the most popular being PMI (Plus, Minus, Interesting), which is used in the classroom to generate thinking about a situation or stimulus material.

[3] Proponents of Community of Inquiry have mapped the thinking moves inherent in the inquiry process. This refers to identifying and marking where critical, creative and caring thinking occurs in the contributions of students in a Community of Inquiry. See, for example, Prior (2007).

CHAPTER 5

CRITICAL ENGAGEMENT: EVALUATIVE THINKING

Education is generally focused on achieving certain basic skills, rather than on the potential that might be achieved through the development of thinking and its improvement. As the previous chapter indicated, generative thinking fosters creativity through freedom of expression, experimentation, scaffolding of ideas, and reconstruction of thought. But generative thinking does not exist in a vacuum, and relies on evaluation in order to give it focus. Put another way, critical and creative thinking are interrelated and complementary aspects of thinking. As Richard Paul (1993) points out, if thinking lacks a purpose it becomes aimless, and if it does become useful it is merely by chance that we stumble across it. If we only employ creative thinking in the classroom it has nothing to keep it in check, and it will diverge and is likely to wander off aimlessly. In other words, if we continue to generate new ideas or come up with original ideas, these may go untested. As noted in the previous chapter, all ideas are generated from existing ideas; from the familiar, new ways of thinking come about. New ideas, however, must go through a process of evaluation and judgment in order for us to question what already exists and to see it in new ways. Reconstruction, as we noted previously, requires the use of both critical and creative thinking. Paul (1993) is worth quoting at length here with regards to what I have just said.

> Creative and critical thinking often seem to the untutored to be polar opposite forms of thought, the first based on irrational or unconscious forces, the second on rational and conscious processes, the first undirectable and unteachable, the second directable and teachable. There is some, but very little, truth in this view. The truth in it is that there is no way to generate creative geniuses, nor to get students to generate highly novel ground-breaking ideas, by some known process of systematic instruction. The dimension of 'creativity', in other words, contains unknowns, even mysteries. So does 'criticality' of course. Yet there are ways to teach simultaneously for both creative and critical thinking in a down-to-earth sense of those terms. To do so, however, requires that we focus on these terms in practical everyday contexts, that we keep their central meanings in mind, and that we seek insight into the respect in which they overlap and feed into each other, the respect in which they are inseparable, integrated, and unitary. (pp.101–102)

The relevance of Paul's words to the topic of this chapter is that creative and critical thinking need to be developed simultaneously and not to be seen as separate in practice. However, in order to discuss critical thinking we need to separate the two concepts. But we should bear in mind their interrelatedness.

So how do we become a critical thinker? Marie-France Daniel (2005) identified that becoming a critical thinker occurs in five stages; anecdotal, monological, non-critical, semi-critical, and critical. In her studies she notes that children slip into one of these categories. Conducting an experiment with children in primary school, Daniel mapped the progression of the thinking processes of children from the beginning stages of development when children share anecdotes to eventually engaging in critical thinking in their dialogues. She observed that under careful facilitation children went from having anecdotal exchanges which involved just speaking regarding personal situations through to monological contributions, but did not as yet engage in dialogical exchanges. Daniel viewed the next stage in the progression which she calls non-critical thinking as students respecting differences of opinion, constructing points of view according to peers, and justifying their remarks. They then moved onto the next stage where they become semi-critical thinkers. They began to question peer statements but engagement was not at a level to be cognitively strong enough to alter the perspectives of others. In other words, there was no self-corrective process occurring. Finally, they moved to the next stage to what a Socratic classroom aims to achieve, i.e., they became critical thinkers, which was indicated by both group-correction and self-correction as a way of moving forward. As Daniel put it:

> When pupils not only improve the group's initial perspective, but they also modify it. They are then capable of considering the other as the bearer of divergence and, as such, as a necessary participant to the enrichment of the community. Momentary uncertainty is accepted as being a part of any interesting discussion, and peer criticism is sought after in itself, as a tool to move forward in comprehension. (p.116)

What Daniel is talking about is that the process of group-correction and self-reflection helps to develop criteria in order to understand better the concepts that are crucial to solving the problem at hand. As Lindop (2002) says, a critical thinker is someone who is sensitive to the criteria of critical thinking. He refers to this as syllogistic thinking. Kennedy (1996) concurs with this view, but he also suggests that children can, from an early age, seek to explain things through syllogistic thinking. Like Lipman, who believes that children have a natural ability to wonder, Kennedy thinks that they also have a natural ability to seek explanations. Kennedy uses an example of a two-year old child who encounters a horse for the first time. The child was familiar with dogs, and so proceeded to point to the animal while uttering the word 'doggie'. It is likely that the child had made the assumption that because the animal had four legs (and other similar features) that it too was a dog. The argument can be set out in syllogistic form as follows:

– All dogs have four legs
– That animal has four legs
– Therefore that animal is a dog.

This is not evidence that the child thinks in syllogisms, but rather that the child is making inferences. Although the inference is invalid, it shows that in some kind of way that the child is sensitive to criteria. If Kennedy is correct, then through their willingness to wonder and explore ideas, children make such connections automatically (pp.6–7).

As with the previous chapter on creative thinking, because we are focusing on the development of thinking and its improvement through Socratic pedagogy, in this chapter I will be concentrating only on the aspects of critical thinking that underpin dialogue. There has been much written on critical thinking in particular stemming from the critical thinking movement and from authors such as Paul (1994), Fisher (1995a; 1995b), Robert Ennis (1993; 1996), and Harvey Siegel (1986; 2004). There is contention over the teaching of critical thinking as skills in isolation. While I acknowledge the significance of critical thinking to good thinking practices, some theorists are sceptical and have voiced their concerns over the promotion of certain approaches to critical thinking. As pointed out previously, most famously is de Bono's criticism of existing models of critical thinking, especially those based on the Socratic Method, for relying on an adversarial model of argument and refutation, especially the kind of logic used which he claims is based on is/is not, true/false, either/or dichotomies. Anecdotal evidence suggests that this kind of attitude to philosophy has meant that some education professionals, including teachers, who are interested in doing philosophy with children have had to resort to calling it by another name; such as introducing it 'in cognito' as a literacy program.[1] Rather than valuing the enhancement of judgment through evaluative thinking, many critics are worried that this may translate outside of the classroom in a negative way by encouraging adversarial behaviour.[2] However, critical thinking should not been seen as adversarial thinking; it should be seen as marked by a readiness to reason, to challenge ideas, and to promote good thinking.

Critical thinking, therefore, has the ability to strengthen children's reasoning abilities and to develop an attitude toward seeking truth. To be a critical thinker is to be what Siegel refers to as having a 'critical spirit', which is best described as a person who has the ability to reason about and question those things around them. It is "the inclination or disposition to think critically on a regular basis in a wide range of consequential circumstances. The spirit cannot be defined by a cluster of skills. It's a way of life" (in Neilson, 1989, p.2). Analogously, it is like putting on a different pair of glasses and seeing things through new lenses that allows the person to uncover fallacies, and bias, and to be reflective and evaluative not only of things presented to him or her, but to self-reflect. It is through such action that the person becomes more thoughtful.

For this chapter our first task, therefore, will be to identify the characteristics or general features of multi-dimensional thinking that are more typical of critical thinking than of creative or caring thinking. We shall see that what is common to these characteristics or central to their meanings is *evaluative thinking*. By evaluative thinking I mean reasoning, analysis, evaluating, valuing and judgment. We shall also explore where evaluative thinking features in each of the models of dialogue to show its practical application.

WHAT IS CRITICAL THINKING?

There is much literature devoted to the development of the critical thinker.[3] Most notably is the author Paul (1993), but also widely recognised are Ennis

(1993; 1996) and Siegel (1986; 2004). While there is not strict consensus on a definition of critical thinking, there is general agreement that it includes reasoning and analysis, argument and formal logic, and that it is both a skill and a disposition. What is significant for philosophical dialogue is that it relies also on creative thinking. Paul's assertion that critical and creative thinking work simultaneously in the development of good thinking and the improvement of it, draws attention to the interplay between convergent and divergent thinking as discussed previously. We have already discussed divergent thinking, so we will now look at the relationship of convergent thinking to critical thinking.

Just as creative thinking has divergent thinking as one of its characteristics, critical thinking could be said to share in the characteristic of convergent thinking. Convergent thinking is thinking that brings together information focused on solving a problem. It is directed towards a conclusion with an emphasis on, but not limited to, searching for truth or finding answers through informed judgments. Concluding could mean arriving at a single correct answer, but it could also mean arriving at different understandings, or dealing with unresolved differences, or accepting that our claims to knowledge are fallible and that truth is provisional requiring an on-going self-correcting process of inquiry. I do not make the connection to convergent thinking to say that all participants in an inquiry will always arrive at the same conclusion, but rather that through critical thinking they can work through agreement and disagreement to come to shared meanings. Critical thinking is largely a rational enterprise with the outcome of knowledge. But this statement needs to be qualified with the understanding that knowledge gained through the process of thinking critically is not treated as a stockpile of inflexible truths awaiting transmission, but rather that all knowledge is in principle provisional and subject to further critical thinking.

Critical thinking is foremost concerned with finding criteria that will allow us to find shared meanings. Cam (2006) describes criteria as decisive reason that we appeal to in making judgments or decisions. Criteria are the tools that need to be examined or referred to in order to come to reasoned agreement through deliberation in dialogue. He uses the following examples.

> In employment, for example, applicants for a position are evaluated against a set of criteria, which are the considerations we appeal to in ranking them in making an appointment. If someone were to dispute a decision, properly speaking that could only be because they thought the stated criteria were not adhered to or because they disagreed with the choice or relative weighting of the criteria. When such disputes arise, we attempt to justify (or sometimes revise) our judgements by reference to the criteria, or to justify or revise the criteria themselves. (p.75)

Criteria enable convergence because there must be agreement on such things as necessary and sufficient conditions, or on whether or not certainty or reliability is required. Moreover, agreed upon criteria necessitates a certain level of procedural consensus, which in turn relies on rigorous processes. No more is this emphasis on convergent thinking evident than in Nelson's Socratic Dialogue, which relies heavily on his philosophical method which he calls regressive abstraction. Nelson (1965) describes the process in the following two passages.

> The function to be performed by the philosophical method is nothing other than making secure the contemplated regress to principles, for without the guidance of method, such a regress would be merely a leap in the dark and would leave us where we were before—prey to the arbitrary. (pp.8–9)

and

> The regressive method of abstraction, which serves to disclose philosophical principles, produces no new knowledge either of facts or of laws. It merely utilizes reflection to transform into clear concepts what reposed in our reason as an original possession and made itself obscurely heard in every individual judgment. (p.10)

What Nelson is talking about here is the development and employment of reasoned judgments through convergent thinking. The metaphor of the hourglass depicts this well. We move from a position of divergent thinking to that of convergent thinking through reasoning, analysing, evaluating, valuing and judgment. This convergence is represented by the narrow waist of the hourglass. Paul's (1994) description of narrow sense logic is also useful here. Simply put, convergence as represented by the hourglass is the drawing of conclusions on the basis of reasons and the principles that apply to the assessment of that process (p.105).

I will have more to say on Nelson's Socratic Dialogue later in this chapter. In this part we will identify the characteristics that are common to most conceptions of critical thinking. We will deal with conceptual exploration which is concerned with thinking categorically. We make conceptual connections through distinction making, criteria making, and categorical thinking which involves classification and taxonomy. We will look at reasoning and its relationship to formal and informal logic. Fallacious reasoning is addressed in terms of evaluating validity and soundness of argument.

Conceptual Exploration

Although critical thinking requires more than the application of thinking tools, in order to think effectively we need to understand how to use these tools and how to use them effectively. Conceptual exploration is an essential tool for the critical thinker. Conceptual exploration relies on categorical thinking, which is primarily a way of making conceptual connections through distinction making, finding and testing criteria, and classification or taxonomy.

Without concepts, knowledge and understanding is not possible. This is because humans need language to communicate and language is underpinned by concepts. But not only do concepts underpin language they inform perception and action (Cam, 1995, p.66). Concepts are general ideas derived or inferred from specific instances or occurrences, and as such are central to the way we understand and make sense of the world. Philosophical concepts, which are inherently contestable and problematic, are embedded in all disciplines. Disciplinary knowledge then flows on to curriculum in the form of syllabus documents for the key learning areas. By understanding how to develop and analyse concepts students learn to question the meaning of seemingly familiar concepts, and thus clarify or change their perceptions, which in turn informs their behaviour.

One way in which we explore concepts is to make distinctions. Distinction-making is discriminating between two or more things that are similar in significant ways but within that similarity display significantly different characteristics. We make distinctions for certain purposes, usually so we can make sense of our world in terms of being able to distinguish between things for the purpose of communicating. Distinction-making is the most common thing that we do, not just in inquiry but in everyday life. However, it is one thing to make distinctions, but it is another thing to understand how distinction-making works and why we make distinctions at all. For example, we make distinctions between different animals; for example, horses and dogs. Kennedy's example highlights the child's initial attempt to make a distinction between one kind of animal, a dog, and other animals, albeit the child mistakenly identified what was actually a horse as a dog. But this could simply have been a matter of the child having insufficient criteria. The child required precise criteria to make the correct distinction.

Criteria are the standards, measures, or expectations used in making an evaluation. Criteria offer decisive reasons that we can appeal to when making evaluations and judgments (Cam, 2006, p.75). Thus criteria are in themselves evaluative. Let's take our example of the dog and horse. What the child is doing is appealing, albeit erroneously, to criteria. One criterion for an animal being a dog is that it has four legs, but so too has a horse. In order to make a further distinction more criteria are needed to distinguish between the two kinds of animals with four legs. As children learn to apply criteria they come to understand the kinds of criteria required for making a judgment or reaching a decision. In the case of the young child, she has yet to learn the difference between necessary and sufficient conditions with regards to something failing to satisfy criteria. One of the aims of critical thinking is to draw out the implicit criteria used in making a judgment, and to examine them and knowingly employ them in ways that make us better informed about our judgments.

Classification or taxonomy provides another way of thinking about how we divide things in order to differentiate characteristic definitions. One way to do this is to make dichotomous divisions. For example we can divide animals into different categories—those that have four legs and those that do not. Under the category of animals with four legs we would include horses and dogs. But we can also make further divisions and sub-divisions. For example, dog can be further classified into breeds: Cocker Spaniel, Maltese Terrier, and Labrador. Whatever the category, it entails differentiating characteristics based on criteria.

Reasoning: Formal and Informal Logic

While Socrates' dialogues were reliant on the production of logical arguments, formal logic as a discipline was not recognised until Aristotle who assigned certain rules to arguments. Argument construction and its development since Aristotle had an emphasis on validity and soundness. Critical thinking is sometimes reduced to mere logic, but this is a very narrow use of the term. Preoccupation with formal logic reduces critical thinking to simply a skill. Nevertheless, logic, both formal and informal, is essential to critical thinking, and reasoning is its subject matter.

Reasoning is the cognitive process of looking for reasons for beliefs, conclusions, actions or feelings. Humans have the ability to engage in reasoning about their own reasoning using introspection. We engage in reasoning in everyday life through making connections. For example, we can say that if it is wet outside, either it rained or someone has watered the grass. It follows from the premise that if it is wet outside that either of these events (or others) could be considered possible causes. To infer correctly we need more information. There are two main kinds of reasoning: inductive and deductive reasoning. Without going into details lest we stray from the topic, both inductive and deductive reasoning are concerned with making correct inferences. Correct inferences could be said to be those that follow the dictates of logic, and have been tested for validity, soundness or strength. Inferences that are incorrect fall into the category of fallacious reasoning.

Formal logic can be used as a way of understanding how to make correct inferences. We use rules as criteria that dictate how we come to conclusions. There are a number of principles that we can follow to make deductions. These are represented often in syllogistic form and may involve symbols or formula. Informal logic, on the other hand, is an attempt to develop non-formal standards, criteria, and procedures for analysis, evaluation, and construction of argumentation to improve everyday reasoning. Informal logic has closer ties, than has formal logic, to the goals of education generally and to critical thinking, which is to improve public reasoning by developing social and intellectual capacities and dispositions necessary for active citizenship. Emphasis on inference and argumentation means that informal logic must rely on formal methods; that is, the rules of logic play an important role in informal logic also. It is the emphasis on natural language that distinguishes the two kinds of logic, and is what makes informal logic more effective as a method for teaching critical thinking.

The differences between formal and informal logic notwithstanding, they are both applicable to Paul's narrow sense of logic and reasoning as they are concerned with procedures for narrowing thoughts down rather than engaging in thinking that is divergent. Recall in the previous chapter that we drew the analogy between logic and reasoning and the process of flying a plane. The narrow sense logic and reasoning does involve using criteria to evaluate arguments, which is analogous to applying the brakes to balance the acceleration when flying a plane.

Fallacious Reasoning

Because critical thinking deals with agreement and disagreement, it has a preoccupation with argumentation, which requires paying attention to the validity and soundness of the reasoning behind the assertions made. To judge an argument as valid requires paying attention to the form of the argument. When a component of an argument is demonstrably flawed in terms of its own logic or form, either formal or informal, we call this fallacious reasoning. In deductive arguments where the conclusion follows with certainty from the premises, validity is derived from its form. Take our earlier example, the child's reasoning came about from the following *invalid* deductive form.

– All dogs have four legs
– That animal has four legs
– Therefore that animal is a dog.

This kind of reasoning, although understandable for a two-year old, is, nonetheless, faulty. The child has only limited criteria and thus when she applies her reasoning she judges what is actually a horse to be a dog.

Informal fallacy, on the other hand, is any other invalid kind of reasoning where the flaw is not in the form of the argument. Informal fallacies are numerous, but it is not important to address each one of them here. We can extrapolate that an informal fallacy does not provide sufficiently good grounds for its conclusion, employs unwarranted, unaccepted, unproven or incorrect premises, and ignores or overlooks relevant information. When we engage in dialogue we must be careful about making correct inferences to avoid falling into the trap of fallacious reasoning.

EVALUATIVE THINKING: A WAY OF THINKING CRITICALLY

Let me spend a few moments to sum up what I have said so far about critical thinking. Whereas in the previous chapter the focus was on the generation, development and extension of ideas, in this chapter it was on the process of evaluating ideas. To summarise, critical thinking is concerned with (1) concept exploration, (2) reasoning in both formal and informal logic, and (3) fallacious reasoning. What is central to critical thinking is the development of criteria and its application to conceptual analysis as well as reasoning and logic. Now that we have identified the characteristics or general features of multi-dimensional thinking that are typical of critical thinking, in this part we shall see that what is common to these characteristics or central to their meanings is *evaluative thinking*. By evaluative thinking I mean the development, application and evaluation of criteria. Many books have been written on critical thinking, but one author who is widely accessed by classroom teachers, is Benjamin Bloom. Bloom's Taxonomy is divided into three categories with regards to the way people learn. One of these, which speaks directly to the aims of critical thinking, is the cognitive domain which emphasises intellectual outcomes. The cognitive domain is divided into further categories with evaluation at the apex of the structure (in Fisher 1995b). This taxonomy is particularly helpful to our understanding of evaluative thinking. Bloom takes evaluation to be the ability to judge, based on definite criteria, the value of something for a given purpose. Understanding is at a meta-cognitive level because the process of evaluation required existing knowledge, the skills of comprehension, application, analysis, and synthesis. Evaluation also includes value judgments, also based on clearly defined criteria. Evaluative thinking, described in this way, is thinking as a kind of reconstruction.

Evaluative thinking concentrates on thinking that allows us to reconsider or evaluate knowledge that we take for granted, essentially breaking down the assumptions that may have informed that knowledge in the first place (a process of elenchus). Recall that reconstruction occurs through generative thinking, from the seeds of wonder that create opportunities for making the familiar strange, and consequently to generate, expand, and develop ideas. Reconstruction, however, also relies on evaluative thinking in order to break down commonly held assumptions and to make reasoned judgments about the ideas that have been generated. Evaluative thinking uses information to make judgments, which also includes using this information to make changes and improvements. In summary, we can say that evaluative thinking is comprised of five interrelated components: (1) reasoning, (2) analysis, (3) evaluation, (4) valuing, and (5) judgment.

To reiterate, reasoning is a cognitive process of drawing a conclusion from a set of premises. Evaluative reasoning focuses on what makes reasoning efficient or inefficient, appropriate or inappropriate, good or bad. Going back to our example, the child encounters an animal, and understands it to be a dog on the basis that it shares in those features from previous, but limited, encounters with dogs. What the child is doing is drawing a conclusion by inferring from previous encounters with dogs, which requires being sensitive to criteria. For the child, what we know to actually be a horse was evaluated as fulfilling such criteria. For a two year old child this would be considered age appropriate reasoning, but the inference itself is not an example of good reasoning. To judge what is good or bad reasoning relies on analysis.

Analysis is the process of breaking a concept down into simpler parts so that its logical structure is revealed. When it comes to testing taken-for-granted knowledge, we must rely on the examination of assumptions as well as the examination of concepts and meanings. This process of examination requires a level of doubt. Let us revisit from Chapter 2 Lipman's (2004) assertions.

> It was doubt that caused us to reflect, to inquire. It was doubt that compelled our attitude to switch from an uncritical one to a critical one. It was doubt that forced us to begin thinking imaginatively, creatively, productively, so as to come up with a hypothesis of what could be done to make our doubt subside. Eventually, with the cessation of doubt, we could relax, secure in the knowledge that our underlying beliefs were once again working well, and were carrying the weight we'd imposed on them. (pp.3–4)

The analysis that comes from breaking down taken-for-granted knowledge can give rise to new ways of looking at things. In the Socratic process this is where the elenchus features; that is, ideas are broken down through a process of doubt, analysis and evaluation.

Recall our discussion on divergent thinking with regards to generative thinking. Evaluative thinking has its own counterpart, convergent thinking. Unlike divergent thinking, which is expansive, convergent thinking is systematic reasoning that focuses on arriving at an answer through logical inquiry. This includes inductive and deductive reasoning. Convergent thinking is regressive insofar as it seeks to narrow down the process of inquiry to finding definitions, applying criteria, and testing for validity, soundness, and strength of argument. That is to say, convergent thinking is generally concerned with evaluation. The hourglass of Socratic Dialogue depicts this process well, whereby ideas and concepts are narrowed down through a continual process of evaluation until all ideas have converged and there is an agreement. However, even within the narrow confines of the hourglass, divergent thinking is not completely absent, as the testing of definitions requires the use of examples and counterexamples, which is a generative process. For example, were an older child come to the same conclusions as the two year old child, we might ask them to think of other instances of animals with four legs that are not dogs, thus asking them to use their imagination in order to find one case that will challenge their own conclusions, in order to examine their criteria and knowingly employ them.

Evaluation requires that we exercise judgment, but in order to do so we must have an awareness of our own position and the assumptions that underpin them. Our assumptions influence the beliefs that we hold dear and the direction of our arguments, and therefore it is crucial that they should also be examined critically (Bohm, 1996). The way we think is influenced by multiple factors, such as parents, friends, formal schooling, religion, and the media. Take this story of a taxi driver who picks up a journalist following the federal election campaign.

> The journalist, ever ready to test the local wisdom on the political story he was pursuing, asked the cabbie how he was going to vote in the forthcoming election. The cabbie was forthright: 'I'm a conservative voter and my father before me was a conservative and his father before him was a conservative, but I have decided the time has come when a man must *put aside his principles and do what is right!*' (Preston, 1997, p.1)

Despite his confusion over moral terms, what the taxi driver was trying to say is that he was reconsidering his moral point of view, and by implication examining his assumptions. Examining assumptions is a key aspect of valuing. Pekarsky (1993) discusses the critical nature of the Socratic Method and contends that by asking questions and being critical of one another, we can break down the assumptions that underpin what we think we know. It is only when we come from a place of Socratic ignorance that we can begin to come to renewed understandings. The notion of Socratic ignorance is vital to the process of evaluative thinking. Shedding assumptions in order to become ignorant about the topic being discussed allows for a process of inquiry to 'find out' by 'thinking through' our reasons. This is the starting point for renewed and reconstructing thinking because we seek to not only examine the arguments of others but to examine our own assumptions about beliefs that were once believed as fact (Reich, 1998). This process requires valuing; an open-mindedness to genuinely weigh-up alternatives in order to cultivate a balanced viewpoint.

The process of evaluative thinking described so far requires participants in a dialogue to make judgments at every stage of the inquiry. Judgment allows us to exercise thoughtfulness when it comes to making decisions. According to Nelson (1949), judgment is guided by principles of logic and is sensitive to criteria, but it also requires independent thinking. Bohm (1996), on the other hand, sees judgment as a source of self-reflection that allows for holistic thinking, to dig deeper into our assumptions and to recognise the interplay between the particular (fragmented) and the universal (cohesion). Lipman (2004) acknowledges the highly complex relationship between reasoning and judgment with regards to cultivating reasonableness. Making judgments means assessing matters within a framework of creative, critical and caring thinking. In order to strengthen judgments in students, teachers "must encourage the three forms of thinking and their convergence" (p.276). Judgment, it seems, requires a level of independent thought, yet it is interdependent as it arises out of the reasoning process. Harold Brown (1988) sums this up as: "judgement is the ability to evaluate a situation, assess evidence, and come to a reasonable decision without following rules" (p.129).

What seems to be common to the thought of all these writers is that judgment is not separate to reasoning, yet it is not restricted to formal judgments only, meaning it is not simply the end product of a formal reasoning process. In other words, judgment is not simply a matter of following formal procedures of logic. Lipman sums this view up aptly.

> The reasonableness we want to cultivate in students is, to be sure, the result of a combination of reasoning and judgment, but the relationship between the two is highly complex. Probably—we are not quite sure how—there is a kind of osmosis by means of which they flow into each other, so that at least some judgment informs all reasonings and at least some reasoning informs all judgments. Or, as Santayana might have put it, all judgments have a kernel of reasoning and all reasonings have judgments as their natural fruition. (p.274)

For Harvey Siegel (1986) what draws all these elements together is reflection. He argues that reflection is at the very heart of judgment because there is a level of thoughtfulness inherent in thinking things through.

> By encouraging critical thinking, then, we teach the student what we think is right but we encourage the student to scrutinize our reasons and judge independently the rightness of our claims. In this way the student becomes a competent judge; more important for the present point, the student becomes an independent judge. That is, the student makes her own judgments regarding the appropriateness of alternative beliefs, courses of action, and attitudes. (n.p)

It seems that Siegel too thinks there is a reciprocal relationship between thinking things through, which in turn allows for autonomous thinking.

Evaluative thinking, which includes reasoning, analysis, evaluation and valuing leads to the making of better judgments, but at the same time the judgments that need to be made at each stage of the process create independent thought for the making of better judgments overall. This brings attention to a distinction made by Siegel (2004) between rational judgment that comes out of rational procedures (reasoning) and irrational judgment (based on evaluating evidence and claims). When couched within a framework of multi-dimensional thinking, judgment need not be expressed in terms of rational and irrational, but rather as an interplay between generative judgments (creative insight) and evaluative judgments (reasoned judgments), and as we shall see in the next chapter, connective judgments (contextual considerations). But in relation to evaluative thinking, judgment requires the consideration of the rules of logic and sensitivity to criteria, as well as relying on our own ability to assess a situation. We can conclude that evaluative thinking in dialogue requires judgment as well as cultivates judgment.

EVALUATIVE THINKING IN DIALOGUE

Let us now explore where evaluative thinking features in each of the models of dialogue to show how it would look in practice. Given that we have identified the characteristics of evaluative thinking, let us see where evaluative thinking features in classroom practice to understand how it will further inform our framework for Socratic pedagogy. We will look firstly at Socratic Dialogue with its significant focus on evaluative thinking through the regressive method represented by the hourglass. Coming to consensus in the dialogue requires convergence, i.e., logic and reasoning and conceptual exploration. Next, we will explore the Community of Inquiry, which emphasises evaluative thinking within a framework of multi-dimensional thinking. Finally, we shall turn to Bohmian Dialogue, in which concentration on evaluative thinking is on the process of breaking-down assumptions and self-reflection rather than in the rules of logic.

Socratic Dialogue

The use of the hourglass as representative of regressive abstraction illustrates its role in the process of Socratic Dialogue; that is, coming to consensus about a definition or conclusion and the application of that definition or conclusion to the wider context of the initial question or stimulus. The various steps in the method of Socratic Dialogue bring participants through a process of narrowing down and applying criteria. It is primarily evaluative because it demands standards and sensitivity to criteria for the purposes of applying them back to the initial question and the concrete example arising from it. That is to say, regressive abstraction is evaluative because it requires critical rigor as criteria are constructed, applied and evaluated. This process forces participants to be precise in their thinking. The characteristics of evaluative thinking are displayed by the hourglass which epitomises how participants progress through the dialogue through a process of narrowing down to concise statements. It should, however, be noted that Nelson's model of dialogue also enlists generative and connective thinking. It employs divergent thinking within the narrow confines of its structure, which is primarily focused on convergence until participants come to a shared understanding of meaning. Nevertheless, it is evaluative insofar as convergent thinking is given priority in terms of the stages of the dialogue. Boele (1998) argues that the rigor required by the process of narrowing down to consensus is where the dialogue gains its depth. If participants arrive at definitions, then they will all have come to agreement based on a common understanding.

Consensus in Socratic Dialogue is a way of enhancing and developing students' skills of evaluative thinking because it requires students to be more critical of their own reasoning, to be precise about what they are saying, and to be self-reflective, but also to be critical of other arguments (Heckmann, 2004). Because students must come to agreement, the first aspect is that they must understand each other clearly (Kessels, 2001). Inquiry is contained within the structure of an hourglass-like flow of dialogue, which is somewhat different to Lipman's idea of letting the argument lead which is still governed by evaluative thinking, but balanced with generative thinking, insofar as there is more room for expanding on ideas in relation to the initial stimulus and the questions and agenda that flowed from it. In a Socratic Dialogue, the structure of dialogue is itself a rigorous facilitator and students must be focused on finding criteria for a definition, or core statement. Socratic Dialogue clearly fits under Paul's category of narrow-sense logic.

It should not be forgotten that Nelson (1965) came from the tradition of critical philosophy. His thinking was that philosophy should be conducted by examining one's own assumptions and being rigorous in argument. Seen in this light, Socratic Dialogue is an exemplar of cultivating evaluative thinking in the classroom. But this statement should be qualified with the rejoinder that Socratic Dialogue fails to position evaluative thinking within the broader context of inquiry and the wider aims of educational theory and practice. Lipman's Community of Inquiry, with its emphasis on multi-dimensional thinking, offers a larger context within which the evaluative principles of Socratic Dialogue could be adopted. But as we will see in the next chapter, connective thinking cannot be ignored if what we seek is a Socratic pedagogy which balances the characteristics of the three modes of multi-dimensional thinking.

The Community of Inquiry

Lipman's model of the Community of Inquiry sits within a broader framework of multi-dimensional inquiry that balances the generative and evaluative dimensions of dialogue. Using Paul's terminology, it employs both the narrow-sense and broad-sense of reasoning and logic. Participants in the dialogue creatively produce and critically assess what is produced in every step of the inquiry. To translate Dewey's pedagogy into an explicit model for philosophical inquiry in the school classroom, Lipman and his colleagues developed an extensive series of curriculum materials. These curriculum materials, which include a series of narratives and teaching manuals, were intended to make explicit the pedagogy of the Community of Inquiry through Philosophy for Children.[4] Most notable in terms of its relevance to evaluative thinking is *Harry Stottlemeir's Discovery* (1974) which concentrates on reasoning and logic. Since the initial publication of these materials there has been a wealth of literature aimed at both theory and practice, including classroom resources and instructional books on thinking tools for inquiry.[5] However, as is the case of most educational programs, teachers do not always come to them via a theoretical understanding or from extensive immersion in the study of the principles underpinning the practice. Unlike Socratic Dialogue which focuses on a specific aspect of inquiry and limited to a series of successive logical steps on how to apply rigorous thinking, the logic embedded within the pedagogy of the Community of Inquiry is not always explicit. It requires a broader understanding of the context within which philosophical inquiry generally takes place and where it is situated in classroom practice. What I propose is that the rigor of philosophical inquiry demanded by Lipman himself be developed by concentrating on evaluative thinking through the principles inherent in the method and pedagogy of Socratic Dialogue.

In order to follow the Socratic maxim inherent in the Community of Inquiry of following the argument where it leads, evaluative thinking must be applied to every step of the dialogue. I repeat that this is not to the neglect of generative thinking but to work in concert with it, to achieve a balance between the creative and the critical. This is important, for attention to generative thinking without 'putting on the brakes' of evaluative thinking is likely to result in poor reasoning and judgment, where students are not sensitive to criteria or not able to identify fallacious reasoning. But evaluative thinking also has another role to play in the Community of Inquiry, i.e., as a kind of self and peer reflection and self-correction at the closure of a dialogue session. Students learn to reflect on and assess the thinking going on in the group, by appealing to criteria for the inquiry skills, reasoning and conceptual skills, and interactive patterns. The self-reflective component works in conjunction with self-correction, which is essential for learning as reconstruction, especially the social aspects of reconstruction, such as making ethical connections and the development of dispositions. With the addition of critically reflecting on their thinking at the end of the dialogue, opportunities are created for students to develop an awareness of how they think together. As we shall see in the next chapter, this can be assisted by Bohm's principle of attentive awareness which is primarily a process for connecting the evaluative and generative aspects with the communal aspects of dialogue.

Bohmian Dialogue

Bohmian Dialogue offers a different kind of evaluative thinking than the other models of dialogue, but which is, nonetheless, significant to Socratic pedagogy. While there is a level of critical reflection required in Community of Inquiry and Socratic Dialogue, it is different to the continual reflection that is required in Bohm's approach to dialogue. Previously we looked at Bohmian Dialogue as the process of the group holding a mirror up to themselves and their own thoughts to gain meaning. The process is genuinely evaluative insofar as students must question their own assumptions. Bohmian Dialogue may not appear on the surface to be Socratic, but Bohm's emphasis on thinking as a system is important for a working understanding of multi-dimensional thinking that is inherent in Socratic pedagogy. The notion of an awakened awareness (discussed in the next chapter) plays large in the dialogue as an evaluative method for self and group reflection; it is reflection through suspending beliefs and examining assumptions. Even before participants contribute to the dialogue, they must go through a thoughtful process of understanding how their opinion or viewpoint has been formed, whether or not those opinions are based on assumptions, unquestioned beliefs or taken-for-granted knowledge. It is curious then that Bohm does not attribute his model to the Socratic tradition, especially since he was not unfamiliar with philosophy. For it is Bohm's attention to connecting community and thought as a system that makes sense of the elenchus and the aporia, by placing the emphasis back on Socratic ignorance as a starting point for an on-going inquiry. Bohm has a lot more to contribute to the nature of thinking and reflective thought, but it is suffice to say at this point that reflection is a necessary component for the cultivation of evaluative thinking.

WHERE ARE WE NOW?

Let us review where we are at this moment before moving to the next chapter. In Chapter 4 we observed that generative thinking, which is the pulse of creative thinking, is concerned with the generation, development and extension of ideas that comes out of wonder. But what have we said in this chapter about critical thinking? There are five characteristics: (1) reasoning, (2) analysis, (3) evaluation, (4) valuing, and (5) judgment that are common to critical thinking. Evaluative thinking is central to the meaning of these five characteristics. Therefore, evaluative thinking is necessary for effective critical thinking. We also identified where evaluative thinking fits into a multi-dimensional framework for Socratic pedagogy by demonstrating how it can be applied to each of the models of dialogue in order to gain a better understanding of its practical application.

We can extrapolate from the analysis in this chapter that evaluative thinking, as a form of narrow sense logic in relation to multi-dimensional thinking, is best described by Nelson's model of dialogue. Socratic Dialogue, which embeds the principle of self-reflection and self-correction as ideas are tested and reflected upon in order to come to some shared understandings, represented by the figure of the hourglass, makes an important contribution to the development of evaluative thinking. This, in turn, is important for the framework for Socratic pedagogy. It is suffice to say that by recognising evaluative thinking as the pulse of critical thinking what we are doing is showing both in theory and in practice what teachers will need to concentrate on when it comes to classroom practice. Teachers should keep in mind Nelson's idea of regressive abstraction because it requires bearing in mind the necessity of being sensitive to criteria to evaluate thinking. Evaluative thinking should be viewed in this way as a disposition and not simply a set of skills to be learnt. Teachers should therefore place an equal emphasis on evaluative thinking, that is, the regressive nature of dialogue, as well as on generative thinking, being the development, building and extending of creative thought.

CHAPTER 5

In the concluding chapter we will further the ideas presented here on how evaluative thinking sits into the Socratic pedagogy framework in relation to multi-dimensional thinking. We have already addressed generative thinking, so let us look at the last domain of thinking that is central to Socratic pedagogy: connective thinking.

NOTES

[1] I refer here to my own experiences and to the anecdotal evidence of other practitioners who have attempted, either successfully or unsuccessfully, to introduce philosophy into the classroom. I was once advised that it would be better to refer to my teaching as literacy and not philosophy.

[2] For more on philosophy as adversarial thinking see de Bono (1994), Slattery (1995), Moulton (1983), Burgh, Field and Freakley (2006).

[3] For critical thinking activities see Splitter (1991), Wilks (1995), Golding (2002).

[4] Lipman explores the nature of critical thinking through both his practical and theoretical publications. For more information see Lipman (1974, 1988, 1991a, 1991b).

[5] See Cam (1995, 2006), Burgh, Field and Freakley (2006), Splitter and Sharp (1995), Golding (2002).

PEDAGOGICAL CARE: CONNECTIVE THINKING

Remember the three friends talking together at a café. I used this scenario in Chapter 1 to distinguish between dialogue and mere conversation. Let us now revisit the concept of dialogue. The three friends engaged in mere conversation could be seen discussing an upcoming wedding. This conversation may surround the chosen flowers or the final details of a wedding dress. Despite the wedding banter that the conversation may consist of, what is important is that the focus is on retaining equilibrium lest the friends break the rules of conversation. A dialogue however, aims at disequilibrium whereby assumptions are explored and both agreements and disagreements examined. The three friends at the café may turn their conversation from wedding dresses and bouquets to topics such as identity and name changing that may require more critical consideration. While it is possible that a dialogue may result from an initial conversation, it is unlikely that the friends would choose to upset the equilibrium that surrounds chatting about the happy event. What is important in this scenario is that the friendship that has brought the three individuals together is based on mutual admiration and fondness. Friendship in this case, is unlikely to allow for a focused dialogue on matters of philosophical importance. However, three people who come together for the purpose of dialogue have a very different connection. Their aim *is* to examine agreements as well as disagreements and to find a balance between equilibrium and disequilibrium. We could say that their connection is based on care for finding truth. They may become friends outside of the dialogue, but their relationship while in the dialogue is one based on care. The three café-going friends could meet for the purpose of dialogue but then the relationship in the dialogical situation is one based on their common commitment of travelling together to find truth.

We will now make further the distinction between friendship and care to define what is important for Socratic pedagogy. When it comes to addressing caring thinking in philosophical dialogue, this is a necessary exploration in order to avoid the promotion of relationships that may be counter to philosophical progress through dialogue. In the previous two chapters we have concentrated on dialogue as a form of intellectual inquiry. In this chapter, we turn our attention to the dialogue as a form of communal inquiry. Because we are addressing relationships, in dialogue it is necessary to understand the kinds of connections we are making with others. The notion of care may depict multiple connections, anywhere from a connection out of duty, to a loving, emotional care that one has for, say, their child or close family member. Care has also come to encompass relationships based on friendship, a distinction I will make clearer in this chapter. In philosophical inquiry, the use of the terms is both vague and ambiguous. Ever since Aristotle drew attention to the connection between friendship and philosophical inquiry a host of writers have revisited the topic (Reed & Johnson, 1999; Roumer, 1994; Badhar, 1993; Lynch, 2005).

Reed and Johnson (1999) trace the history of the role of friendship in philosophy. The most notable of these examples is C.S. Lewis's imagery of two friends sitting side by side, looking out in the same direction. This image reflects Lewis's definition of friendship; of two people with common views finding the same point upon which to fix their gaze. Reed and Johnson use Lewis's imagery to compare friends with lovers.

> The lover simply delights in the other, while the friend, it may be said, delights in the delight the other takes in the shared activity, delights in the way the other "cares for the same truth". In Lewis's telling image,—"we picture lovers face to face but friends side by side; their eyes look ahead". (p.169)

Lewis's friends have in common something substantive; they are friends because they have common interests. Lewis was not the first to make such connections. Aristotle claimed common interest to be the basis of friendship, albeit he recognised the volatility of friendship. Immanuel Kant also was "aware of the fragility of relationships given the difficulties between individuals and the potential for conflict which difference entails" (in Lynch, 2002, p.9). We must, therefore, consider the impact of such difficulties on a dialogue in which difference is imminent.

Reed and Johnson (1999) give an example of the Dodgers baseball team—a group of men from different cultures, of different race and socio-economic status placed in a team as an experiment to see what would ensue. Sharing a commitment to baseball resulted in these individuals being friends, and subsequently, becoming a very successful baseball team. No doubt, friendship was important in this case, but it was a consequence of the team mates having an interest in common, i.e., the commitment to baseball. Recall that Reeve (2005) analogises that the relationship in a Bohmian Dialogue, which is based on impersonal fellowship, was like a group of people supporting a sporting team. It is important not to confuse this with what Reed and Johnson (1999) are pointing to. For participants in Bohmian Dialogue, their common interest *is* dialogue and the search for truth rather than a separate interest that does not underpin inquiry. Genuine dialogue requires a commitment to the process of inquiry. Common interest may, therefore, not be enough to sustain such an inquiry unless the common interest is dialogue itself. Friends may avoid voicing different opinions that could cause disagreement, and this could disrupt the natural dialogue. Disagreement should instead be seen as a catalyst for strengthening dialogue through the sharing of different points of view. The dialogue engages people in critical inquiry, whereby the ideas, and not the people who express the ideas, are open to criticism. This does not, of course, discount the possibility of a friendship founded on a common interest or commitment to dialogue.

Snyder and Smith (1986) suggest that friendship can be either shallow or deep. By shallow they mean that a person enjoys the company of another, and has a fondness or liking for the other person. This is a social relationship that is not necessarily based on anything substantial between the friends except that they share common experiences together. Could this be what Lewis meant by lovers simply delighting in each other? Lewis's lovers face each other, which connotes a fondness between them. I suggest that the image of Lewis's lovers facing each other is synonymous with Snyder's and Smith's description of shallow friendship, albeit that linking the two broadens Lewis's description to incorporate both lovers and friends. But this need not be a problem if a defining feature of (shallow) friendship and of being lovers is having a fondness for one another. A deep friendship, on the other hand, is one in which two or more people share the same attitudes and values (p.69). This is an important difference, as it is not the feelings that friends have for one another that defines the friendship, but that they have attitudes and values in common. Snyder's and Smith's deep friendship echoes Aristotle's, Kant's, and Lewis's definition of friendship as that of sharing common interests. In the case of the Dodgers, they shared a deep friendship based on their attitudes and values with regards to baseball.

Plato's definition of friendship is somewhat different. He defined a 'true' friendship as being the common search for knowledge; to get to truth. David Allman (1988) describes the Platonic view of friendship as "two people sharing the experience of contemplating the universal quality of truth" (pp.113–26). Note that the quest for universal truth is what defines Platonic friends. Turning again to Lewis's imagery, we might want to say that Plato's definition of friendship qualifies as deep friendship. However, it is also something more. The point at which Platonic friends are gazing is unchangeable, beyond the material world. Deep friendship, as characterized by Snyder and Smith, is far less demanding. Having a common interest, such as an interest in baseball, or a concern for ecological sustainability, is enough to qualify for a deep friendship. The friends need not be concerned over any progress toward truth, or the process of dialogue, let alone the quest for universal truth. On the Platonic account of friendship, these are necessary requirements. It is possible to also interpret Reed and Johnson's view of friendship in this way especially if we concentrate on their words in relation to a friend who cares for the same truth (although the Dodgers analogy suggests otherwise). However, if this is the case, it is not an appropriate metaphor for philosophical dialogue. The quest for truth in the Socratic pedagogy I propose here is not for universal truth as described by Plato, but in the valuing of, or being motivated by, the progress toward truth (I use the term as attributed to Gardner earlier).

The question that we need to ask is whether or not the literature devoted to the importance of friendship in dialogue uses the term in the same way as Plato did in his dialogues. Reed and Johnson acknowledge the significance of the qualities that Plato tried to capture in his view of friendship, but, as we have seen, their use of the term is somewhat ambiguous to say the least. To avoid confusion between the Platonic view of friendship and Snyder and Smith's deep friendship, I suggest that a fundamental quality of Platonic friendship is 'caring'. To put it another way, dialogue requires a caring for progress toward truth, rather than friendship as Reed and Johnson, and others claim. However, in the case of Platonic friends, their quest is for universal truth.

Reed and Johnson (1999) acknowledge the problem that friendship poses for philosophy. If people are closely aligned, they have the power to sabotage inquiry, e.g., through exclusion or by bullying others. Recall the discussion in Chapter 1 on technologies of silence, particularly coercion and friendship. If friends shut themselves off from the rest of the group, then they cannot be fully immersed in group dialogue. They may be in agreement with each other based on their relationship as friends, but not on reflecting upon their own beliefs and values. It may be more difficult for individuals to express their views, especially if their beliefs and values differ to that of their friends. This may also be intimidating to others in the dialogue. As for the whole group being friends, this may well prove to be impossible in a philosophical dialogue in an educative setting. It would be unlikely that all members would agree with each other on all aspects of a particular issue of concern. Friendship may well be detrimental to the success of philosophical inquiry. However, if the focus is not on friendship in dialogue, but on *caring thinking*, then this trap may be avoided. Even if friendship between some members does develop over the course of the dialogue, or exist beforehand as was the case of the café friends, if the dialogue is founded on care, then the care that each participant has for the outcome of the dialogue would not allow groups or individuals to hinder the course of dialogue and can avoid some of the technologies of silence.

If a defining feature of friendship is the sharing of common interests, then difference, conflict, and change may pose difficulties for such a relationship. Would a friend necessarily be honest about a difference of opinion if it is likely to cause considerable problems with the friendship? This, of course, is a matter for empirical investigation. However, I maintain that a dialogue based on care ensures that at least all beliefs and values are respected equally as we shall see in this chapter. Reed and Johnson (1999) argue that in a dialogue, "we create an environment in which children become friends in virtue. Those virtues include respect for truth, respect for evidence, respect for other persons and so on" (p.193). Again, I question Reed and Johnson's use of the term friendship. Children do not necessarily become friends based on these virtues. Indeed, it is more likely that childhood friendships are based on common interests or interpersonal qualities, or what the children themselves may describe as a 'liking for each other'. What Reed and Johnson define as friendship based on virtues can only be described as what I shall refer to as care, provided friendship in this case is defined as having a common interest in the quest for truth. Otherwise, it is no more than Snyder and Smith's deep friendship, like the friendship shared by the players in the Dodgers. If we only have respect for others out of friendship, then respect may well be given to a friend in dialogue but may not be given to others.

An analysis of friendship and caring can help to understand better the sort of relationship required, in order for progress to occur in dialogue. From here on in, this chapter will explore only caring thinking. I will be concentrating only on the aspects of caring thinking that are important for dialogue. Because a precise definition of care is unlikely given its multiple meanings, mostly built around the everyday sense of the term as meaning an affective state linked to cognate terms such as fondness, compassion, empathy, and so forth, there is often confusion over what the term stipulates when it comes to pedagogy. Therefore our first task is to highlight what is important about caring thinking with regards to multi-dimensional thinking and Socratic pedagogy. What is common or central to the meaning of caring thinking is *connective thinking*. By connective thinking I mean collective thinking, impersonal fellowship, and awakened attentiveness. We will explore where connective thinking features in each of the models of dialogue to show its practical application.

WHAT IS CARING THINKING?

Caring thinking is a contentious term, even more so than its counterparts, creative and critical thinking. In the context of dialogue where we engage with others not only intellectually but collectively in a communal inquiry the term is vague. Because the environment that we come together in dialogue must be one that is conducive to inquiry, it is important to specify how care can inform effective dialogue. An obvious starting point is with Gilligan's ethic of care as it is her empirical studies into moral development that have laid the foundations for further research on care and caring thinking. Gilligan (1993) was a student of Lawrence Kohlberg (1981). Kohlberg proposed a stages theory of moral development to explain the development of moral reasoning.[1] His theory holds that moral reasoning has six identifiable developmental constructive stages that are each more adequate at responding to moral dilemmas than the previous stage. Gilligan has argued that Kohlberg's theory is not only overly andocentric but that it also emphasises justice to the exclusion of other values such as caring. Because Kohlberg's theory is based on the results of empirical research using only male participants, Gilligan argued that it did not adequately describe women's concerns. Instead of focusing on the value of justice, she developed an alternative theory of moral reasoning that is based on the ethic of care. Her studies found that women (or mainly women) base their decisions on care which has a focus on relationships and real-life situations, whereas men (or mainly men) base their decisions on a justice approach taking principles and rules of logic as paramount to ethical decision-making. It is interesting to note that after Gilligan's initial studies, other psychologists have also questioned the assumption that moral action is primarily reached by formal reasoning, and therefore that moral reasoning is less relevant to moral action than Kohlberg's theory suggests.

Gilligan's ground breaking research has had an influential and sustained effect on feminine and feminist ethical theory, philosophy, and through Nel Noddings, on education. The literature on care I draw on owes much to Gilligan, especially her emphasis on maintaining relationships, connections, and context. My concern is not with an ethic of care or even with care generally, but with caring thinking in relation to dialogue. Caring thinking is distinct from caring as emotional attachments, and cognate terms such as love or friendship. If we think of care as caring thinking, this puts it into the context of critical thinking and creative thinking—both of which have contexts outside of inquiry. By defining care as a thinking process, we can look at it in the context of dialogue, or more specifically philosophical inquiry.

According to Ann Sharp (2004), caring thinking "suggests a certain view of personhood and pedagogical process" (p.9). I concur with Sharp, but she does not make it clear as to how caring as a pedagogical process could inform Socratic teaching. Pedagogical caring, a term used by Hult (1979, pp.237–43) gives us some insight as to what it means to display caring in the classroom.[2] In an educational setting, caring appropriately refers to students being provided with opportunities to receive the best possible education. In his article, 'I teach you not love you', teacher Michael Blumenthal (2001) stresses that practising teachers should place importance on caring about the education that is being provided to the student, which is different from any personal caring for individual students. If we incorporate Hult's term to Blumenthal's claims about teaching, we can say that pedagogical caring is necessary to student-learning, and should not be mistaken for personal bonds or concern, friendship or other emotional connections, which have the potential to be obstacles to productive inquiry or dialogue. It is important, therefore, to make a distinction between caring *for* and caring *with* in relation to caring in inquiry. It is far more meaningful in terms of Socratic pedagogy and as a description of the communal aspects of dialogue to think of caring as 'caring with each other' rather than 'caring for each other'. The nature of the 'care of' the child has implications for educational relationship between teacher and student and for this chapter our exploration will focus only on the relationship *between* participants in an inquiry.

In this part of the chapter we will identify the characteristics that are most common to caring thinking as it relates to dialogue. There are many authors who have written on care, most notably in psychology is Gilligan (1993), in philosophy Annette Baier (1986), and in education Nel Noddings (1984). While all agree that care and caring is in some way about connections between people, there is much to say on how caring contributes to effective communal dialogue. Sharp (2004), a colleague of Lipman, directly addresses the relationship between 'caring thinking' and dialogue in the classroom. Sharp is, therefore, an obvious starting point for our discussion on care as a way of organising how caring thinking fits into Socratic pedagogy. She places caring thinking in four categories. They are: (1) their care for the tools of inquiry, (2) their care for the problems they deem worthy, (3) their care for the form of dialogue, and (4) their care for each other (p.14). While Sharp certainly has more to say on the wider application of care as another dimension of thinking, these categories point to the experience of inquiry as embedded in care. She notes:

> This deeper dimension of meaning is not something of which they are always totally aware. The dimension lies not only in what they say to each other, how many problems they solve, what questions they decide to take on, but in the aesthetic and intersubjective form of the dialogue as a whole as they experience it. (p.14)

Sharp's categories of caring thinking offer a useful starting point for a discussion on care in dialogue. However, I will adapt them to make them applicable to Socratic pedagogy. Rather than speak of caring for the tools of inquiry and for the form of discussion I will refer to both as care for inquiry. Caring for inquiry includes paying attention to interactive patterns of inquiry, such as listening, turn-taking, and contributing, as well as caring for the tools of inquiry, such as the use of reasoning, conceptual exploration, asking questions, and making judgments. Note that I will refer to 'care with others', rather than retain Sharp's category of 'care for each other', as I think this is a more accurate description of what is necessary to dialogical inquiry. Moreover, we should not be concerned primarily with caring for one another, whether emotionally or in the sense that we have a concern for others, but that engaging in dialogue is something that we do with others together. I will, therefore, be examining: (1) care for inquiry, (2) care with others, and (3) care for problems deemed worthy.

Care for Inquiry

Care for the inquiry itself is what motivates participants in a dialogue. This aspect of caring thinking gives rise to the other aspects of care that Sharp (2004) mentions, namely, care for others, and care for the topics that students deem worthy. Caring thinking also motivates students to enlist critical and creative thinking. In Chapter 1 I discussed that the purpose of inquiry is to uncover truth, or at least to make some progression towards it. This view is particularly poignant here as it is caring for truth that gives inquiry its purpose. Without valuing truth or a greater knowledge, an inquiry does not have a purpose. One way to put this is that care is the facilitator of inquiry. If participants care for inquiry, then the other tools and requirements of inquiry will be carried through. For example, there may be disagreement on a matter of importance that has the potential to block the flow of dialogue. A group of students who care for the inquiry itself will put the energy into moving through this potential obstacle by engaging in thinking activities aimed a resolving the matter. On the other hand, a group that does not place any value on inquiry may quickly tire, and as a result may not have the desire to explore disagreements through reasoning or exploring alternatives in order to move forward. The teacher's role is to facilitate inquiry, but care is the primary facilitator that motivates the group and compels them to explore the matter further. If care is the facilitator of inquiry, then students will be more inclined to take risks rather than hold back. If this is so then care for the inquiry should be paramount and foremost in the minds of teachers as a virtue that requires nurturing. While there is no scope to address it here, surely caring for inquiry must come from the students themselves and through exposure to inquiry. It is suffice to say that if students are aware of the inquiry process and their active role as participants then emphasis should be placed on developing an awareness in students of different ways of knowing, meaning an emphasis on caring thinking in addition to the cognitive dimensions of thinking.[3]

Care with Others

While I have categorised care for inquiry and care with others separately, I acknowledge that they are interrelated. For it is out of care for inquiry that we care with others in the inquiry. I reiterate that care in this instance is care with the individuals in the inquiry as fellow inquirers, not as an emotional connection outside of those relationships that already exist or may exist in the future. It is important to note at this stage that when I refer to caring with others, I am referring to care as pedagogy not as affective thinking or as an emotional process or state. I, therefore, make a distinction between caring *with* and caring *for.* Engaging in philosophical inquiry requires that participants care with others. Caring with others involves the connections that we make in the dialogical community in our common journey towards greater understandings through inquiring together. The connection is one of impersonal fellowship, or pedagogical care. It is not an emotional connection to others and hence in the dialogue we do not care *for* others (despite the fact that this may occur outside the dialogue) but we care with each other in the dialogue as we progress towards reaching truth. On the other hand, we can care *for* the connections that we make and this requires us to listen, accept difference, and contribute to the dialogue. In this case, we are caring for the relationships and connections. We can also care for individuals outside of the dialogue in much the same way. For example, I could say that I care for humanity and hence I care for my neighbour as she is part of a global citizenship. While I may not have a friendship with my neighbour, I would treat that person with respect because of the care that I have for humankind rather than because of my personal relationships with a particular person.

Burgh, Field and Freakley (2006) offer a list of criteria for caring thinking: (1) being aware of the context in which discussion takes place, (2) sharing discussion, (3) welcoming and respecting each other's views, and (4) engaging in self-correction. Under each of these categories they list their essential characteristics.[4] A cursory glace at the categories and their characteristics suggests that what they have in mind is caring as pedagogy. However, they do not make this distinction themselves, but I mention it here as their list goes some of the way to illustrate what I mean by pedagogical care as dispositions that lend themselves to interactive patterns of inquiry necessary for engaging in dialogue. I think that Reich (1998) alludes to something similar with regards to what he calls Socratic Virtues for inquiry, which includes postponing judgment, trusting one's doubts, and patience. What I want to say is that these dispositions, virtues, or skills (whatever they may be) should be made explicit because caring thinking is an insurance against the risks inherent in the inquiry process; it connects participants through trust, reciprocity, and acceptance of difference, within the context of an inter-subjective community of people engaged in dialogue together.

The notion of caring as the facilitator of dialogue is tied to Dewey's notion of the Greater Community and the relationship between thinking together, social communication, and mutual interest necessary for supporting democratic ways of life. Pedagogical caring supports an educational arrangement suitable for democracy for it develops the social dispositions needed for active citizenship, as well as the environment to nurture the intellectual dispositions and capacities for students to think for themselves. Viewed in this way pedagogical care could be considered to liberate the powers of the individual because the emphasis is on the cultivation of participatory and deliberative virtues. As Lipman (1998) points out, there are certain dispositions needed in a participatory democracy that favours deliberation such as trust, fair-mindedness and tolerance. These virtues are at the heart of a caring relationship in the inquiry. Without a certain regard for others and for the inquiry social communication in both the dialogue and the Greater Community is not possible. By enabling students to volunteer their beliefs, values, and opinions on issues in an environment of a communal dialogue they learn to transfer an attitude of respect for others and confidence in their own perspectives to their general dispositions (Vicuna Navarro, 1998, pp.23–6). If students have no regard for others and for inquiry then the inquiry will not be meaningful, and consequently will not support democratic ways of life (Sharp, 2004, p.9).

The overarching purpose of engaging in philosophical dialogue in the classroom is for the cultivation of democratic dispositions. The type of democracy I am advocating is a deliberative form of democracy which is participatory and requires a commitment by individuals. If inquiry is to reflect a form of deliberative democracy then care is foundational because individuals must have a connection to the process of communal deliberation and a connection to meaningful topics that may go some way to solving societal and environmental problems. Engaging in inquiry is, as Cam (2006) suggests, one way of enhancing a democratic way of life.

> This kind of collaborative inquiry encourages social communication and mutual recognition of interests that Dewey identifies with a democratic way of life. Such an engagement develops the social and intellectual dispositions and capacities needed for active citizenship, while liberating the powers of the individual. (p.8)

The connections Cam highlights are made possible through dialogue where emphasis is on care with others for the inquiry. Not only is caring thinking necessary for dialogue, but what I have said so far also acknowledges the UNESCO report's aims for creating democratic dispositions in students.

Because dialogue is a communal activity, caring thinking cannot be overemphasized. Participants *must* care with others in order to be a dialogical community and must care for the inquiry itself. Otherwise the notion of community would be reduced to interactions among individuals who do not relate to each other beyond mutual self-interest or adversarial negotiations. Community steeped in dialogue is founded on both a caring interrelationship (caring with others) and a care for inquiry itself (deliberation over matters of common concern). A community neighbourhood watch, for example, is a group of citizens concerned for their own safety and the safety of the community in which they live—a reciprocal connection as one relies on the other. Each person shares a caring relationship with others in the neighbourhood as part of a community, hence their coming together as a group. Perhaps these neighbours are acquainted on a personal level, which is likely, but they have a caring regard for each other as neighbours. They also have a care for matters of concern to all of them, namely safety—this is the primary reason that brings the neighbours together. Similarly, in an inquiry, a community engages in dialogue because participants want to inquire into matters of concern to all within a communal environment (which brings perhaps previously unacquainted individuals together).This means that participants must care with others in their interactions on matters of mutual concern for the group.

The notion of intersubjectivity is important to community. Below I will discuss further Buber's I/thou dichotomy, but suffice it to say that a community is made up of individuals who act both as 'I' and 'thou'. Intersubjectivity implies a collective process in which all participants volunteer, and contribute to, arguments on matters of concern. The emphasis is placed on the participants in the dialogue to move towards an understanding that has been reached through the contributions of all participants. This does not necessarily mean that there has been no disagreement during the inquiry, as disagreement is inevitable, especially when dealing with matters of ethical concern, but instead, as a community, participants move together towards a common goal of seeking truth. When an individual reflects on his or her own argument, that contains his or her perspective as well as the views of others, it becomes clear that this perspective has been shaped by all members of the inquiry. There may still be disagreement amongst the community members, but if, after reflection, the group decides to accept the different opinions, they have come to this conclusion collectively. Care in this sense allows for community by enhancing thinking as collaborative. Let us now look at the specific elements that contribute to thinking collaboratively.

Care as Reciprocity: The Temple of Hearing Petra von Mornstein (2005) addresses intersubjectivity in terms of its relation to Martin Buber. She takes Buber's theory of the I/thou relationship and applies it to philosophical dialogue. Von Morstein says that in an inquiry we are both object and subject. Because we are both object and subject at the same time, this is the state in which we can say we are 'intersubjective'—both individual (I) and opposite of others (thou). She argues that in an inquiry we base our experiences on being a subject. But we must also know each other (hence, the I/thou relationship). This is bound up in concepts of empathy. By knowing others in an inquiry we must empathise with them (to put our feet in their shoes to try to understand their viewpoint). But to allow us to be truly intersubjective we must have trust. We need to trust in order to be trusted. She argues that in philosophical inquiry "our individual boundaries are transcended when we are I/thou" (n.p). However, the I/thou relationship is not always sustainable for long and she warns against the perils of becoming a 'we'. If her warning is understood as becoming friends then this supports my earlier claim that it is care and not friendship that is necessary for dialogue, and that friendship could become an obstacle to effective inquiry.

Integral to von Mornstein's theory on the I/thou relationship and inquiry, and to the definition of care presented here, is the notion of a 'Temple of Hearing'. What von Mornstein is referring to is reciprocity in terms of language. Much like the question of a tree falling in a forest, she questions whether a word is indeed a word until someone receives it. The hearer has to attend to the speaker and also suspend their own meanings of the word in order to actually hear. She asserts that it is love that allows this process. It is not the word but the ear that allows communication to happen. The speaker trusts in being heard. Although von Morstein uses the term 'love', given our discussion so far, a more suitable term is care. In a dialogue our actions have to be reciprocal because if we don't create an environment that is conducive to others' inquiry, then our own inquiry will suffer. In a dialogue we listen and attend because that is what we would hope for when we are the person in a position of speaker. This is trust, as we only speak when we trust that we will be received. In relation to my assertion that participants must care for the inquiry to make it truly meaningful, von Mornstein is relevant insofar as she pays attention to participant's care for words. We must care for our words in order to care for each other (i.e., care for what we are saying). We must have a commitment to the dialogue that comes from being part of an 'I/thou' relationship. This is the 'Temple of Hearing', a process of being both interconnected and different in the dialogue, in which we are both hosts and guests together.

Noddings (1984) also describes caring as having a regard for the views and interests of others, and that it requires reciprocity (p.9). For caring to be fulfilled, the 'one-caring' must receive some sort of validation from the 'cared-for', in order for the act of caring to be complete. Caring, argues Noddings, "must somehow be completed in the other if the relationship is to be described as caring" (p.4). Dialogue requires reciprocity, as well as a regard for the views and interests of others, which entails trust, tolerance, and fairmindedness.[5] Opinions or points of view can be truly received only when others engage with those opinions or points of view as we discussed earlier. Regardless of disagreement, if the relationship is a caring one, then a commitment to the process of inquiry becomes paramount. Caring is, as Noddings says, integral to the success of the dialogue, as it is this element that helps participants to accept different views.

> Through such a dialectic, we are led beyond the intense, and particular feelings accompanying our deeply held values and beyond the particular beliefs to which these feelings are attached *to a realization that the other who feels intensely about that which I do not believe is still to be received.* (p.186, *emphasis* my own)

In sum, caring helps participants value and accept different points of view. Instead of placing importance on common interests, caring accommodates for differences. In an inquiry where participants may not share the same beliefs or values, they can still follow the dialogue from their own perspective and from the perspectives of others. In such cases, while participants acknowledge disagreement, they also are learning that the beliefs and values of the participants must be given equal respect and attention.

John Thomas (1997) says something similar to Noddings. Although he talks specifically of the Community of Inquiry, his argument applies equally to dialogue and inquiry generally: "[t]he idea of the community of inquiry in which people come together for the common purpose of thinking rationally together has the potential to bridge the difference between individuals such that a deeper understanding of their differences and mutual respect for them can happen" (p.42). Thomas talks of differences being "transcended and yet retained" in the community set up (p.43). Rather than agreeing with the views of a participant in the inquiry, we can perhaps say that we value what an individual brings to the group inquiry. When we engage with the viewpoints of others in a dialogue, this shows that we value what that person has to contribute to the development of the argument. We may not always come to an agreement in inquiry and it is this aspect that gives us greater understanding of the topic being inquired into. It is also this aspect that makes philosophical inquiry intrinsically democratic. Students are allowed to voice our viewpoints and to actively disagree or agree on a topic.

Coming together for a common purpose and acceptance of difference requires empathy. Empathy should not be mistaken for or should not imply compassion because the capacity for empathy can be present in other contexts such as cruelty. Rather, empathy is to recognise or understand someone else's state of mind or emotion. It is not in itself an emotion, but a kind of reflective disagreement insofar as it allows for the exploration of disagreement through 'putting yourself into another's shoes'. This is consistent with pedagogical care, and requires the ability to listen attentively to others, to imagine, to think analogously, and to be open to possibilities and different perspectives. As such, empathy is integral to caring thinking as it allows us to connect to the experiences of others. The presence of empathy as integral to dialogue would also satisfy the concerns of critics such as de Bono's regarding philosophy as adversarial. If not, then perhaps the critics should heed Pitchard's warning: "If people are not convinced that one can learn through reflective disagreement, then perhaps what is called for is some discussion of what learning involves and why it is important to explore our disagreements as well as out agreements" (in Power, 1999).

Care as Trust   The cooperative nature of dialogue described so far is not possible without trust.[6] In a philosophical inquiry, we enter into a kind of contract i.e., we are committed to seeing an inquiry to its completion, and, hence, there is a certain amount of trust involved that participants of the inquiry will respect the contract that they have entered into and will behave accordingly. According to Baier (1986) "[i]t seems fairly obvious that any form of co-operative activity ... requires the cooperators to trust with one another to do their bit" (p.232). In a cooperative endeavour such as a philosophical inquiry, it is imperative that each participant 'does their bit' and contributes to the dialogue or the inquiry itself could not ensue. We must all contribute ideas and also engage with the ideas of others or we risk the inquiry becoming a series of monologues. This reciprocal arrangement that we agree to when we enter into dialogue is founded on our caring for the process of inquiry.

The reciprocal relationship between caring and trusting when engaging in dialogue together requires that we trust people with 'things we care about'. When we enter into dialogue we not only agree to care for the inquiry but we trust that others will share a reciprocal care for inquiry. But we also care about our ideas in inquiry. It is the contribution that we make to inquiry that makes us vulnerable, but it is also the production of ideas that shows that we care for what we are saying. This brings us back to von Mornstein (2005) and our discussion on caring for our words. When we care enough about developing our own and others' ideas, then we enter into dialogue. This is where trust must be enlisted. At the time of being most vulnerable (or at the time of greatest risk), we trust that "the trusted will not harm one, although one could harm one" (Baier, 1986, p.235). It is possible that our ideas may not be received in an inquiry and it takes courage to voice viewpoints to a group of people (hence why some participants may take some weeks to find confidence to contribute to a dialogue). We trust that these ideas will be met with openness. In doing so, we have, according to Baier, a reciprocal relationship of one-trusting to the trusted, which creates unequal power. We give the trusted power and trust that they will not do ill to us (such as laughing out loud at an idea rather than treating it with respect). In a caring inquiry, these power relations become less threatening. All participants in the inquiry are in a position of power as the trusted, but also in the vulnerable position as the truster. Because we must treat each other with respect, not only out of care, trust is necessary for a successful dialogue. The teacher must facilitate the inquiry by creating an environment where care is ever-present, by modelling appropriate connections and encouraging the building of a classroom community alongside building critical and creative thinking skills.

In Chapter 4 we touched briefly on the idea of creativity as risk. It is undeniable that the exploration of new or innovative ideas in a group can be confronting to some students. Were this to go undetected, then the very environment which was intended to develop students' ability to think well, could itself become a technology of silence. But risk also plays a role in the broader context of inquiry, as dialogue requires participants to be intellectual risk-takers. Caring thinking creates opportunities for students to take risks; to be creative in their thinking, to generate, expand and develop their ideas, but also to be critical, to challenge their own ideas and those of others. Caring thinking allows the participants in the dialogue to take risks in an environment that is intellectually safe (Miller, 2005). In other words, the presence of caring thinking in inquiry may 'soften the fall' so to speak, in terms of taking risks as creative and critical thinkers. It seems that risk and trust go hand-in-hand; we cannot have one without the other. The transition between risk and taking the step forward in creating intellectually safe environment is the act of trusting. Baier (1986) sees this process as:

> ... the natural order of consciousness and self-consciousness of trust, which progresses from initially unself-conscious trust to awareness of risk along with confidence that it is a good risk, on to some realization of why we are taking this particular risk, and eventually to some evaluation of what we may generally gain and what we may lose from the willingness to take such risks.

The ultimate point of what we are doing when we trust may be the last thing we come to realize. (p. 236)

Baier's words remind us of the interplay between risk and trust, and how we move from unconscious awareness of trust at the moment of taking a risk to eventually feeling confident about the risks we take, which we ultimately do not recognise as an act of trusting. This process could be made more explicit in an intellectually safe environment.

The conception of philosophical dialogue as an intellectually safe educational environment rests on two presuppositions in relation to distribution of power, in that it requires openness to inquiry and readiness to reason, and mutual respect of students and teachers towards one another. However, these presuppositions are dependent upon the ability of participants to share power (Yorshansky, 2007; Burgh & Yorshansky, 2008). To introduce an intellectually safe environment requires that the participants within that environment behave accordingly, but this is the very thing that the safe environment is supposed to bring about. Turgeon (1998) recognises that there are many factors that contribute to some students' lack of openness to inquiry and readiness to reason, or lack of mutual respect of students and teachers towards one another. Students may have personal reasons or deep seated reasons for not actively engaging in learning regardless of whether or not it is a safe intellectual environment (p.11). However, she points out that some of these problems can be overcome through the creation of such an environment.

> Before one can do philosophy, one must have the sense that one's ideas will be listened to, taken seriously, and respectfully responded to. This does not mean that you must have a fully developed community of inquiry as a pre-requisite for doing philosophy but it does point to the important need to focus on the nature of community and its importance in knowledge building from the start. (p.14)

In other words, there are distinct aspects of dialogue to which we must be alert in order to develop and maintain a safe environment. If taken into consideration with the processes Baier describes on the emergence of trust then it seems that a safe intellectual environment is possible through caring thinking. I am not offering this as a solution, but as a way of illustrating that the idea of a safe intellectual environment should not be discounted with regard to developing the relationship between risk and trust.

Despite what I have said, I also offer a caution that we should not discount the practicalities of students' unwillingness to openness or mutual respect. As Burgh and Yorshansky (2008) point out:

> It is not clear how dispositions towards sharing power necessarily develop in the course of the inquiry process. This prevalent assumption overlooks the possibility that sharing power, opinions, and other resources could cause strong emotional responses, which are often manifested as resistance, among participants in a community of inquiry. For example, certain members who

are prone to silence or who dominate discussion might not be receptive to changing their patterns of behaviour. (p.10)

What this passage suggests is that blocked inquiry is an indication that something is wrong. But blocked inquiry should not always be interpreted as a potential obstacle to dialogue. Some behaviours, typically seen as blocked inquiry, could be interpreted as providing opportunities for growth. The following comment by Turgeon (1998) suggests this should be the case.

> Paradoxically we might also re-examine the whole dilemma of the recalcitrant classroom as a sign of health, rather than as something that must be 'fixed' or eliminated. Perhaps such conflicts and protestations against philosophy reveal a more honest engagement within the classroom than is generally found in the traditional room. (p.14)

Turgeon's comments bring us back full circle to the relationship between risk and trust and the facilitation of an intellectually safe environment built on care. The absence of caring thinking can only result in a lack of trust and a reluctance to take intellectual risks. Caring thinking is, therefore, necessary, although I stress not sufficient, for the creation of opportunities to participate in the generation of innovative ideas and their evaluation in order to develop the intellectual and social dispositions and capacities for active citizenship. This, in turn, also liberates the individual and subsequently furthers the growth of an intellectually safe environment.

Care for Problems Deemed Worthy

Sharp (2004) argues that students may engage on a deeper level if what they are inquiring into is meaningful. This is reflective of Dewey's thinking that learning should be connected to the students' own lives in order for them to make substantive connections to what they are learning about or inquiring into. If students care for the process of inquiry, then their engagement will no doubt be deeper if what they are inquiring into is meaningful to them. The stimulus need not be a text, narrative, or other resource but an actual situation. For example, in a school classroom, a teacher may use some of the concerns that students raise in a weekly class meeting as stimulus for dialogue. A scenario could, for instance, arise out of student concerns that bullying is being disguised as 'just a joke'. While both bully and victim may have different views on what constitutes a joke, the situation could be addressed through inquiring into the meaning of the word joke. Conversely, if students are handed down ready-made topics to study that have either no connection to the students' own lives and experiences or do not spark their interest in any way, then they are less likely to become involved in moving through the process of inquiry. This is not to say that all students will necessarily be more interested in a topic through the process of inquiry, to which the reasons stated in the section above attest.

There are various ways of setting an agenda and these vary depending on the model of dialogue being used. For instance, in Socratic Dialogue the initial question to be explored throughout the dialogue is generally brought to the group by the facilitator (although this may be changed if the group has a different question or if they agree that another question needs to be addressed first). In Bohmian Dialogue, the group sets the agenda based on what is of interest to the group. This eventuates out of the initial discussion that precedes the dialogue. In the Community of Inquiry stimulus material can elicit questions, but this ultimately is decided on by the students themselves. This occurs in two ways; by making connections between questions by the students in order to arrive at an agreed upon question, or by voting to decide what question is of most interest. Caring thinking is particularly important in the initial stage of inquiry, where the use of the stimulus, the raising of the questions, and the setting of the agenda create the tone for whether or not students will consider a topic to be worthy of further exploration and analysis. Despite differences about what should count as stimulus material for inquiring, how to address questions, or set an agenda for inquiry, by focusing on what matters to students and inviting them as a group to problematise a situation, that is, by creating a caring environment that connects the social and intellectual aspects of inquiry, this will create opportunities to elicit thinking that is both transformative and substantive. Above all, it will be meaningful dialogue which in turn will create further connections and more opportunities for facilitating social communications and mutual recognition which underscores caring thinking.

CONNECTIVE THINKING: A WAY OF THINKING WITH CARE

We are in a position now to sum up what we have said so far about caring thinking. In Chapter 4 we explored the production, development, and extension of ideas as a way of thinking creatively that has application to the world, to situations, or problems. In the previous chapter the focus was on the development, application, and evaluation of criteria through conceptual analysis, reasoning, and logic. In this chapter caring thinking was described as the connections between individuals and thoughts in the communal dialogue. It is a process of: (1) caring for inquiry, which motivates students throughout the dialogue, (2) caring with others, which emphasises the connections between students through reciprocity, and an acceptance of difference, trust, and hearing, and (3) caring for problems deemed worthy, or those problematic situations that warrant further inquiry. Now that we have identified the characteristics or general features of caring thinking that are important for dialogue, in this part we can see that what is common to these characteristics or central to their meanings is *connective thinking*. By connective thinking I mean the connections between students in the dialogue as well as the connections inherent in multi-dimensional thinking. Connective thinking is comprised of three interrelated components: (1) collective thinking, (2) impersonal fellowship, and (3) awakened attentiveness.

Before we move on to our discussion we need to be clear about the distinction between care as affective thinking or as an emotional process or state, and care as caring thinking. Care is usually thought of as an affective state, which includes love, liking, friendship, and other emotional attachments, as well as compassion, sympathy, and nurturing. Lipman (2004) is more specific and uses the term 'caring thinking', which he says is comprised of appreciative, active, normative, affective, and empathic thinking, each of which has their own characteristics (p.271). The list of characteristics attests to Lipman's intention to purposely conflate the distinction that we wish to make here. The way that caring thinking is presented here is that it is a kind of thinking that is necessarily connective. Connectivity, simply put, is the messages that are sent between different conduits that connect fragmented elements to create a greater understanding and allows for coherence that comes from wholeness. This connection is one of an impersonal fellowship or pedagogical care. It is the interaction between the participants in the inquiry (between teacher and students, and students and students as co-inquirers) and the content of the inquiry through a relationship of intersubjectivity. Participants follow the inquiry where it leads through a complex process of interactive patterns of inquiry conjointly guided by generative and evaluative thinking.

A necessary condition of connective thinking is that it is collective thinking. This is because engagement in dialogue is a shared activity where participants collaboratively exchange and explore ideas, and where the process of dialogue—its patterns of thinking, inquiry, and interactions—are internalised by the group. They are continual connections. The connection between the individual and the idea, and the individual and the group is a series of connections that occur when there is a communal dialogue. There is a level of disassociation from ego as thought becomes, as Bohm suggests, collective or participatory thought. Collective thinking is, therefore, intersubjective. Bohm's (1991) description of intersubjectivity may be helpful.

> As sensitivity and experience increase, a perception of shared meaning emerges in which people find that they are neither opposing one another, nor are they simply interacting. Increasing trust between members of the group—and trust in the process itself—leads to the expression of the sorts of thoughts and feelings that are usually kept hidden. There is no imposed consensus, nor is there any attempt to avoid conflict. No single individual or sub-group is able to achieve dominance because every single subject, including domination and submission, is always available to be considered. (n.p)

The impersonal fellowship, as Bohm prefers to call it, is an intersubjective connection between the participants in the dialogue and their ideas, and their inner thoughts and feelings as individuals and as a group.[7] The idea of the relationship as being both impersonal and a fellowship is important to connective thinking. A relationship that is founded on a connection between participants in the dialogue for the common purpose of inquiring together takes away the need to care *for* others, and instead puts the emphasis on caring *with* others as a way of engaging in dialogue. Recall the three café friends that we discussed at the beginning of this chapter. Their connection was an emotional connection based on fondness for each other and would likely support the retaining of equilibrium. However, if the three friends were to come together for the purpose of dialogue, their relationship would be connected by a fellowship rather than a friendship. This allows for a genuine commitment to the inquiry with the aim of progressing toward truth of finding meaning together. This is not to deny that friendships may result from the inquiry process but they are not necessary to effective dialogue.

Interconnected with collective thinking and impersonal fellowship is awakened attentiveness, which is a kind of collective self-awareness. It is notable that the impersonal fellowship may be mistakenly depicted as 'uncaring' but it is far from that. What underpins it is *attending* to emotions and feelings, but rather than letting these emotions or feelings guide the dialogue, what is required is purposeful reflection in order to gain an understanding the feelings, assumptions, judgments, and thoughts that underpins emotion. This involves engaging in continual meta-dialogue. Because participants gain an awareness of what and how they are thinking they internalise this process and apply their awareness outside of the dialogue, effectively reconstructing thinking as a system, instead of remaining fragmented. The participants begin to develop group thinking attitudes rather than seeing problems exclusively from their own perspective. To understand this better it will be helpful to revisit the idea of proprioception.

> The body can perceive its own movement. When you move the body you know the relation between intention and action. The impulse to move and the movement are seen to be connected. If you don't have that, the body is not viable. (Bohm, 1991)

Being aware of movement can be applied to dialogue as an awareness of how we think through dialogue. To use Bohm's favoured analogy, the awareness of movement is like a collective dance of the mind.[8] In a dialogue participants must be aware of their connections to others and how their movements, or thoughts, impact on the movements of others, and how both the connection between movement and each other propels them further in collective dialogue. Bohmian dialogue is fundamentally connective as it is a continual process of reflection through a collaborative process in order to progress toward coherence.

CONNECTIVE THINKING IN DIALOGUE

We can now move on to where connective thinking features in each of the models of dialogue to show its practical application. So that we have a better understanding of how connective thinking features in Socratic pedagogy, we will explore how it has been employed in Bohmian Dialogue, Community of Inquiry, and Socratic Dialogue. Firstly we will look at Bohmian Dialogue and the metaphor of a collective dance of the mind. We will concentrate also on agenda setting and self-reflection as significant for connective thinking. Next, we look at the Community of Inquiry and Lipman's various approaches to caring thinking that have implications for generative thinking. Lastly, we will see how Socratic Dialogue also utilises connective thinking because there is a focus on meta-dialogue and personal anecdotes.

Bohmian Dialogue

In Bohmian dialogue, connective thinking is not simply present but is the very foundation of dialogue. Bohm's description of dialogue as a collective dance of the mind was intended to illustrate that participants need to look inwards at the way in which they interact with others, and reciprocally how others interact with them. He described this process as an awakened attentiveness. This means that the dialogue should be slow enough so that the participants can observe how they were actually thinking and how their interactions and the interactions of others impacted on their own thoughts, in order to experience thinking as a system rather than as instrument for tackling a problem. This process rests on a level of reciprocity that comes out of having an impersonal fellowship or cohesive bond. In an impersonal fellowship speech and silence are interwoven insofar as the distinction between speaker and listener tends to disappear. This allows for the dialogue to slow down so that careful attention can be paid to the interaction patterns of the dialogue and the internal thoughts and feelings of the participants revealed to themselves. Bohm envisaged that by enabling participants to concentrate on the connections that they make through collective thought, that there may be a greater level of self-awareness. This relies on connectivity through a process of awakening, being attentive to what is happening in the dialogue and the internalization process. The dialogue itself occurs out of collective thought that is informed by an intersubjective awareness; how our own movements in inquiry impact on others (a concentration on relationships) and how our own thoughts impact on the movements we make. If we do not engage in a collective dance of the mind, then there is no dialogue.

The metaphor represents the connections between individuals and to thinking that are made when steps are being followed: individuals must be aware of their movements. It places the emphasis on both thinking and collaborating. The metaphor of a collective dance of the mind is significant because it puts the focus not on the content of dialogue but on the very process of how dialogue features in a collaborative context, which is lost if the emphasis on thinking in dialogue remains only an intellectual process. While self-reflection has a role to play in the other models of dialogue, in Bohmian Dialogue reflection is a paramount feature and of utmost consideration as it places emphasis on *how* we inquire rather than on the content of the discussion. If in the dialogue there is disagreement, contention, or ill-feeling participants are encouraged to examine their assumptions, opinions, judgments, and feelings in order to awaken their awareness and to engage in meta-dialogue. In doing so, they engage in an internal dialogue within the dialogue itself.

The idea of 'no agenda' is also significant for our discussion on how connective thinking applies to Bohmian Dialogue. Not only should students be connected to each other through dialogue, but must also have some connection to matters of importance to the participants. Like arriving at a cocktail party, the group gathers around in conversation, but unlike a cocktail party the conversation inevitably leads to substantive topics of concern in order to begin the dialogue proper. Through this process, the individuals will be able to address topics that are meaningful to them. Only those topics that are worthwhile being inquired into will be addressed in a successful inquiry. Because of this, it is likely that most or all participants would become interested in the content of the dialogue as it was generated by the interests of the participants themselves.

Let's revisit the three friends featured at the beginning of this chapter. The three friends who come together for the purpose of conversation may turn their conversation on wedding flowers towards identity and hence their connection moves from one based on friendship and equilibrium to fellowship, based on dialogue. This is Bohm's point about dialogue. While some critics have argued against Bohm on this issue, theorists and practitioners who have continued with Bohm's work on dialogue have found that participants do eventually engage in effective dialogue. Because there is no agenda, topics for dialogue can be many and varied. For Bohm, the group chooses the topic based on what is meaningful that comes out of conversation. Bohm notes that by having no set purpose this allows for topics that are meaningful to naturally make their way into the conversation that leads to dialogue. Bohm essentially shows us that a conversation may not remain as a 'mere conversation' but that it may be facilitated towards something more meaningful. We must therefore find an approach to agenda setting that allows for topics that resonate with the participants if we are to have proper connections to what we are inquiring into.

Bohm is important to our definition of connective thinking because he places reflection at the forefront of dialogue rather than as a 'meta-dialogue'. It *is* the dialogue. If we are to have a model of collective thought that gives rise to an awakened attentiveness to our own assumptions within the connections we have with others, then Bohm is integral to the connections that we should be making in a Socratic classroom.

The Community of Inquiry

According to Sharp (2004) Lipman has not given enough attention to caring thinking in the Community of Inquiry. She argues that while Lipman recognises the role of care in the Community of Inquiry, it is not given the same level of description and importance in Lipman's theory of educational philosophy than the other dimensions of multi-dimensional thinking. However, in the second edition of *Thinking in Education* Lipman made several substantial and significant revisions, including a full chapter devoted to caring thinking, and its relationship to critical and creative thinking. It appears that Sharp's concentration of caring thinking had an effect on Lipman. Nevertheless, Lipman's approach to caring thinking needs clarification.

Lipman (2004) offers five criteria for caring thinking, which he calls value-principles. They are: (1) appreciative thinking, (2) affective thinking, (3) active thinking, (4) normative thinking, and (5) empathic thinking. The criteria are intended to be used as an inventory of varieties of caring thinking rather than a precise definition, which he states he is not in a position to offer. He does mention that caring unavoidably creates a struggle to balance our propensity toward emotional discriminations and our normative tendencies to place all humans on an equal standing (p.264). I think Lipman is correct in his stipulation, but it is the continual process of finding this balance which suggests to me that caring thinking is something more than what Lipman suggests on his inventory. For me this is pedagogical caring which is a kind of connective thinking, or at least underpinned by it. It is connective thinking because it links all of Lipman's categories.

First on the rank of Lipman's inventory is appreciative thinking. By appreciative thinking, he means paying attention to the things that matter. Examples of appreciative thinking are doctors who care for health, or judges who care for the law, and relevant to our discussion teachers who care for education. These people are in a position of care, who attend to what matters to them rather than act out of an emotional attachment or connection. Appreciative thinking could be said to be a feature of pedagogical caring. That is to say, teachers who care for education attend to what matters to them as professionals, for example, the development of social and intellectual dispositions and capacities required for active citizenship. But they do this because of the concern for the education of students generally. Similarly, participants in a dialogue who care for inquiry attend to what matters to them as a group not because they care for anyone in particular but because they are motivated out of their concern for the topic.

Affective thinking connects the affective and the cognitive. Some emotions are themselves judgments, or to put it another way the emotion itself has judgment built into it. Some examples are: guilt, shame, indignation, pity, and sympathy. These emotions carry with them an awareness of the event or action that prompted the emotion. Lipman claims that affective thinking is important for moral education. To this there can be no doubt. However, without pedagogical caring, i.e., being a teacher who cares for education and pays attention to what is required to meet the goals of education, teaching runs the risk of being tainted with inappropriate judgments in any given context. Connective thinking, i.e., making connection to broaden the scope of our thinking, allows teachers to judge what is or what is not misplaced emotion within the context of education.

Active thinking has an inbuilt reflective component that connects action and caring. According to Lipman, when talking about care in terms of caring *for* or *about*, this means having an affectionate feeling for someone that this is affective thinking. However, when we use the term caring *for* in the sense of taking care or looking after someone this is better described as active thinking. It is active because it is a way of thinking that implies an action. What mediates thinking and action is judgment. The judgment is an appraisal of the situation and how one feels about it. Pedagogical caring can assist in preventing us from acting in ways that are not pedagogically appropriate, meaning that when we are caring for the inquiry or for the problem deemed worthy then it is appropriate to act accordingly, as we are caring for something because we aim to calculate its worth as educationally useful. However, this is not so when we care for others as it could result in taking care of students or looking after them in ways that have no pedagogical value. Pedagogical caring asks teachers to think about the situation differently as caring with others. This still implies action, but a different kind of action. It requires empathy and caring for the things they care for as a group, caring for outcomes, and other things considered educationally valuable.

Normative thinking refers to caring conduct; that someone who cares about something would behave in a certain way. It is thinking about what we ought to do. Since it is reflective it is also cognitive. It makes us pay attention to how we act in the world and makes us reflect on the sort of person we would like to be, or more importantly who we ought to be. Normative thinking, therefore, has a crucial role to play in pedagogical caring. Pedagogical caring, by definition, is defined by its attention to the role of ethics, i.e., it asks us as professionals to reflect on what it means to be a professional in an educational context, and to pay attention to what matters in regard to teaching practices. It is therefore underpinned by appreciative thinking. Normative thinking is also crucial to the progress of the dialogue as it facilitates the social aspects of engaging in dialogue.

Empathic thinking is about putting ourselves in another person's situation in order to experience that situation and the emotions as if they are our own. I note that under empathic thinking Lipman lists 'sympathetic'. This is a contentious use of the term. Whereas empathy is to consider how others might feel in a given situation or vicarious experience of another's emotions, sympathy evokes an emotional response toward another person. Empathy is caring *with* someone, to feel as they do. Sympathy is both caring *for* someone, meaning having an affectionate feeling, and caring *about* someone, meaning a sense of wanting to look after them or aid them in some way. Empathy is necessary for pedagogical caring, as it can broaden our understanding of the different way in which different people experience situations, but it also makes a logical connection as it allows us to compare and contrast situations, to see things analogously. Again, pedagogical caring helps teachers to discern between misplaced emotions that arise out of affection for someone or a wanting to look after them, and empathy.

Because of Lipman's emphasis on multi-dimensional thinking, connective thinking has a ready-made place in the Community of Inquiry. While is it right at home in Bohmian Dialogue, in the Community of Inquiry it has a natural connecting role. Connective thinking compels students to follow the argument where it leads by caring for the inquiry, caring with others, and caring for the problems deemed worthy. It requires participants to think appreciatively, to pay attention to matters of concern, especially important in relation to caring for the problems deemed worthy. Normative thinking is also vital to connective thinking as that is what we are doing when we care with others. Empathy is another crucial element of connective thinking, and is central to caring for the inquiry. In order to develop innovative thinking and to care for the logic of inquiry, including the content and form of the dialogue, requires a level of empathetic thinking when welcoming, respecting, and considering other people's point of view, or considering alternatives. Connective thinking by its very nature is complex as it makes existing connections, links new pathways, but also discovers new ones. The educational setting within which it operates is facilitated by: collective thinking, connecting people and ideas; an impersonal fellowship, caring with others; and awakened attentiveness, and being aware of our intersubjective connection to others.

Socratic Dialogue

Connective thinking can be easily identified in the beginning stages of Socratic Dialogue. Firstly, a number of participants must volunteer a personal experience that acts as an example for the topic question. Entering into dialogue brings with it some level of risk, but particularly in Socratic Dialogue, where the information we give up can be personal and in some cases, can be emotional. In order to feel able to take that risk, trust must already be present in the group in order for the environment to be intellectually safe. Such an environment could be described as an impersonal fellowship. In an impersonal fellowship, we may trust that others will take the same sort of risk and in doing so that these experiences will be accepted with the same respect that is given to them.

Secondly, participants must choose an example from the volunteered experiences. We have already acknowledged that volunteering an example involves some kind of risk for the participant. When each example is scrutinised, it must be done with a level of sensitivity, but in keeping with the process of dialogue, it is done with the intention to further the dialogue. In order to find the example, to allow for a genuine dialogue, participants must act both through a connection with the process of inquiry and through connections of other participants in the group. That is to say, if we have a connection to the dialogue we care with others in the dialogue, and subsequently provide a safe intellectual environment for rigorous inquiry. Each example must be examined carefully in order to provide a foundation as a focus for dialogue. This is paramount for the progress of the dialogue. Unlike friendship, which can act as an obstacle to genuine dialogue, an impersonal fellowship keeps us intellectually rigorous.

The idea of an impersonal fellowship underpins collective thinking and goes someway to define the relationship that participants can expect in a Socratic Dialogue. While participants should not be concerned over the impact that dialogue could have on the feelings of others, lest we avoid any sensitive topics, these feelings should be taken into consideration. Respect must be shown to each participant who has volunteered an example and this respect must be retained throughout the dialogue. Showing respect is integral to the wellbeing of the participants and the health of the inquiry, as in the long term trust can be built that will allow participants to feel comfortable in the future to volunteer their examples. In other words, an impersonal fellowship can contribute to the creation of an intellectually safe environment, which in an inquiry where logical rigor and consensus is demanded, is necessary.

In some variations of Socratic Dialogue participants have the opportunity to break into meta-dialogue. The purpose of the meta-dialogue is to resolve any problems, differences, or confusions that arise from the relationships between the participants in the dialogue. This is integral to creation of an intellectually safe environment. Moreover, because Socratic Dialogue requires a deep level of rigor throughout the dialogue, which means that participants have to explore each of the disagreements, an emphasis on connective thinking is imperative. What is required is a commitment to collective thinking in order to sustain the rigor required to come to consensus, but also in order to 'weather the storm', so to speak, when students have to examine their disagreements deeply.

WHERE ARE WE NOW?

Before moving on to the next chapter we need to pause for a moment to review where we are. In Chapter 4 we saw that generative thinking, which is the pulse of creative thinking, is concerned with the generation, development and extension of ideas that comes out of wonder. Subsequently, Chapter 5 focussed on evaluative thinking, which is central to critical thinking, is concerned with reasoning and analysis, criteria and judgment. So, what have we said about caring thinking in this chapter? There are three characteristics: (1) collective thinking, (2) impersonal fellowship, and (3) awakened attentiveness, common to caring thinking. Connective thinking is central to the meaning of these three characteristics. Therefore, connective thinking is necessary for effective caring thinking. We also identified where connective thinking fits into a multi-dimensional framework for Socratic pedagogy by demonstrating how it can be applied to each of the models of dialogue in order to gain a better understanding of its practical application.

We can extrapolate from the analysis in this chapter that connective thinking, in relation to multi-dimensional thinking, is best described by Bohm's model of dialogue. Bohmian Dialogue embeds the principle of connection to others, an awareness of self, and attendance to thought, all represented by the metaphor of a collective dance of the mind. Because Bohmian Dialogue has a concentration on the connective elements of dialogue, it has much to contribute to the development of connective thinking in Socratic pedagogy. It is suffice to say that by acknowledging connective thinking as the defining feature of caring thinking it illustrates the connections between the intellectual and social aspects of dialogue.

Connective thinking connects much more than just relationships between people. It sets standards by engaging in normative thinking, analogous reasoning, empathy, and attentive awareness through listening and questioning. In concert with generative thinking connective thinking creates new ways of making connections. It connects the social with the mental, the generative and evaluative aspects of thinking, the cognitive and the affective, risk and trust, and rationality and empathy. Lipman's description below offers a context from which connective thinking flows.

> [E]very mental act actualizes a mental move; every thinking skill actualizes a thinking move; every connection of mental acts has already been made possible as a mental association or bridging. In other words, any particular thinker is the site of an enormous number of paths, roadways, avenues, and boulevards that crisscross the terrain that is already familiar through constant

use, and that suggests hitherto unrelated connections or clusters of connections to those adventurous thinkers who are looking to explore new terrains. Due to ignorance or prejudice, certain connections are deemed unachievable or improbable, but often it is just these that the inventive or creative or imaginative mind will select for a breakthrough. (2004, p.255)

This passage by Lipman describes what it means to think beyond the familiar, to see good thinking as more than evaluative thinking. Good thinking also requires generative thinking to make intellectual connections that would otherwise not be made possible by evaluative thinking alone. But it is connective thinking that makes this possible as it is the social dimension of thinking. Because we think together in dialogue, through wondering and evaluation we are able to make the familiar strange and see old patterns in new ways. Without connective thinking we will, as Bohm says, remain fragmented in both our thinking and in our social connections.

We are now ready to move on to the final chapter where I shall outline the framework for Socratic pedagogy.

NOTES

[1] For more on Kohlberg, see *Essays on Moral Development, Vol. I: The Philosophy of Moral Development, 1981.*

[2] For more on pedagogical care, see Davey (2004, 2005).

[3] For further exploration of this idea, see Mia O'Brien who argues that students do have an awareness of their own ways of knowing and reflect on ways of learning (2000).

[4] The characteristics as listed under each of the categories are: (1) alert listening for clues to understand the context of the community, constantly reminding and reshaping self and others, and an attitude of openness and willingness for genuine inquiry, (2) asking questions, giving reasons, commenting on the whole group, listening attentively and actively, using silence for listening and thinking, and not opting out of discussion, (3) being open to possibilities and different perspectives, exploring disagreements, helping each other build on ideas, responding to the idea and not the person, and openness to alternatives, and (4) accepting fair criticism, being prepared to have ideas challenged, and being precise not vague (Burgh, Field & Freakley, 2006, p.113).

[5] See Lipman (1988); Cam (1995).

[6] Trust is not a new concept to the history of philosophy. Plato's 'Gyges' Ring' suggests that morality is being able to trust in one another that we will all act ethically in times of invisibility. Thomas Hobbes' idea of 'social contract' is one based on setting up conditions to enable trust in the community.

[7] The idea of an impersonal fellowship was originally used to describe the early form of Athenian democracy in which all the free men of the city gathered to govern themselves (Bohm, Factor & Garrett, 1991).

[8] Bohm argues that we should try to distance ourselves from our deeply held opinions and notice how these have been formed rather than try to argue them.

SOCRATIC PEDAGOGY

This book, simply put, explored the potential of Socratic pedagogy as an effective educational strategy for developing the social and intellectual capacities and skills for active citizenship in a democratic society. As we have seen from the preceding chapters, philosophical dialogue is about reconstruction, or as Fisher puts it, making the familiar strange. This involves both evaluative and generative thinking as we challenge our assumptions about taken-for-granted knowledge and then begin to seek alternatives to come up with new knowledge. It also involves connective thinking as we inquire within a communal dialogue. However, theorists and practitioners who advocate the teaching of philosophy or philosophical inquiry in schools need to also engage in professional dialogue on matters of concern with regard to educational philosophy, in particular philosophical pedagogy. Professional discussion must also occur in communities. In the previous chapter, I pointed to Lewis' imagery of two friends looking forward, out to the horizon, in the same direction. This metaphor is particularly poignant for this book because it reflects what I consider to be a common practice among practitioners of Socratic education. They are friends who walk side by side down the same pathway. They look forward in the same direction and follow each other down well-trodden paths. These pathways may have proven in the past to be reliable, predicable and unchanging. The friends, however, may discover new horizons, so to speak, by looking sideways to other pathways well-worn by other friends. By diverging onto other pathways, the friends may gain a new outlook. While the friends may choose to remain on their chosen paths, it will be with the added perspective of new pathways.

For friends and indeed practitioners of philosophical dialogue who diverge to other pathways, the initial encounter will be novel. Well-worn paths are, hence, only familiar to the proponents that frequent them. Yet, not often enough do these proponents diverge from the pathways that they have chosen. Socratic pedagogy, on the other hand, is where models of dialogue can converge and diverge. This opens up the opportunities for new roads to follow—to follow the argument where it leads! This book does not make the claim that any proposed framework for Socratic pedagogy will offer something entirely new, or that they should act as a substitute for alternative teaching methods. Socratic pedagogy is a philosophic tradition with a diverse history that can be traced back to Ancient Greece.[1] However, by concentrating on generative, evaluative, and connective thinking, we can look at Socratic traditions of education in new ways. The framework for Socratic pedagogy I am about to describe here, opens pathways between well-trodden, and perhaps familiar, practical models of dialogue in the form of the Community of Inquiry, Socratic Dialogue, and Bohmian Dialogue. I have highlighted the essential feature of Socratic pedagogy common to all of these models of dialogue that can take us in many different directions if we start the exploration. The end point is not what is important. What is important for Socratic pedagogy is that we continually arrive at a new beginning. This is what we have done here.

At the outset of this book recall that we pointed to the importance of the UNESCO study which highlights the need for pedagogy that supports democratic ways of life. The report states that philosophy and philosophical inquiry is the road to freedom. What is limited in the initial report is the concentration on Lipman's Philosophy for Children program as a model suited to that need. This is, for some, a well trodden pathway to freedom. The need that is highlighted in the UNESCO study provides the impetus for philosophers and educators to seek alternative pathways so that we are able to evaluate current models of philosophical pedagogy, generate new models, and connect to existing practices which may lead to a reconstruction of what is already familiar, in order to suit the needs of the context in which these models are intended. Hence, if we are to satisfy some of the basic rights afforded to students through education, as described in the Universal Declaration of the Rights of the Child, we can ascertain that engaging in thinking of a philosophical kind could lead to freedom, which is foundational to active citizenship in a democracy. This view is also reflected by Cam (2000) who argues that the role of education is to have an emphasis not only on producing numerate and literate students, but also on producing Socratic students. What he proposes is that educators change their focus towards a thinking curriculum based on collaborative, inquiry-based teaching and learning. Guided by the UNESCO study, and innovators such as Dewey, Lipman, Nelson, and Bohm, as well as scholars and practitioners who continue to explore the field of reflective education, this book provides a foundation for Socratic pedagogy.

Before we move on let us take a moment to reflect on the road so far. Fundamental to this journey is dialogue. In Chapter 1 we saw dialogue as a specific form of engagement whereby individuals can test ideas against others to create better outcomes than thinking alone can achieve. Dialogue is specifically for the purpose of travelling together to achieve a better understanding of matters that concern the participants in the dialogue. Moreover, dialogue is essential to freedom, a place where individuals can explore ideas together and where they are free from being forcibly silenced. Silence, however, is also viewed as a probing questioner and may be a component of dialogue. As such, silence and speech work hand-in-glove in the interaction between thinking and dialogue. Fundamental to this is Socratic Method. Socratic pedagogy is underpinned by dialogue that is Socratic in tradition, which is not just any dialogue, but it is a communal dialogue. In order to understand what Socratic pedagogy might look like, we identified three models of dialogue that are typically Socratic in form, and, hence, have implications for the framework of Socratic pedagogy that is proposed herein. While Lipman's Community of Inquiry and Nelson's Socratic Dialogue may be traced back to the Socratic Method, these are modern interpretations of the tradition. Bohm's Dialogue, on the other hand, does not have Socratic roots but can inform us about the communal aspects of dialogue. By exploring the metaphors used to depict each of the models, we have opened up possibilities for a greater understanding of how each of the models can contribute individually and simultaneously to a productive pedagogy.

While Socratic Method has been described variously as midwifery, as gadfly, and as a kind of self-stinging-ray, what is central to the literature on Socratic Method in the classroom is its pedagogy based on the intellectual and the social elements of inquiry. Where the intellectual inquiry mediates between critical and creative thinking, the social inquiry is the experience of the communal aspects of dialogue. By its very nature a dialogue must be situated in a community for it to be a genuine dialogue, and consequently if it is to satisfy the overall aim of the UNESCO study, as well as go some way towards cultivating the social and intellectual abilities required for active citizenship. Hence, Socratic pedagogy is concerned with critical and creative thinking as well as caring thinking as the ingredients for thinking democratically.

Recall that we also explored creative, critical and caring thinking. As this book focused on the development of thinking and its improvement through Socratic pedagogy, we concentrated only on the aspects of these three dimensions of thinking that underpin dialogue. As pointed out, there is a proliferation of literature and research in these areas coming out of the disciplines of philosophy, psychology, and education, especially in relation to the thinking curricula at all levels of education. Simultaneously, this has led to the development of many thinking programs and classroom strategies for developing students' thinking capacities. However, the vast literature has caused confusion over the various ways these dimensions of thinking are employed in theory and in practice. Consequently, the characteristics or general features of multi-dimensional thinking that are more typical of these three modes of thinking were identified. What is common to these characteristics or central to their meanings is generative, evaluative, and connective thinking. We have not simply replaced or substituted the terms creative, critical, and caring thinking, nor offered a new definition, nor proposed synonyms. The terms generative, evaluative, and connective thinking highlight the thinking that is vital for dialogue. What is common to conceptions of creative thinking is generative thinking, which includes the generation of hypothesis and conjectures, and giving rise to divergent ideas. Generative thinking is the production, development, and extension of ideas that can in some way be applied to the world, to situations or problems. Critical thinking is a form of evaluative thinking. Evaluative thinking is characterised by reasoning, analysis, evaluating, valuing, and judgment. In caring thinking, what most of the literature suggests is that it there is some sort of connectivity. Connective thinking is collective thinking, impersonal fellowship, and awakened attentiveness. With all this in mind, I have illustrated where these dimensions of thinking feature in each of the models of dialogue to show their practical application. To preface my proposal for Socratic pedagogy, I will now briefly give an account of the philosophical and educational qualities of these models.

Lipman's model of dialogue is steeped in the pedagogy of the Community of Inquiry, which is based on an epistemology of community as reflective equilibrium. This equilibrium is suitably described as fallibilistic because the community is constantly open to new ideas, to revision, to improvement, and most of all to self-correction. Rejected in practice is the search for foundational knowledge and absolute truth. Lipman's analogy of the Community of Inquiry as chamber music, where the musicians embellish on an original score, describes the centrality of creative inquiry to collectively following the argument where it leads. The musicians display a commitment to entering into musical dialogue together. Their appreciation or concern for the process is displayed in their actions, which can be found in the application of their skills, knowledge, and valuing of their contributions. The process is connective; each musician is engaged in an intersubjective experience. They generate ideas that flow from the original music, but simultaneously the original music, their musical skills, and knowledge of their instruments act as evaluative criteria. The analogy also represents an essential process of the Community of Inquiry; that is, the interplay between equilibrium and disequilibrium that is necessary to dialogue. In terms of usefulness for Socratic pedagogy, it describes how generative thinking works in concert with evaluative and connective thinking to create new meanings or understandings, in order to appreciate the different perspectives of any given situation as a way of problem-solving and moving forward. As a metaphor it serves the purpose of giving us a broader understanding of dialogue as a collaborative, reflective process, and more specifically of generative thinking as a creative yet focused process.

Unlike Lipman who wrote volumes on his theory and practice of educational philosophy, including a complete set of curriculum materials comprised of narratives and teacher's manuals, Nelson left only implicit pedagogical guidelines for Heckmann and others to develop into the model of Socratic Dialogue practiced today. Socratic Dialogue owes its epistemology to the critical philosophy movement founded by Kant and developed by Fries and Nelson himself. The pedagogy that underlies Socratic Dialogue is founded on the method of regressive abstraction, which has a very specific symmetric structure, expressed explicitly in the shape of an hourglass. It is widest at the top and bottom, and narrowest at the waist, stressing its logical rigor. The inquiry starts with a broad question, which is then examined in search of a core statement (represented by the narrowest section), and this statement is then subject to further examination until consensus is reached over a definition. The structure is convergent stressing its attention to reasoning and logic. Within this structure, following the argument where it leads is primarily an evaluative process of testing and retesting of ideas through the dialogue. Regressive abstraction shares the logic of falsification, and, therefore, avoids the pitfalls of verification. While Nelson did not acknowledge it, by relying on falsification Socratic Dialogue accepts the notion of fallibilism and truth as provisional. The analogy informs Socratic pedagogy by drawing attention to the importance of evaluative thinking. Whereas philosophy begins in wonder, a phenomenon that Lipman reminds us is natural to the human mind, philosophising must also critically evaluate and judge what wonder creates. The hourglass demonstrates how every relevant question, doubt, insight, observation, or objection offered by participants must be considered by the group, until everyone is satisfied with the outcome of deliberative process. As metaphor, it stands as a reminder that dialogue is also an evaluative process of drawing conclusions on the basis of reasons and applying the principles of logic to assess the stages as well as the whole of the dialogical process.

Bohm does not reference the Socratic Method as having influence on his method of dialogue, yet the method itself affirms the importance of Socratic ignorance as a starting point for dialogue. This is achieved through the suspension of beliefs that permits a 'free space' for communication and the appreciation of differing personal beliefs. Ultimately, the dialogue enables inquiry into the sorts of processes that fragment genuine social communication between individuals in a group, which is a 'microculture' of the kind of fragmented social communication that makes up society. The pedagogy, while not explicit, is the impersonal fellowship; a way of participating in collective self-reflection. It is a meta-dialogue which reveals an epistemology of collective proprioception—the process of self mirroring back through dialogue to come to renewed understandings. Like the Community of Inquiry, it is a dialogic epistemology that rests on reconstruction. Bohm uses the metaphor of dialogue as a sort of collective dance of the mind to highlight the awareness of the associations and connections during dialogue. In terms of its contribution to Socratic pedagogy, Bohmian Dialogue stresses the social aspect of dialogue as a kind of connective thinking out of which trust and openness emerge.

Let us finally elucidate what we mean by Socratic pedagogy. The framework is multi-dimensional; comprised of generative, evaluative and connective thinking. By describing each of the dimensions of multi-dimensional thinking in terms of the function they perform, in conjunction with their accompanying metaphors, we are able to escape the confusion created by the vagueness of the terms critical, creative and caring thinking. When we look at creative thinking as generative thinking, represented by chamber music, and critical thinking as evaluative thinking, represented by an hourglass, and caring thinking as connective thinking, represented by collective dance, we move away from the prejudices and disagreements that surround the previously adopted terms. This allows for a greater understanding of the kind of contribution they offer Socratic pedagogy, which in turn informs classroom practice. It also offers a renewed understanding of Socratic pedagogy and a new starting point for discussion on theory and practice.

A PRACTICAL APPROACH TO SOCRATIC PEDAGOGY

Let us now turn to the framework for Socratic pedagogy. The diagram in the following section illustrates this framework, which is comprised of: (1) two distinct but partially overlapping phases—the creative and critical phases, (2) the basic pattern of inquiry is made up of six features, which broadly speaking are progressive steps in a dialogue, and (3) multi-dimensional thinking. The generative and evaluative dimensions of multi-dimensional thinking are at play in each of the features in the basic pattern of inquiry. These features, again broadly speaking, are the intellectual steps of the inquiry described by their function. At the centre of the framework is connective thinking, represented by the hub and the movement across the critical and creative phases. Connective thinking could be described as the communal aspect of dialogue; the interaction patterns that inextricably link the intellectual steps of the inquiry.

Note that the pattern of inquiry embedded in the creative and critical phases moves progressively through each feature in a clockwise direction and concludes where it began, by reconstructing the initial problematic situation into a meaningful experience. Nevertheless, the framework is not intended to represent an inflexible procedure for classroom practice. Depending on the circumstances an inquiry may commence at different points. For example, an inquiry may not have arrived at a conclusion, and thus at the subsequent session would need to scaffold off the previous session. As another example, take a case of a teacher who uses Nelson's Socratic Dialogue only. The pattern of inquiry will focus primarily on the critical phase and move to and fro within it, depending on whether or not consensus is attained. In other words, the framework allows for the various ways in which inquiry may occur.

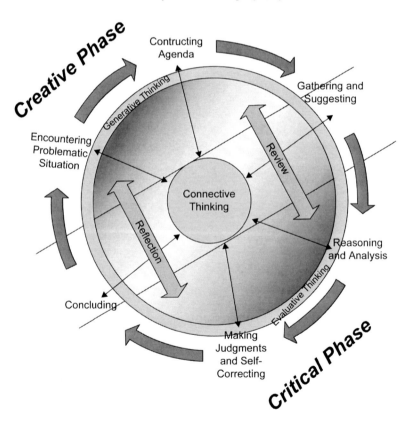

Figure 1. A practical approach to Socratic pedagogy

Socratic pedagogy could be broadly described as having two phases: the creative phase and the critical phase. This distinction is not only a useful mechanism for drawing attention to what point in the inquiry the discussion is placed, but also for understanding which inquiry tools would be required to facilitate the progress of the dialogue. The creative phase is characterised by the initial steps of inquiry that are to a large extent divergent, such as identifying a problem, asking questions, offering suggestions, creating hypothesis. The critical phase is, in turn, characterised by the refining of ideas and examining assumptions. In this phase, there is an attendance to both the logic of inquiry and also a level of self-reflection. Conceiving of inquiry as having distinctly creative and critical phases is, however, somewhat artificial. As Cam (2006) points out:

> We may begin by raising questions, respond with suggestions, and go on to reason about them and explore them conceptually, until by a process of evaluation we arrive at a conclusion. However, we may need to explore the central concepts that lie behind a question before we go on to make suggestions, or find that exploring a concept only raises further questions. Just as obviously, questions may arise at any point in the inquiry, distinctions may need to be made at various times, and we may need to attend to assumptions built into questions or reason about examples. (p.29)

Hence, while we can say primarily that inquiry is either creative or critical, it is much more complex. By employing the terms generative and evaluative thinking to describe the function each of the dimensions of thinking perform, we are able to see how each functions within the creative and critical phases. To explain this further we need to revisit the basic pattern of inquiry.

The six features of the basic pattern of inquiry are: (1) encountering a problematic situation, (2) constructing an agenda, (3) gathering and suggesting, (4) reasoning and analysis, (5) making judgments and self-correcting, and (6) concluding. The first three features sit within the creative phase, as it is here that ideas are built, and meanings created and explored. The movement from one feature to the next in the inquiry provides both the foundation and the direction for the critical phase after an initial review and reflection. During this phase it is primarily generative thinking that comes into play, characterised by wonder, production, synectics, and fluency. The second three features sit within the critical phase, because there is a concentration on the use of conceptual tools and reasoning. This phase could be considered evaluative, primarily because it is reliant on reasoning, analysis, evaluating, valuing, and judging. However, the degree to which the inquiry is generative or evaluative heavily depends on the feature of inquiry and its position in the creative or critical phase. For example, the process of asking questions that has been stimulated by encountering a problematic situation sits neatly in the creative phases because it requires primarily generative thinking. But, to explore the central concepts that lie behind a question before we go on to make suggestions requires evaluative thinking. Thus, asking questions that arise out of an encounter with a problematic situation or other stimulus is prominently creative, but it relies primarily on generative thinking, with evaluative thinking having a subsidiary role.

We now come to the hub of the framework, which is central to the diagram. This represents connective thinking. Note that two of the features of inquiry, 'gathering and suggesting' and 'concluding', are situated inside the overlap that flows between the creative and critical phases. It is here that the participants review or reflect on what has already been done in order to determine the direction of the dialogue, for example, by deciding on whether further exploration is required or if it is time to move on to the critical phase of inquiry. The shaded area and open-ended arrows indicate a flow and ebb or overlap of the two phases, and the smaller arrows indicate fluency between the features of inquiry through the connective thinking process. By implication it connects variously each of the features of inquiry, which dictate if more or less generative or evaluative thinking is required. For example, the feature of gathering and suggesting requires the generation of hypothesis and therefore emphasises generative thinking. However, the group must also decide on whether or not to test the hypothesis or develop it further. This requires the group to review its position in terms of whether or not further exploration is required or to move into the critical phase and test the hypothesis. Similarly, before making judgments at the conclusion of the discussion, the group must decide through reflection or some other method of evaluation (depending on the kind of inquiry), on whether or not further analysis or evaluation is required (and remain in the critical phase), or to conclude discussion and pursue other questions that have arisen from the conclusion reached which will require further exploration, development or generation of ideas (and move on to the creative phase).

A Framework for Dialogue: Generative and Evaluative Thinking

Now that the framework has been broadly described in relation to the critical and creative phases, the pattern of inquiry, and multi-dimensional thinking, in this section we will attend to each of the features in the pattern of inquiry.

Encountering a Problematic Situation The pattern of inquiry begins in the creative phase with a problematic situation. By problematic I don't mean that the stimulus gets presented as a pre-existing problem, but rather that the students are able to encounter it as problematic. This may be due to any number of reasons, such as being puzzled, or an inability to fully comprehend the situation, or various members of the group seeing things from different points of view. Regardless of the reason, at this initial point in the inquiry the group encounters a problematic situation that arises from a sense of wonder that arouses its members to seek answers or solutions that require them to think. What gives the dialogue its richness is that there is some sort of contention with which the group must grapple, be it an ethical dilemma, a matter of fact, or a definition. Whatever the problematic situation, what is important is that the students are driven by a sense of curiosity.

An encounter with a problematic situation may occur in various ways that may send the dialogue down various pathways. For example, for a Community of Inquiry this happens through the reading of a philosophical narrative or other material that can stimulate philosophical discussion. In a Socratic Dialogue, this may occur with a pre-set question or a question arising from the group. For Bohmian Dialogue, the problematic situation naturally occurs out of mere conversation. Regardless of how the dialogue begins, there is a requirement at this point in the inquiry that the problem is articulated. This could be described as generative thinking, as a question needs to be generated. Even in Socratic Dialogue, where in some cases it is recommended that the teacher formulates the question, the group will still need to decide if it resonates with them or if there should be a subsidiary question asked first. From this point, the group needs to separate out the issues. This primarily requires evaluative thinking in order to make distinctions and engage in categorisation.

Constructing an Agenda The next feature is constructing the agenda. This feature requires a level of organisation and teasing out of the issue at hand. It could be purposefully constructed and require identification, clarification and ordering, but this will be ultimately dependant on why people came to the dialogue. If the overall purpose is finding a definition, then the agenda will be set according to finding definitions through what is common or uncommon for each individual in the community. For other kinds of inquiry, it may be a matter of simply finding what needs to be said. It will also be dependant on the context in which the dialogue is conducted. In early childhood classrooms, for example, the teacher may subtly determine how the dialogue must proceed by scaffolding with suggestion questions. In some cases, like Bohmian Dialogue, there may be no agenda, but a natural flow of dialogue may come out of mere conversation.

There are various ways in which agendas may be set. According to Dewey, defining the problem allows for some decisions to be made on how best to proceed. For the Community of Inquiry, agenda setting comes out of reading a narrative that provides the catalyst for further agendas to be set. Students are required to engage in identification, clarification, and ordering in order to set an agenda for inquiry. I view these aspects as being evaluative. On the other hand, agenda setting requires elaboration and the adjustment of scope which are primarily generative. For Bohm, there should be no agenda set upfront but this should emerge naturally from the conversation. In some Community of Inquiry classroom practices, although I don't recommend it, agendas are set by a majority vote. However, a recommended model is to find out what is most common to all. In a Socratic Dialogue, the agenda is naturally set by the process of dialogue whereby the group must journey towards the narrow waist of the hourglass before elaborating on these ideas as the hourglass widens again.

Gathering and Suggesting   The third feature of the pattern of dialogue is gathering and suggesting. It is through this feature of the dialogue that generative thinking has its main focus. This is where participants generate ideas, hypotheses and conjectures. Throughout this process, ideas are generated and explored as participants are encouraged to think divergently as they follow the argument where it leads. At this stage the flow of the inquiry is structured by a broad sense logic and reasoning to 'figure things out', albeit this is subtly balanced by evaluative thinking, in order to provide a foundation for further review in the subsequent stages. This enables the group to explore meanings and values. Because each participant could come with different perspectives and perceptions, in this feature of the dialogue they can explore their ideas by elaborating and clarifying meanings, or comparing the different conceptions they bring to the discussion. Ideas in this case are provisional answers or initial suggestions to some of those things that the participants wonder about. This is an inherently risky part of the process, as ideas are generated that are likely to diverge from the main ideas, in order to explore multiple possibilities to provide a foundation for further discussion. This is, nevertheless, an important feature of dialogue, as it allows for the exploration of alternatives and different perspectives, and for elaborating and building on ideas, including the generation of hypothesis and conjectures.

More than any of the other models of dialogue, the Community of Inquiry places greater value on this stage of the inquiry, as it appeals to a much broader conception of inquiry than, say Socratic Dialogue. It is here that Lipman's dictum of following the argument where it leads and his understanding of inquiry can make a valuable contribution in both theory and practice. The importance of exploring innovative ideas and allowing time to do so cannot be over-emphasised. This requires flexibility as well as deferring judgment. This is not to be confused with an unstructured discussion as the inquiry still needs direction. The logic of inquiry also cannot be ignored, otherwise if fallacious reasoning is to go undetected, it may be seen by the participants as valid or sound reasoning.

Inbuilt into this feature of the inquiry is the preliminary review. The balance between generative and evaluative thinking, or to use Paul's (1994) terms, the broad and narrow sense reasoning and logic, is maintained by a review process of evaluating the progress of discussion or assessing the efforts that are the result of generative thinking. It is a review of what has already been done and deciding on the merits of the review whether further exploration is required, or if it is time to move on to the critical phase (Burgh, Field & Freakley, 2006, p.116). This is not a simple matter of the group deciding, but requires some kind of consensus. By consensus I don't mean an absolute or unanimous consensus, but that there has been some resolution in relation to the task that has to be performed. This does not mean unreflectively moving on. If there are unresolved disagreements or different understandings, this is itself an indication that evaluative thinking is required and that it is time to make some initial moves into the critical phase.

Reasoning and Analysis   The fourth feature, the first in the critical phase, follows immediately from the initial review and reflection, and, therefore, builds on the creative phase of inquiry. The flow from one feature to the next is transformative and relies on both generative and evaluative thinking. Once in this stage of the pattern of inquiry, reasoning and logic play heavily in order to progress in the dialogue. Participants may be required to employ a variety of conceptual tools, as well as reasoning and evaluative tools that rely on criteria or logic. Because of its emphasis on conceptual exploration, and on reasoning and logic this stage of the inquiry is primarily evaluative. But with this narrow sense reasoning and logic, there is still a requirement for generative thinking. The use of examples, counterexamples, making generalisations and employing analogous reasoning all, to some extent, require thinking that is divergent, innovate, novel, or flexible.

It is undeniable that much of Socratic Dialogue is played out in this feature of the pattern of inquiry. This is not to say that the Community of Inquiry or Bohmian Dialogue do not take evaluative reasoning seriously. To the contrary, it is just that it is not emphasised as the primary goal of inquiry as in Socratic Dialogue. Rather, Socratic Dialogue can make a significant contribution insofar as it is an exemplar of evaluative thinking, and, therefore, can inform the structure of this stage of Socratic pedagogy. It is illustrated by the narrow waist of the hourglass, where definitions are explored and reasoning tested. It could also be said that this stage is defined by the notion of regressive abstraction, not necessarily to the extent that the actual stages of Socratic Dialogue must be adhered to, but in the spirit of Nelson's attention to the detail of logic and reason, which emphasises abstraction from the particular to test for validity, soundness and strength of the argument, and then to be evaluated again by the particular circumstances.

Making Judgments and Self-correcting   A defining feature of this stage in the inquiry is judgment, which is informed by self correction and also flows from it. There is a level of weighing-up that occurs in this feature as it precedes the final stage of inquiry—the conclusion. It relies heavily on evaluative thinking and the appropriate thinking tools for inquiry. Criteria are subject to further logical rigor, which along with logic and reasoning will inform all judgments. It is important to note that the Community of Inquiry and Socratic Dialogue use student experience as a resource, especially counterexamples. Thus, while this stage of the inquiry is primarily evaluative, generative thinking has an important function to perform.

For Nelson and Lipman, self-correction is an integral part of this feature of inquiry. It is more than simply following the dictates of logic or reason. By referring to the students' own experiences, they come to understand that the validity or soundness of the inferences also impact on their beliefs. The more familiar they become with this process the more they engage in self-correction, and the more likely that the whole process becomes internalised. This internalisation leads to habits of mind or the development of dispositions, rather than students simply becoming familiar with the tools of inquiry as if they were applying a skill.

Bohmian Dialogue is particularly poignant here too; the dialogue itself is self-corrective through the requirement that participants stand aside from assumptions. This requires that the participants suspend their judgment in order to arrive at a collective kind of judgment.

Concluding The final feature could be said to be both generative and evaluative. In this feature generative thinking is subsidiary to evaluative thinking because participants need to reflect on whether or not there is agreement, if disagreement prevails or if further evaluation is required. It is noteworthy that concluding means the end point in the dialogue itself or the end point for the initial activity. Because every conclusion is open for further review, after coming to an initial conclusion, there may be a need for the dialogue to begin the process again if further counterexamples or other perspectives require exploration. A conclusion in this case is a tentative or provisional end point.

In some contexts, this is actually the end of the dialogue if the stages in pattern of inquiry have been followed, or could signal the conclusion of one stage of inquiry. Once the reflection and review has been conducted, further inquiry may be required, in which case the pattern is repeated. This noted, it is still a conclusion, which may be better described as closure. At this stage of dialogue there should be a level of resolution of the initial problem. This may be heralded, for example in Socratic Dialogue, by reaching consensus. Regardless of the model of dialogue, this part of the pattern requires a level of closure. Closure in this case, may still be open-ended. However, the end of an inquiry may leave the students in a state of confusion, but in a form of 'happy confusion' after exploring ideas and making progress.[2] According to the Pragmatists, this part of the dialogue would be where we declare we have a 'warranted assertion'. As we can never find certainty or absolute truth the conclusion is always treated as fallible, malleable and changing. But this is what makes the dialogue Socratic, as we must always be vigilant about what we claim to be true and be open to the possibility that we don't know what we think we know—hence, the appeal to Socratic ignorance as necessary to effective dialogue. For Nelson, it is the point that there can be no further inquiry. Conclusions are also points in the dialogue that could be said to have reconstructed the previously problematic situation. The notion of reconstruction, as discussed previously, is integral to Vygotsky's notion of internalisation, which is necessary for the development of dialogical dispositions. This brings us once again to the Review and Reflection stage of the diagram where decisions must be made about the direction of the inquiry. The dialogue may be complete for the time being, or the process may begin again.

Reflecting and Review: Connective Thinking

Let us now look at the feature of the inquiry that overlaps both the creative and critical phases of inquiry that are characteristic of two of the features of the dialogue: Review and Reflection. Review and reflection refers to the self and group reflection required throughout the dialogue, but also to a continual understanding of the requirements of the dialogue that need attending to. For example, we could ask: Do we need to go back and think of further definitions in order to move on from this point? Have we sufficiently explored alternatives? There are a number of ways that reflection functions. We have explored this variously throughout the book. For Lipman, this is metacognition. For Nelson, it is the metadialogue that could occur at anytime throughout dialogue upon a student's request. Reflection and review also provides the foundation for Bohm. What he calls proprioception is an awareness of the obstacles and assumptions that require constant reflection and awareness by individuals in the community. Values, beliefs, and prejudices are all considered throughout the dialogue in order to develop and maintain an impersonal fellowship.

Let's take a moment to reiterate the contributions that Bohm makes for Socratic pedagogy. He takes the focus of dialogue away from the content to make us aware of the connections between individuals in a dialogue, between individuals and their own thoughts, and the connectivity of our thinking. Dewey, on the other hand, was interested in content but also in acknowledging the pragmatist need to collaborate to come closer to truth. Bohm emphasises this aspect of Dewey for Socratic pedagogy. This links further to Vygotsky's idea of intersubjectivity and socio-cultural learning which we have also discussed. Connective thinking has an important function to perform in Socratic pedagogy. It is for this reason that it is situated at the heart of the framework. It is illustrated by the arrows that connect the creative to the critical phase, and it is also the community (comprised of individuals in the group) though which all thinking must pass; or as Fisher suggests, it is the fluency between thinking. Theorists often overlook the importance of caring thinking, hence, by redefining this feature in terms of its function as connective thinking, it is my intention that the communal process of dialogue is recognised for its contribution to Socratic pedagogy.

Note the arrows that move between the different features of the pattern of dialogue. This is what Gardner (1995) refers to when she says that we follow the argument where it leads. In this case the teacher is facilitator and may guide the direction of dialogue between the features and phases depending on the requirement of the dialogue. Finally, this diagram represents pedagogy because it may be adapted for use in various educational contexts as a process but also as an underpinning philosophy of learning. It should not, as has happened to other models of dialogue, be seen only as a methodology but as an approach to the philosophy of teaching and learning that is primarily dialogical and communal.

A MODEL OF SOCRATIC PEDAGOGY FOR CLASSROOM PRACTICE

What I have described so far is a framework for Socratic Pedagogy that has been informed by the Socratic Method, but that also has been heavily influenced by three familiar methods of dialogue. Various philosophical traditions have influenced the way these models have been reconstructed as curriculum or pedagogy for practical use. Subsequently, all three models have been variously adapted to suit the needs of teachers and educators in various educational settings around the world. Regardless of any intentions the founders of these models may have had, the more widespread the model the greater likelihood of a gap between their intentions and the actual practice.

This gap may indeed be one of improvement. This, arguably, is the case with Lipman's Philosophy for Children curriculum, which may have remained no more than implicit guidelines for practice had Lipman not come along and developed his extensive educational philosophy and curriculum. But, on the other hand, also arguable, is whether or not the current way his curriculum and pedagogy has been adapted and practiced around the world has reached his own standards or indeed has fallen short. The gap between intended practice and actual practice can be exacerbated by the lack of professional development programs for practising teachers, and the lack of interest from Education Faculties to introduce philosophical education or educational philosophy into pre-service degree programs. (Burgh, 2008)[3]

I do not signal out Lipman, but simply point out that this is an issue that all proposals for philosophising in education must face. Like all attempts to adapt theory to practice there will be successes, a fact to which all of these models can attest. But also, all of these models have been criticised for their shortfalls. But the shortfalls are measured by actual practice. This in itself is not a problem, unless the shortfall gets erroneously attributed to the theory or principles of intended practice. This can sometimes go undetected in empirical studies conducted by researchers who themselves don't have the necessary understanding of the principles of practice or the theories that underpin them. It is to the shortfalls I would like to now turn, but I want to place my discussion in the broader context of educational philosophy, rather than speak to a specific model. I will draw from some of these criticisms and pre-empt what I consider to be a possible objection to Socratic pedagogy generally, and particularly to the model I have proposed. The shortfall, simply put, is that philosophy as a curriculum and pedagogy for schools fails to deliver in practice on their promises.

Oscar Brenefier (2005) is vocal in his concern about the practice of philosophising with children, and the ways in which the pedagogy of philosophy has been interpreted. He worries that students may generate ideas as opinions or give rise only to creative ideas without the balance of the rigor required through critical thinking. The facilitator's role is to make sure that there is a balance between the dimensions of thinking. While generative thinking is important to inquiry, the facilitator must, as Brenifier suggests, promote critical rigor to balance the generation of ideas, lest the inquiry simply becomes a session of opinion-sharing. The dialogue, in Brenifier's case needs to spend more time in the critical phase rather than simply building through the creative phase. Sometimes the evaluative aspects of inquiry fall by the wayside, as is Brenifier's main concern.

Brenifier is concerned over the requirement of reflection and discussion between practitioners. He notes that practitioners need to be reflective of their practice. Brenifier says that educators are unable to engage in critical discussions surrounding the very practice of philosophy in the classroom. He proposed that what is required is a forum by which ideas can be explored in terms of how to go about engaging in philosophy in the classroom. In effect, this was what the UNESCO study called for. I have shown that Lipman's Community of Inquiry is not the only way by which we can satisfy the UNESCO report and Cam's request that education find ways to keep students from being 'insocratic'. If we do not pay attention to Nelson, Bohm, and indeed other models of dialogue, then we fail to do what philosophy in general aims to do – engage in self-reflection and examination. What this requires us to do is explore alternative pathways, not to follow them strictly, but so that our own pathway is informed. We may choose to both diverge and converge from the pathways that we are used to. We cannot deny that the UNESCO report reflects a move around the world towards a 'thinking curriculum'. What is needed now is a further emphasis on philosophy in the classroom through Socratic pedagogy in order to draw out the practical aspects of a curriculum that attempts to align with the principles of the UNESCO report. It requires us, however, as educators and philosophers, to continue the dialogue regarding the implementation of Socratic pedagogies and how this may look in the classroom. I contend that it may look something like a collective dance of the mind, an hourglass, and a chamber orchestra.

SOCRATIC PEDAGOGY: DIALOGUE AS A DEMOCRATIC WAY OF LIFE

As we come to the close of our discussion on an appropriate educational philosophy that satisfies the goals of education in a democracy, and which may also be suitable for or satisfy the recommendations of the UNESCO study, it will be pertinent to again ask why a Socratic classroom would be worthwhile? No matter what the question, underpinning Socrates' curiosity was the question 'what is a good life?' As this book is a reply to the question of what kind of education would support the development of skills and dispositions necessary to active citizenship, it must at least attempt, in some way, to justify how it can make a contribution to the Socratic question. I'm reminded again of Cam's observation that education is preoccupied with literacy and numeracy, but is negligible with regard to developing a citizenry required for active citizenship. If the good life is a democratic one then what is needed is an inquiring society, which requires citizens with the appropriate dispositions and capacities to continually ask questions about accepted moral opinion and to question democratic structures and the institutions and organisations that function within them.

What is implied by my argument for Socratic pedagogy is that Socratic pedagogy is integral to the on-going maintenance of a good life. It has not only an emphasis on constructing thinking in students, but also *reconstructing* thinking in order to constantly question our own thinking, which is at the heart of judgment; what Lipman, Nelson and Bohm all argue is central to their methods. What we are attempting is the reconstruction of thinking, which in turn may lead to the reconstruction of society and the development of an active citizenship. According to Dewey, reconstruction is reliant on being open-minded, dialogical and community minded. Cam concurs with Dewey's call for education as reconstruction. I shall quote him here at length, for what he has to say is worthwhile and speaks to the overall aim of the book.

> If we believe that our educational institutions should not help merely to perpetuate existing social conditions, but should be a means of making them more democratic, then they must not be places where students are weighed down by the legacy of the past or indoctrinated with prevailing attitudes, beliefs and values. Instead, as Dewey says, we should establish in our schools 'a projection in type of the society that we should like to realize, and by forming minds in accord with it gradually modify the larger and more recalcitrant features of adult society'. Insofar as we are talking about a projection of the democratic society, this means that we need to turn our schools into communities, in Dewey's sense. Among other things, this would require that we foster communication among our students instead of isolating them from one another; that we engage them in open inquiry rather than simply teaching them by authority; that classroom activity and school life should expand students' interests by building upon them; that schooling should build on cooperation and reciprocity of interest rather than focusing upon competition and social division; and that many and varied forms of association should be developed within the school, and between the school and the wider community, so as to enable children in groups and as individuals to develop socially intelligent attitudes and approaches to one another. In sum, we should do all that we can to turn schools into communities through which we can liberate the powers of those that inhabit them and develop their capacities for growth. If Dewey is right, then schools must practice the virtues of community if they are to project democracy and to provide the society at large with better prospects for progress in that direction. (Cam, 2000b, pp.165–166)

I argue that Socratic pedagogy above all is dialogical. When we are dialogical, the way that we think through dialogue is the way we think in our everyday lives. It is not about transferring what students have learned in the classroom to their lives outside of the classroom. If Socratic pedagogy achieves its goal of an education of reconstruction then it will have contributed to social reconstruction; that is, the creation of an inquiring society. It could be said that "just as philosophy begins in wonder, an inquiring society begins in dialogue" (Burgh, 2008). This is because it allows us to see outside of the confines of our own minds and perspectives by exploring ideas in the context of other ideas – we diverge off our own well-travelled pathways. To think philosophically is more than acquiring a set of skills, it emerges out of dialogue. To think dialogically is to care for what is meaningful, but as dialogue happens in communities perhaps participants will also come to think of community-mindedness as meaningful. Community-mindedness is what informs democratic citizenship. In order to develop such a citizenry education needs to create thoughtful students capable of generating new ideas, evaluating their own assumptions and opinions, and connecting their thoughts and actions.

I would like to conclude this book with a passage from T.S. Elliot that depicts the process and outcome of Socratic pedagogy: it is a journey along new pathways as well as a reconstruction of well-trodden pathways. The journey that T.S. Elliot describes below reflects what is central to a Socratic classroom. It represents both the process of Socratic pedagogy that aims to reconstruct thinking, but this passage is also important in representing how practitioners should approach the pedagogies that are adopted in both theory and practice. The journey includes experiences of various pathways. It is an experience of an orchestra whereby new ideas are created through following reasoned arguments and the wonder inherent in creating new ideas. It also includes an hourglass, where ideas are analysed and critical evaluation is enhanced. Finally, it is the experience of a collective dance of the mind, where the dancers are compelled to follow their own movements and the movements of each other, but motivated by the importance of the collective dance itself. Above all, experiencing Socratic pedagogy is a journey of reconstruction for the purpose of arriving at thoughtfulness.

We shall not cease from exploration
And the end of all our exploring
Will be to arrive where we started
And know the place for the first time.
(T.S. Elliot)

NOTES

[1]   I am referring here to what is commonly called the Western tradition of philosophy, which grew out of rational thought. There is, of course, as wealth of history, equally as ancient, that emerged from Eastern traditions, as well as from other parts of the globe, such as African philosophy. The UNESCO study is to be applauded for bringing together such a diverse range of philosophical practices from around the world.

[2]   The term happy confusion is used by Golding (2002).

[3]   This quote and others elsewhere in this chapter were taken from an unpublished manuscript by Burgh (2008) which has since then been revised as a conference paper. Permission was given to include the quotes in this book. Pages numbers have been omitted as they no longer reflect the current manuscript. Note also that this section is the result of previous discussions with Burgh on the content of the manuscript.

REFERENCES

Abbot, C., & Wilks, S. (1997). *Thinking & Talking Through Literature: Using the Philosophical Approach in the Middle Years of Schooling*. Cheltenham, Victoria: Hawker Brownlow Education.

Allen, T. (1998). Being an Individual in the Community of Inquiry'. *Critical and Creative Thinking: The Australasian Journal of Philosophy for Children, 6*(1), 28–36.

Allman, D. (1998). Ancient Friends, Modern Enemies. *The South Atlantic Quarterly, 97*(1), 113–126.

Amir, L. (Ed.). (2001). *Don't Interrupt my Dialogue*. Surrey, United Kingdom: Practical Philosophy Press.

Aristotle. (2000). Rhetoric. *The Philosophy Source* [CD-Rom]: Wadsworth.

Badhar, N. (1993). *Friendship: A Philosophical Reader*. Ithaca, New York: Cornell University Press.

Baggini, J., & Fosl, P. (2003). *The Philosopher's Toolkit; A Compendium of Philosophical Concepts and Methods*. Malden: Blackwell Publishing.

Baier, A. (1986). Trust and Antitrust. *Ethics, 96*, 231–260.

Barnett, R. (1995). Reflections on Electronic Frontiers in Education Retrieved 9 December, 2005, from http://www.eric.ed.gov/ERICDocs/data/ericdocs2/content_storage_01/0000000b/80/22/95/83.pdf

Bashford, C. (2003). *The string quartet and society*. Cambridge: Cambridge University Press.

Berk, L. (2000). *Child Development* (5th ed.). Massachussetts: Allyn & Bacon.

Birnbacher, D. (2005). *The Socratic paradigm of Ethics teaching in a multicultural society*. Paper presented at the 5th International Conference, The Challenge of Dialogue, Society of the Furtherance of Critical Philosophy, Berlin.

Blanshard, B. (1965). Foreword. In L. Nelson (Ed.), *Socratic Method and Critical Philosophy*. New York: Dover Publications.

Bleazby, J. (2005). *Reconstruction in Philosophy for Children*. Paper presented at the Creative Engagements: Thinking with Children Conference, Oxford.

Blumenthal, M. (2001, 17 Oct). I Teach You, Not Love You, *The Australian*.

Boele, D. (1998). The "Benefits" of a Socratic Dialogue Or: Which Results Can We Promise? *Inquiry: Critical Thinking Across the Disciplines, 17*(3), 48–70.

Bohm, D. (1996). *On Dialogue*. London: Routledge.

Bohm, D. (1996b). *On Creativity*. London: Routledge.

Bohm, D., Factor, D., & Garrett, P. (1991). Dialogue- A Proposal Retrieved 3 June, 2004, from http://www.infed.org/archives/e-texts/bohm_dialogue.htm

Brenifier, O. (2005). A quick glance at the Lipman method: Reflections on a Conference. *Critical & Creative Thinking: The Australasian Journal of Philosophy for Children, 13*(1&2), 114–138.

Brown, H. (1988). *Rationality*. London: Routledge.

Brown, T. (1965). Introduction (T. K. Brown III, Trans.). In L. Nelson (Ed.), *The Impossibility of the "Theory of Knowledge*. Dover.

Brune, P. (2004). The Methodology of the Socratic Dialogue. In P. Shipley & H. Mason (Eds.), *Ethics and Socratic Dialogue in Civil Society* (pp. 148–168). New Brunswick, USA: Transaction Publishers.

Burgh, G. (1998). *Is Demarchy Possible: A Case for Ruling and Being Ruled In Turn*. PhD, University of Queensland, St Lucia, Qld.

Burgh, G. (2003a). Philosophy in Schools: Education for Democracy or Democratic Education. *Critical & Creative Thinking: The Australasian Journal of Philosophy for Children, 11*(2), 18–30.

Burgh, G. (2003b). Democratic Education: Aligning Curriculum, Pedagogy, Assessment and School Governance. In P. Cam (Ed.), *Philosophy, Democracy and Education*. Seoul: Korean National Commission for UNESCO.

Burgh, G. (2008). *Reconstruction in Philosophy Education: The Community of Inquiry as a Basis for Knowledge and Learning*. Paper presented at the Philosophy of Education Society of Australasia Conference, Brisbane.

REFERENCES

Burgh, G., & Davey, S. (2004, 6–8 December). *Learning for Democracy: Caring, dialogue and deliberative communities.* Paper presented at the Education and Social Action Conference, Centre for Popular Education, University of Technology, Sydney.

Burgh, G., & Davey, S. (Forthcoming). *Critical Thinking and Thoughtful Writing.*

Burgh, G., Field, T., & Freakley, M. (2006). *Ethics and the Community of Inquiry: Education and Deliberative Democracy.* Melbourne, Victoria: Thomson Social Science Press.

Burgh, G., & O'Brien, M. (2002). Philosophy & Education: Integrating Curriculum, Teaching and Learning. *Critical & Creative Thinking: The Australasian Journal of Philosophy for Children, 10*(1), 45–58.

Burgh, G., & Yorshansky, M. (2011). Communities of Inquiry: Politics, power and group dynamics. *Educational Philosophy and Theory, 43*(5), 436–452.

Button, G., & Sharrock, W. (1993). A Disagreement over Agreement and Consensus in Constructionist Sociology. *Journal for the Theory of Social Behaviour, 23*(1), 1–25.

Cam, P. (1993, 1994, 1997a). *Thinking Stories 1–3: Philosophical Inquiry for Children.* Sydney, NSW: Hale & Iremonger.

Cam, P. (1993, 1994, 1997b). *Thinking Stories 1–3: Teacher Resource/Activity Book.* Sydney, NSW: Hale & Iremonger.

Cam, P. (1994). A Philosophical Approach to Moral Education. *Critical and Creative Thinking: The Australasian Journal of Philosophy for Children, 2*(2), 19–26.

Cam, P. (1995). *Thinking Together; Philosophical Inquiry for the Classroom.* Sydney, NSW: Hale & Iremonger.

Cam, P. (2000). Philosophy and Freedom. *Thinking: The Journal of Philosophy for Children, 15*(1), 10–13.

Cam, P. (2000b). Philosophy, Democracy and Education: Reconstructing Dewey. In S. Cha (Ed.), *Teaching Philosophy for Democracy,* (pp. 158–181). Seoul,: Seoul University Press.

Cam, P. (2006). *Twenty Thinking Tools.* Camberwell, Victoria: Acer Press.

Catrambone, R., & Holyoak, K. J. (1989). Overcoming contextual limitations on problem-solving transfer. *Journal of Experimental Psychology, 15*(6), 1147–1156.

Chaffee, J., McMahon, C., & Stout, B. (2005). *Critical Thinking, Thoughtful Writing: A Rhetoric with Readings* (3rd ed.). Boston: Houghton Mifflin Company.

Comte-Sponville, A. (2005). *The Little Book of Philosophy.* London, United Kingdom: Vintage.

Cooper, R. (2007). An Investigation into Constructivism within an Outcomes Based Curriculum. *Issues in Educational Research, 17*(1), 15–39.

Costa, A. (2001). *Developing Minds: A Resource Book for Teaching Thinking, Association for Supervision and Curriculum Development* Alexandria, VA.

Csikszentmihalyi, M. (1997). *Creativity: Flow and the Psychology of Discovery and Invention.* New York: Harper Perennial.

Cummings, N. (1981). Analytical Thinking for Children: Review of the Research. *Analytic Teaching, 2*(1), 26–28.

Curnow, T. (2000). The Value of Dialogue. *Thinking: The Journal of Philosophy for Children, 15*(3), 37–40.

Curnow, T. (2007). Thinking about Dialogue. *The Society for Philosophy in Practice* Retrieved 6 June, 2007, from http://philosophicalcounselling.org.uk/Articles/General/ThinkingAboutDialogue.htm

Curnow, T. (2001). Thinking About Dialogue. In T. Curnow (Ed.), *Thinking Through Dialogue* (pp. 234–237). Surrey, United Kingdom: Practical Philosophy Press.

Daniel, M. (2005, 14–16 July). *Learning Philosophical Dialogue in Preschool.* Paper presented at the Creative Engagements Conference; Thinking with Children Conference, Oxford.

Davey Chesters, S. (2008). *In Pursuit of Knowledge: Socrates Vs The Thinker.* Paper presented at the Philosophy of Education Society of Australasia Conference, Brisbane.

Davey Chesters, S. (2010). Engagement through dialogue : an exploration of collaborative inquiry and dimensions of thinking. In Brune, Jens Peter, Gronke, Horst, & Krohn, Dieter (Eds.) *The Challenge of Dialogue : Socratic Dialogue and Other Forms of Dialogue in Different Political Systems and Cultures* (pp. 73-96). LIT-Verlag, Munster.

Davey Chesters (2009, 3-6 December) *Technologies of Silence*. Paper presented at the Dialogue and Difference Conference, Philosophy of Education Society of Australasia, Hawaii.

Davey, S. (2004). Consensus, Caring and Community: An Inquiry into Dialogue. *Analytic Teaching, 25*(1), 18–51.

Davey, S. (2005a, 14–16 July). *Creative, Critical and Caring Engagements: Philosophy through Inquiry.* Paper presented at the Creative Engagements Conference; Thinking with Children Conference, Oxford.

Davey, S. (2005b). *Engaging through Dialogue: comparing Socratic Dialogue with other forms (philosophy in schools and Bohmian Dialogue).* Paper presented at the 5th International Conference, The Challenge of Dialogue, Society of the Furtherance of Critical Philosophy, Berlin.

Davey, S. (2005). Socratic Dialogue in Education Review of Saran, R & Neisser (eds), Enquiring Minds: Socratic Dialogue in Education in Analytic Teaching. *The Community of Inquiry Journal, 25*(2), 78–79.

Davis, D. (2002). The Adventure of the Discussion Board Retrieved 9 December 2005, from http://www.eric.ed.gov/ERICDocs/data/ericdocs2/content_storage_01/0000000b/80/27/fb/2a.pdf

Dawid, J. (2005). A report into the effects of a project using story-telling and the Community of Inquiry in Six Primary Schools. *Critical and Creative Thinking: The Australasian Journal of Philosophy for Children, 13*(1&2), 34–66.

de Bono, D. (1994). *Parallel Thinking: From Socratic Thinking to de Bono Thinking.* Australia: Penguin.

de Bono, E. (1976). *Teaching Thinking.* London: Temple Smith.

de Haan, C., McCutcheon, L., & MacColl, S. (1995). *Philosophy with Kids: Books 1–3.* South Melbourne, Victoria: Longman.

De Maré, P., Piper, R., & Thompson, S. (1991). *Koinonia: From Hate, through Dialogue, to Culture in the Large Group.* London: Karnac Books.

Dewey, J. (1966). *Democracy and Education: An Introduction to the Philosophy of Education.* New York: Free Press.

Duemler, D., & Mayer, R. (1988). Hidden costs of reflectiveness: Aspects of successful scientific reasoning. *Journal of Educational Psychology, 80*(4), 419–423.

Eikin, S. (2000). Giants of American Education: John Dewey, the Education Philosopher. *Technos, 9*(4), 4.

Ennis, R. (1993). Critical Thinking Assessment. *Theory into Practice, 32*(3), 179–186.

Ennis, R. (1996). Critical Thinking Dispositions: Their Nature and Assessability. *Informal Logic, 18*(2&3), 165–182.

Facione, P. (2000). The Disposition Toward Critical Thinking: Its Character, Measurement, and Relationship to Critical Thinking Skill. *Informal Logic, 20*(1), 61–84.

Facione, P., & Facione, N. (1994). *The California Critical Thinking Skills Test: CCTST Test Manual.* California: California Academic Press.

Fearnley-Sander, M. (1998). Care and the Force of the Argument in Respecting Difference. *Thinking: The Journal of Philosophy for Children, 14*(1), 24–28.

Field, T. (1995). Philosophy for Children and the feminist critique of reason. *Critical and Creative Thinking: The Australasian Journal of Philosophy for Children, 3*(1), 9–12.

Field, T. (1997). Feminist Epistemology and Philosophy for Children. *Thinking: The Journal of Philosophy for Children, 13*(1), 17–22.

Fisher, R. (1995a). Socratic Education. *Thinking, 12*(3), 23–29.

Fisher, R. (1995b). *Teaching Children to Learn.* Cheltenham, England: Stanley Thornes Ltd.

Fisher, R. (1995c). *Teaching Children to Think.* Cheltenham, England: Stanley Thornes Ltd.

Fisher, R. (1996). Socratic Education: A New Paradigm for Philosophical Enquiry? *Critical and Creative Thinking: The Australasian Journal of Philosophy for Children, 4*(1), 1–13.

Foucault, M. (1975). *Discipline and Punish: the Birth of the Prison.* New York: Random House.

Freakley, M., & Burgh, G. (2000). *Engaging with Ethics: Ethical Inquiry for Teachers.* Katoomba, NSW: Social Sciences Press.

REFERENCES

Freakley, M., Burgh, G., & Tilt-MacSporran, L. (2008). *Values Education in Schools: A resource book for student inquires*. Victoria: Camberwell.

Freire, P. (1970). *Pedagogy of the Oppressed* (B. Ramos, Trans.). New York: Herder and Herder.

Freire, P. (1998). *Pedagogy of freedom: ethics, democracy, and civic courage* (P. Clarke, Trans.). Oxford: Rowman & Littlefield Publishers.

Gardner, S. (1995). Inquiry is no Mere Conversation (or Discussion or Dialogue): Facilitation is Hard Work! *Critical and Creative Thinking: The Australasian Journal of Philosophy for Children, 3*(2), 38–49.

Gavin, W. (1970). Neutrality. *Religious Humanism, 4*, 128.

Gilligan, C. (1993). *In a Different Voice: Psychological Theory and Women's Development*. Cambridge, Massachusetts: Harvard University Press.

Glass, R. (2000). Education and the Ethics of Democratic Citizenship. *Studies in Philosophy and Education, 19*, 275–296.

Golding, C. (2002). *Connecting Concepts: Thinking Activities for Students*. Melbourne, Victoria: Australian Council for Educational Research Ltd.

Golding, C. (2004). Philosophy for Children and Multiple Intelligences. *Critical and Creative Thinking: The Australasian Journal of Philosophy for Children, 12*(1), 16–31.

Golding, C. (2005). *Truth or Making Sense*. Paper presented at the Philosophy of Education Society of Australasia Conference, Hong Kong.

Golding, C. (2008). *Teaching Philosophy for Democracy*. Paper presented at the The Asia-Pacific Philosophy Education Network for Democracy Conference, Ewha Women's University, Seoul.

Govier, T. (1999). *Rosebuds, Judgment and Critical Thinking, The Philosophy of Argument* Newport News: Vale Press.

Gregory, M. (2001). Curriculum, Pedagogy and Teacherly Ethos. *Pedagogy, 1*(1), 69–89.

Gregory, M. (2002). Constructivism, Standards, and the Classroom Community of Inquiry. *Educational Theory, 53*(5), 397–408.

Hanus, J. (1973). Friendship in Aristotelian Ethics. *Modern Schoolman, 50*, 351–365.

Haynes, F. (1997). Teaching to Think. *Australian Journal of Teacher Education, 22*(1), 1–22.

Heckmann, G. (1989). Socratic Dialogue. *Thinking, 8*(1), 34–37.

Heckmann, G. (2004). Six Pedagogical Measures and Socratic Facilitation. In S. R & N. B (Eds.), *Enquiring Minds: Socratic Dialogue in Education* (pp. 107–120). Trent, UK: Trentham Books Ltd.

Honderich, T. (Ed.). (1995). *The Oxford Companion to Philosophy* (Vol. Oxford): Oxford University Press.

Howells, J., & McArdle, M. (2007). *P4C in the Early Years*. Paper presented at the Federation of Australasian Philosophy in Schools Association Annual Conference, University of Melbourne, Melbourne.

Hult, R. (1979). On Pedagogical Caring. *Educational Theory, 29*, 237–243.

Imbrosciano, A. (1997). Philosophy and Student Academic Performance. *Critical and Creative Thinking: The Australasian Journal of Philosophy for Children, 5*(1), 35–41.

Irigaray, L. (1985). This Sex Which Is Not One (C.Porter, Trans.) *This Sex Which is Not One*. =New York: Cornell University Press.

James, W. (1993). What Education Can Be: Education for Judgment. In M. Lipman (Ed.), *Thinking Children and Education* (pp. 701–704). Dubuque, Iowa: Kendall/Hunt Publishing Company.

Jayakar, P. (1986). *Krishnamurti: A Biography*. San Francisco: Harper & Row.

Kagan, J. (1989). *Unstable Ideas: Temperament, Cognition and Self*. Cambridge, Massachusetts: Harvard University Press.

Kalantis, M., & Cope, B. (2008). *New Learning; Elements of a Science of Education*. Melbourne: Cambridge University Press.

Kelley, L. R. (2006). Logical Issues: Justification (quid facti), First Principles and Socratic Method after Plato, Aristotle, Hume, Kant, Fries, & Nelson Retrieved 1 January, 2008, from http://www.friesian.com/foundatn.htm

Kennedy, D. (1996). Forming Philosophical Communities of Inquiry in Early Childhood Classrooms. *Early Childhood Development and Care, 120*(1), 1–15.

Kessels, J. (2001). Socrates Comes to Market. *Reason in Practice, 1*(1), 49–71.

Kirk, J., & Orr, R. (2003). A Primer of the Effective use of Threaded Discussion Retrieved 9 December, 2005, from http://www.eric.ed.gov/ERICDocs/data/ericdocs2/content_storage_01/0000000b/80/28/24/10.pdf

Kletschko, D., & Siebert, U. (2004). Socratic Dialogue and Democratic Development in the Republic of Belarus. In P. Shipley & H. Mason (Eds.), *Ethics and Socratic Dialogue* (pp. 112–128). New Jersey: Transaction Publishers.

Kohlberg, L. (1981). *Vol. I: The Philosophy of Moral Development*. San Francisco: Harper & Row.

Krohn, D. (2004). Theory and Practice of Socratic Dialogue. In S. R & B. Neisser (Eds.), *Enquiring Minds: Socratic Dialogue in Education* (pp. 15–24). Trent, UK: Trentham Books Ltd.

Laird, R. (1993). Philosophy for Children in Remote Aboriginal communities. *Critical & Creative Thinking: The Australasian Journal of Philosophy for Children, 1*(1), 38–44.

Laverty, L. (2002). Philosophy and Pedagogy in Australian Schools. *Critical & Creative Thinking: The Australasian Journal of Philosophy for Children, 10*(1), 29–43.

le Caze, M. (2004). *Michèle Le Dœuff's The Sex of Knowing: Philosophy of the unthought*. Paper presented at the University of Queensland, Brisbane.

Lee, S. (2005, 14–16 July). *Creative Engagement: Where Teaching and Learning Meet*. Paper presented at the Creative Engagements Conference; Thinking with Children Conference, Oxford.

Lessing, R. (1993). Is it Possible to Teach Socratically? In M. Lipman (Ed.), *Thinking Children and Education* (pp. 444–457). Dubuque, Iowa: Kendall/Hunt.

Levi, I. (1985). Consensus as Shared Agreement and Outcome of Inquiry. *Synthese, 62*, 3–11.

Lindop, C. (2002). Plato's Legacy: How to Do Philosophy. *Critical & Creative Thinking: The Australasian Journal of Philosophy for Children, 10*(2), 36–45.

Lipman, M. (1974). *Harry Stottlemeier's Discovery*. Upper Montclair: Institute of the Advancement of Philosophy for Children.

Lipman, M. (1988). *Philosophy Goes to School*. Philadelphia: Temple University Press.

Lipman, M. (1991). *Thinking in Education*. New York: Cambridge University Press.

Lipman, M. (1991b, July 12–16). *Strengthening Reasoning and Judgment (Keynote Address)*. Paper presented at the Philosophy for Children and the Teaching of Thinking Conference, University of Melbourne, Melbourne.

Lipman, M. (1993). Developing Philosophies of Childhood. In M. Lipman (Ed.), *Thinking Children and Education*. Dubuque, Iowa: Kendall/Hunt Publishing Company.

Lipman, M. (2004). *Thinking in Education* (2nd ed.). New York: Cambridge University Press.

Lipman, M. (2004b). Philosophy for Children's Debt to Dewey' Critical & Creative Thinking. *The Australasian Journal of Philosophy for Children, 12*(1), 1–8.

Lipman, M., & Sharp, A. (1975). *Instruction Manual to Accompany Harry Stottlemeier's Discovery*. Upper Montclair: Institute of the Advancement of Philosophy for Children.

Lipman, M., Sharp, A., & Oscanyan, F. (1977). *Philosophy in the Classroom*. Upper Montclair: Institute of the Advancement of Philosophy for Children.

Lipman, M., Sharp, A., & Oscanyan, F. (1980). *Philosophy in the Classroom* (2nd ed.). Philadelphia: Temple University Press.

Lipman, M., & Sharp, A. M. (1994). *Growing Up With Philosophy*. Dubuque, Iowa: Kendall/Hunt.

Lynch, S. (2003). Friendship, Ethics and Democracy. In P. Cam (Ed.), *Philosophy, Democracy and Education*. Seoul: Korean National Commission for UNESCO.

Lynch, S. (2005). *Philosophy and Friendship*. Britain: Edinburgh University Press.

MacColl, S. (1994). Opening Philosophy. *Thinking: The Journal of Philosophy for Children, 11*(3&4), 5–9.

MacKnight, C. (2000). Teaching Critical Thinking through Online Discussions. *Educause Quarterly, 4*, 38–41.

Marinoff, L. (1999). *Plato, not Prozac: Applying Eternal Wisdom to Everyday Problems*. New York: Quill.

REFERENCES

Marinoff, L. (2005). *Distinguishing between therapeutical and philosophical dialogue.* Paper presented at the 5th International Conference, The Challenge of Dialogue, Society of the Furtherance of Critical Philosophy, Berlin.

Matthews, G. (1999). *Socratic Perplexity and the nature of philosophy.* Oxford: Oxford University Press.

McInerney, D., & McInerney, V. (2006). *Educational Psychology: Constructing Learning* (4th ed.). Australia: Pearson.

Medoca, D. (1997). Reading Vygotsky. *Critical and Creative Thinking: The Australasian Journal of Philosophy for Children, 5*(1), 30–33.

Millar, C. (2005, 14–16 July). *The impact of Philosophy for Children in a high school English class.* Paper presented at the Creative Engagements Conference; Thinking with Children Conference, Oxford.

Mohr, A. (2002). Consensus Conference: Of Being Seen to do the Right Thing: Provisional Findings From the First Australian Consensus Conference on Gene Technology in the Food Chain. *Science and Public Policy, 29*(1), 2–12.

Monro, D. (1950). Subjectivism Versus Relativism in Ethics. *Analysis, 11,* 19–24.

Morgan, N., & Cook, J. (no date). Teaching Cycles in the Creative Community of Inquiry Retrieved 2 January, 2008, from http://www.palatine.ac.uk/files/747.pdf

Moulton, J. (1983). A Paradigm of Philosophy: The Adversary Method. In S. Harding, M. Hintikka & D. Reidel (Eds.), *Discovering Reality. Feminist Perspective on Epistemology, Metaphysics, Methodology and Philosophy of Science.* Holland: Dordrech.

Murris, K., & Haynes, J. (2001). Philosophical Enquiry with Children. In T. Curnow (Ed.), *Thinking Through Dialogue* (pp. 159–164). Surrey, United Kingdom: Practical Philosophy Press.

Needham, D. R., & I. R., B. (1991). Problem-oriented Training Promotes Spontaneous Analogical Transfer: Memory Oriented Training Promotes Memory for Training. *Memory and Cognition, 19,* 543–557.

Neilson, A. (1989). *Critical Thinking and Reading: Empowering Learners to Think and Act.* Bloomington, Indiana: ERIC Clearinghouse on Reading and Communication Skill.

Nelson, L. (1965). Socratic Method (T. Brown III, Trans.). In S. M. a. C. Philosophy (Ed.). New York: Dover Publications Inc.

Nelson, L. (1965b). The Impossibility of the "Theory of Knowledge (T. Brown III, Trans.) *Socratic Method and Critical Philosophy.* New York: Dover Publications Inc.

Nelson, L. (1993). The Socratic Method. In M. Lipman (Ed.), *Thinking Children and Education* (pp. 437–444). Dubuque, Iowa: Kendall/Hunt.

Nevill, I. *Feldenkrais Learning and David Bohm's Dialogue Model.*

Niklasson, J., Ohlsson, R., & M, R. (1996). Evaluating Philosophy for Children', vol. no *Thinking: The Journal for Philosophy for. Children, 12*(4), no page number.

Noddings, N. (1984). *Caring: A Feminine Approach to Ethics and Moral Education.* California: The Regents of the University of California.

Noddings, N. (1994). Conversation as Moral Education. *Journal of Moral Education, 23*(2), 107–117.

Norris, S. (1992). Testing for the Disposition to Think Critically. *Informal Logic, 14*(2&3), 156–164.

Nussbaum, M. (1993). Philosophical Books vs Philosophical Dialogue. In M. Lipman (Ed.), *Thinking, Children and Education.* Dubuque, Iowa: Kendall/Hunt Publishing Company.

O'Brien, M. (2000). Developing Thinking and Knowing. *Critical and Creative Thinking: The Australasian Journal of Philosophy for Children, 8*(2), 19–28.

Odedouin, R. (2000). Overlapping Consensus: Objectivising a Subjective Standpoint. *Journal of Philosophical Research, 25,* 323–343.

Ohlsson, R. (1998). An Early Form of the Community of Inquiry: The Study Circle. *Thinking: The Journal of Philosophy for Children, 14,*(2), 27–29.

Ostrow, R. (2005, August 27–28). Untitled. *The Weekend Australian Magazine, 20.*

Overold, G. (1973). Subjective Truth: A Critique. *The Journal of Value Inquiry, 7,* 1–16.

Pardales, M., & Girod, M. (2006). Community of Inquiry: Its past and present future. *Educational Philosophy and Theory, 38*(3), 299–309.

Paul, R. (1994). Critical Thinking: What Every Person Needs to Survive in a Rapidly Changing World. In J. Willsen & A. Binker (Eds.). Victoria: Hawker Brownlow Education.

Paulus, P. (2000). Groups, Teams, and Creativity: The Creative Potential of Idea-generating Groups. *Applied Psychology, 49*(2), 237–262.

Pekarsky, D. (1994). Socratic Teaching: A Critical Assessment. *Journal of Moral Education, 23*(2), 119–133.

Philips, J. (1994). *The Debating Book*. Kensington, NSW: UNSW Press.

Philips, R. (1994). A Sincere Word for the Devil's Advocate. *Critical and Creative Thinking: The Australasian Journal of Philosophy for Children, 2*(1), 15–20.

Piaget, J. (1926). *The Language and Thought of the Child* New York: Brace & World.

Pierce, C. (1955). *The Philosophical Writings of Pierce*. New York: Dover.

Pierce, C. (2000). Some Consequences of Four Incapacities. *The Philosophy Source* [CD-Rom]: Wadsworth.

Plato. (2000a). Apology. *The Philosophy Source* [CD-Rom]: Wadsworth.

Plato. (2000b). Republic. *The Philosophy Source* [CD-Rom]: Wadsworth.

Plesk, P. (1997). *Creativity, Innovation and Quality*. Wisconsin: ASQC Quality Press.

Pope, R. (2005). *Creativity; Theory, History, Practice*. London: Routledge.

Portelli, J. (1990). The Philosopher as Teacher: The Socratic Method and Philosophy for Children. *Metaphilosophy, 21*(1&2), 141–161.

Powell, G., & Connor-Greene, P. (2004). Discussion-based Classes: Challenges and Solutions. *Academic Exchange Quarterly, 8*(3), 163–169.

Power, N. (1999). Meno Stottlemeier: Linking Socratic Methods with Socratic Contents. *Thinking, 14*(3), 20–23.

Prawda, G. (2000). Authenticity: Is It Possible to be Authentic? Retrieved 4 January, 2005, from http://www.philodialogue.com/Authenticity.html

Preston, N. (1997). *Understanding Ethics*. Leichhardt, NSW: The Federation Press.

Pring, R. (2001). Education as Moral Practice. *Journal of Moral Education, 30*(2), 101–112.

Prior, S. (2007). *Defining Multidimensional Thinking*. Paper presented at the Federation of Australasian Philosophy in Schools Association Conference, Melbourne, Australia.

Rabe, C. (2006). *The Innovation Killer*. New York: AMACOM.

Reed, R. (1991). On the Art and Craft of Dialogue. In R. Reed & A. Sharp (Eds.), *Studies in Philosophy for Children: Harry Stottlemeier's Discovery*. Philadelphia: Temple University Press.

Reed, R., & Johnson, T. (1999). *Friendship and Moral Education: Twin Pillars of Philosophy for Children*. New York: Peter Lang.

Reeve, H. (2005). *No Agenda*. Paper presented at the 5th International Conference, The Challenge of Dialogue, Society of the Furtherance of Critical Philosophy, Berlin.

Reich, R. (1998). Confusion about the Socratic Method: Socratic Paradoxes and Contemporary Invocations of Socrates. *Philosophy of Education Society Yearbook* Retrieved 2 June, 2005, from http://www.ed.uiuc.edu/EPS/PES-yearbook/1998/reich.html

Rohmann, C. (2000). *The Dictionary of Important Ideas and Thinkers*. London: Arrow Books.

Roumer, L. (1994). *The Changing Face of Friendship*. Notre Dame, Indiana: University of Notre Dame Press.

Roy, B. (2001). On Becoming and Being Hospitable: The Modern Socratic Dialogue and the Hospitality Industry. In T. Curnow (Ed.), *Thinking Through Dialogue* (pp. 228–232). Surrey, United Kingdom: Practical Philosophy Press.

Ruggiero, V. (2007). *The Art of Thinking: A Guide to Critical and Creative Thought*. New York: Pearson Longman.

Ryle, G. (1971). Thinking and Self Teaching. *Journal of Philosophy of Education, 5*(2), 216–228.

Santi, M. (1993). Philosophising and Learning to Think. *Thinking: The Journal for Philosophy for. Children, 10*(3), 17–23.

REFERENCES

Saran, R., & Neisser, B. (2004). Socratic Dialogue in Teaching Ethics and Philosophy: Organisational Issues. In R. Saran & B. Neisser (Eds.), *Enquiring Minds: Socratic Dialogue in Education* (pp. 29–39). Trent, UK: Trentham Books Ltd.

Schuster, S. (1999). *Philosophy Practice: An Alternative to Counseling and Psychotherapy*. Westport: Praeger Publishers.

Seixas, P. (1993). The Community of Inquiry as a Basis for Knowledge and Learning: The case of history. *American Educational Research Journal, 30*(2), 305–324.

Sharp, A. (1993). Pierce, Feminism, and Philosophy for Children. *Analytic Teaching, 14*(1), 51–62.

Sharp, A. (2004). The Other Dimension of Caring Thinking. *Critical & Creative Thinking: The Australasian Journal of Philosophy for Children, 12*(1), 9–14.

Shephard, D. (2005, 14–16 July). *Introduction.* Paper presented at the Creative Engagements Conference; Thinking with Children Conference, Oxford.

Shipley, P., & Mason, H. (2004). *Ethics and Socratic Dialogue in Civil Society*. New Brunswick, USA: Transaction Publishers.

Siegel, H. (1986). Critical Thinking as an Intellectual Right. *New Directions for Child and Adolescent Development, 33*, 39–49.

Siegel, H. (2004). Rationality and Judgment. *Metaphilosophy, 35*(5), 597–613.

Slade, C. (1992). Creative and critical thinking. An evaluation of Philosophy for Children. *Analytic Teaching, 13*(1), 25–36.

Slattery, L. (1995, 8–9 April). Sophie Meets Socrates. *The Weekend Australian Magazine* 20–24.

Snyder, M., & Smith, D. (1986). Personality and Friendship. In Derlega & Winstead (Eds.), *Friendship and Social Interaction* (pp. 63–80). New York,: Springer-Verlag.

Splitter, L. (1991). Critical Thinking: What, Why, When and How. *Educational Philosophy and Theory, 23*(1), 89–109.

Splitter, L., & Sharp, A. (1995). *Teaching for Better Thinking: The Classroom Community of Inquiry*. Melbourne, Vic: The Australian Council for Educational Research Ltd.

Sprod, T. (1993). *Books into Ideas: A Community of Inquiry*. Melbourne, Victoria: Hawker Brownlow Education.

Sprod, T. (2001). *Philosophical Discussion in Moral Education. The Community of Ethical Inquiry*. London: Routledge.

Sternberg, R. (2000). Creativity is a Decision. In A. Costa (Ed.), *Teaching for intelligence II*. Thousand Oaks, CA: Corwin Press.

Sternberg, R. (2005). The Role of Creativity in the Dialectical Evolution of Ideas Retrieved 4 June, 2005, from http://www.apa.org/divisions/div10/articles/sternberg.html

Stowell, R. (Ed.). (2003). *The Cambridge Companion to the String Quartet*. New York: Cambridge University Press.

Sunderland, N. (2002). *Silence, Silencing, and the Silenced.* Paper presented at the Towards Human Technologies Conference, University of Queensland, Ipswich. University of Queensland, St Lucia.

Tanner, L. (1997). *Dewey's Laboratory School: Lessons for Today*. New York: Teachers College Press.

Temmerman, N. (2008, January 23). Challenging a school of thought, *The Courier Mail*, p. 28.

Thomas, J. (1997). Community of Inquiry and Differences of the Heart. *Thinking: The Journal of Philosophy for Children, 13*(1), 42–48.

Turgeon, W. (1998a). Metaphysical Horizons of Philosophy for Children: A Survey of Recent Discussions Within the Philosophy for Children Community. *Thinking: The Journal of Philosophy for Children, 14*(2), 18–22.

Turgeon, W. (1998b). The Reluctant Philosopher: causes and cures. *Critical and Creative Thinking: The Australasian Journal of Philosophy for Children, 6*(2), 9–17.

UNESCO. (2007/2008). Philosophy: A School of Freedom, Teaching Philosophy and Learning to Philosophize: Status and prospects. Paris, France: UNESCO Publishing.

Valentino, F. (1998). The Thought of the Heart and Philosophy for Children. *Thinking: The Journal of Philosophy for Children, 14*(2), 29–32.

Van Der Leeuw, K. (2004). Philosophical Dialogue and the Search for Truth. *Thinking: The Journal of Philosophy for Children, 17*(3), 17–23.

van Gundy, A. (1995). *101 activities for teaching creativity and problem solving*. San Francisco: Wiley Imprint.

van Hooft, S. (1995). *Caring: an Essay in the Philosophy of Ethics*. Niwot, Colorado: University Press of Colorado.

van Hooft, S. (1999). Socratic Dialogue as Collegial Reasoning Retrieved 2 June, 2004, from http://www.pantaneto.co.uk/issue10/vanhooft.htm

van Hooft, S. (2001). Overcoming Principles: Dialogue in Business Ethics. *Teaching Business Ethics, 5*, 89–106.

van Hooft, S. (2005). *What can Dialogue or Socratic Dialogue Contribute or Not Contribute in Different Political and Cultural Contexts*. Paper presented at the 5th International Conference, The Challenge of Dialogue, Society of the Furtherance of Critical Philosophy, Berlin.

van Luijk, H. (1996). *Dilemma Training as a Way to Moral Awareness and Moral Competence. Experiences with the Implementation of an Integrity Programme*. Breukelen, The Netherlands: Jijenrode University.

Vicuna Navarro, A. M. (1998). Ethical Education Through Philosophical Discussion. *Thinking: The Journal of Philosophy for Children, 14*(2), 23–26.

Villa, D. R. (1999). *Politics, Philosophy, Terror: Essays on the Thoughts of Hannah Arendt*. Princeton, New Jersey: Princeton University Press.

von Morstein, P. (2005). *Life as philosophical practice: philosophical dialogue for goodness' sake*. Paper presented at the 5th International Conference, The Challenge of Dialogue, Society of the Furtherance of Critical Philosophy, Berlin.

Vygotsky, L. (1962). *Thought and Language*. Cambridge, Massachusetts: The MIT Press.

Vygotsky, L. (1987). Thinking and Speech. In R. Reiber & A. Carton (Eds.), *The Collected Works of L.S. Vygotsky: Vol. 1. Problems of General Psychology* (pp. 37–285). Plenum, New York.

Wellman, C. (1975). Ethical Disagreement and Objective Truth. *American Philosophical Quarterly, 13*(3), 211–221.

Whitehead, A. N. (1934). *Nature and Life*. Chicago: Chicago *University* Press.

Wiegner, A. (2005). The Problem of Knowledge in Light of Nelson's Critical Philosophy. In I. Nowacowa (Ed.), *Observation, Hypothesis, Introspection* (pp. 37–90): Rodop.

Wilks, S. (1995). *Critical & Creative Thinking. Strategies for Classroom Inquiry*. Armadale, Victoria: Eleanor Curtain.

Wren, T. (1991). *Caring About Morality: Philosophical Perspectives in Moral Psychology*. Cambridge, Massachusetts: MIT Press.

Yorshansky, M. (2007). Democratic Education and the Concept of Power. *Critical and Creative Thinking: The Australasian Journal of Philosophy in Education, 15*(1), 15–35.

INDEX

Printed by BoD™in Norderstedt, Germany